NEUROSCIENCE RESEARCH PROGRESS

HANDBOOK OF NEUROPSYCHIATRY RESEARCH

NEUROSCIENCE RESEARCH PROGRESS

Additional books in this series can be found on Nova's website under the Series tab.

Additional E-books in this series can be found on Nova's website under the E-book tab.

NEUROSCIENCE RESEARCH PROGRESS

HANDBOOK OF NEUROPSYCHIATRY RESEARCH

REBECCA S. DAVIES
EDITOR

Nova Science Publishers, Inc.
New York

Copyright © 2010 by Nova Science Publishers, Inc.

All rights reserved. No part of this book may be reproduced, stored in a retrieval system or transmitted in any form or by any means: electronic, electrostatic, magnetic, tape, mechanical photocopying, recording or otherwise without the written permission of the Publisher.

For permission to use material from this book please contact us:
Telephone 631-231-7269; Fax 631-231-8175
Web Site: http://www.novapublishers.com

NOTICE TO THE READER

The Publisher has taken reasonable care in the preparation of this book, but makes no expressed or implied warranty of any kind and assumes no responsibility for any errors or omissions. No liability is assumed for incidental or consequential damages in connection with or arising out of information contained in this book. The Publisher shall not be liable for any special, consequential, or exemplary damages resulting, in whole or in part, from the readers' use of, or reliance upon, this material. Any parts of this book based on government reports are so indicated and copyright is claimed for those parts to the extent applicable to compilations of such works.

Independent verification should be sought for any data, advice or recommendations contained in this book. In addition, no responsibility is assumed by the publisher for any injury and/or damage to persons or property arising from any methods, products, instructions, ideas or otherwise contained in this publication.

This publication is designed to provide accurate and authoritative information with regard to the subject matter covered herein. It is sold with the clear understanding that the Publisher is not engaged in rendering legal or any other professional services. If legal or any other expert assistance is required, the services of a competent person should be sought. FROM A DECLARATION OF PARTICIPANTS JOINTLY ADOPTED BY A COMMITTEE OF THE AMERICAN BAR ASSOCIATION AND A COMMITTEE OF PUBLISHERS.

LIBRARY OF CONGRESS CATALOGING-IN-PUBLICATION DATA
Available upon request.

ISBN: 978-1-61668-138-8

Published by Nova Science Publishers, Inc. ✦ *New York*

CONTENTS

Preface		**vii**
Chapter 1	Prolactinomas, PRL & Weight Gain *Erika C.O. Naliato*	**1**
Chapter 2	Clinical and Pathological Characteristics of Pick's Disease and Frontotemporal Lobar Degeneration with TDP-43-Positive Inclusions *Osamu Yokota and Kuniaki Tsuchiya*	**39**
Chapter 3	Interventions for Affective and Behavioural Disturbances in Acquired Brain Injury: A Conceptual Framework based on the Stages of Change Theory *Erin M. Warriner, Hiten Lad and Diana Velikonja*	**71**
Chapter 4	Sequential Expression of Impaired Psychomotor and Sensorimotor Activities in Rodents during Amphetamine Withdrawal *Junichi Kitanaka, Nobue Kitanaka and Motohiko Takemura*	**97**
Chapter 5	Association Between Salivary Amylase, Cortisol and Stress *Koichi Isogawa, Jusen Tsuru, Yoshihiro Tanaka, Yoshinobu Ishitobi, Tomoko Ando, Hiroaki Hanada, Kensuke Kodama and Jotaro Akiyoshi*	**113**

Chapter 6	Serotonergic Receptors in the Central Nervous System – A Brief Review *L.Y. Yeung, Ross Y.Y. Lee and D.T. Yew*	**125**
Chapter 7	The Next Major Neuropsychological and Neuropsychiatrical Breakthrough: Alzheimer's Disease *Heather Pedersen and F. Richard Ferraro*	**137**
Chapter 8	Neurology, Psychiatry and Genetics: Interrelationship *Viroj Wiwanitkit*	**145**
Chapter 9	How Can Bioinformatics Help Studies in Neuropsychiatry? *Viroj Wiwanitkit*	**153**
Chapter 10	Extracting Discriminant Information from Neuroimages: A Multivariate Computational Framework to Analyze the Whole Human Brain *Carlos E. Thomaz, Rafael D. Leão, João R. Sato and Geraldo F. Busatto*	**159**
Index		**193**

PREFACE

Neuropsychiatry is the branch of medicine dealing with mental disorders attributable to diseases of the nervous system. This new book presents topical data relating to neuropsychiatry including: interventions for affective and behavioral disturbances in acquired brain injury; prolactinomas, PRL and weight gain; the clinical and pathological characteristics of Pick's disease; the association between salivary amylase, cortisol and stress; serotonergic receptors in the central nervous sytem; and the quest for a major neuropsychiatrical breakthrough in Alzheimer's disease.

Chapter 1 discusses prolactinomas, tumors that produce prolactin (PRL), which are one of the most frequent pituitary tumors and the main cause of pathological hyperprolactinemia. These tumors are more frequently diagnosed in women and usually affect the reproductive axis, leading to secondary hypogonadism. The diagnosis of prolactinoma is based on the presence of clinical features – such as menstrual irregularity, erectile dysfunction, galactorrhea, and infertility – and the detection of elevated serum PRL levels and confirmed by the existence of a pituitary tumor on magnetic resonance imaging.

As a consequence of secondary hypogonadism, hyperprolactinemia can affect body composition by reducing bone density. Moreover, data have suggested that lean mass reduction might not be the only way in which hyperprolactinemia may interfere with body composition. Clinical studies have reported that patients with prolactinoma may present with weight gain, indicating that PRL could also alter body fat content. In obese women without prolactinoma, PRL secretion is enhanced in proportion to their body mass index and particularly associated with the size of visceral fat, considered more metabolically active than subcutaneous fat. A few studies have also concluded that normalization of PRL levels in patients with prolactinoma has beneficial effects on body fat distribution. The presence of four PRL receptor (PRLR) isoforms in the human abdominal adipose tissue reinforces the potential role of PRL on fat tissue metabolism and the expression of PRLR has been reported to influence adipocyte differentiation and fat tissue development. Additionally, PRL might interfere with adipose tissue metabolism in an indirect form through the regulation of affinity and concentration of the insulin receptor. Studies of seasonally obese animals have brought up another mechanism for the increase in adipose tissue content in subjects with hyperprolactinemia. In these animals, increased PRL levels lead to hyperphagia and consequent weight gain. PRL has also been reported to interfere with body weight control through the regulation of leptin and adiponectin synthesis and secretion. Interestingly, the prolactin-leptin interaction is reciprocal, since other studies have demonstrated that leptin is capable of inducing PRL secretion.

However, in studying the effects of hyperprolactinemia on body composition, the role of type D2 dopamine receptors (D2R) must be taken into account. It is well known that dopamine exerts the main inhibitory control of PRL secretion, which provides the basis for dopamine agonist treatment in patients with prolactinoma. Furthermore, the D2R gene has also been reported to play a major role in the regulation of appetite, weight, and energy expenditure. Consequently, some studies have suggested that hyperprolactinemia *per se* is not a cause of obesity but only reflects the reduction in D2R activity, which is supposedly the real source of metabolic dysfunction and weight gain in patients with prolactinoma.

Frontotemporal lobar degeneration (FTLD) is a clinical syndrome of dementia that is composed of three clinical subtypes, frontotemporal dementia (FTD), progressive aphasia (PA), and semantic dementia (SD). The underlying pathologies in FTLD patients are variable, including FTLD with tau-positive Pick bodies (Pick's disease), sporadic and familial FTLD with TDP-43-positive inclusions (FTLD-TDP), FTLD with tau gene mutations, corticobasal degeneration/progressive supranuclear palsy (CBD/PSP), argyrophilic grain disease, basophilic inclusion body disease (BIBD), neuronal intermediate filament inclusion disease (NIFID), and Alzheimer's disease with atypical cerebral atrophy. To infer more precisely the underlying pathologies in FTLD patients during life, differences in the clinical characteristics of pathological substrates have been explored, and recent studies support the possibility that the clinical pictures are not necessarily identical between the major pathological substrates. In the authors' autopsy series, early impairment of speech output was more frequent in Pick's disease, and early impairment of semantic memory and auditory comprehension was more frequent in sporadic FTLD-TDP. Asymmetric motor

Preface

disturbances during the course (e.g., pyramidal signs, parkinsonism, and contracture) were more frequently observed in sporadic FTLD-TDP. The most frequent first syndrome in Pick's disease was FTD followed by PA or speech apraxia, while that in sporadic FTLD-TDP was SD followed by FTD. Interestingly, the most frequent clinical syndrome in familial FTLD-TDP cases with progranulin gene mutations was reported to be FTD followed by PA, which differs from those in sporadic FTLD-TDP. In Chapter 2, we review recent findings regarding clinical symptoms, biochemical markers, and quantitative radiological findings revealed by MRI in two major pathological substrates of FTLD, FTLD-TDP and Pick's disease.

High rates of psychiatric difficulties and poor psychosocial and emotional adjustment occur in ABI. Chapter 3 briefly summarizes the prevalence and common presentations of emotional disturbances in ABI and reviews the current literature on treatment interventions. While there is general consensus on the utility of psychological treatment in ABI, the research remains less clear on the effectiveness and timing of different types of interventions for specific symptom presentations. The authors describe a theoretical framework based on the Stages of Change model that offers a way to conceptualize readiness for change and how specific strategies/approaches may be most beneficial to facilitate change in the ABI population.

Abusers of amphetamines and related drugs need to be treated effectively for any withdrawal symptoms (i.e. depression, anxiety, anhedonia, severe fatigue, and apathy) observed after drug abstinence in order to start pharmacotherapy for drug abuse. However, no effective treatment for amphetamine abuse has been established. The withdrawal symptoms are thought to be strongly associated with decreased motor activity and impaired sensorimotor accuracy observed in animal models. In Chapter 4, the authors will review some of the evidence for specific behavioral alterations in rodents chronically treated with amphetamines followed by a drug abstinence period in order to consider which treatment schedule (especially postdrug period) could lead to better understanding of the molecular basis of amphetamine withdrawal in humans.

The role of the Hypothalamus-Pituitary-Adrenocortical (HPA) system in depression and anxiety disorders has been investigated for decades. Depression is associated with elevated blood cortisol levels. The dexamethasone-suppressed corticotropin-releasing hormone (DEX/CRH) stimulation test is used to demonstrate the failure of negative feedback mechanisms in depression. Both cortisol- and ACTH-responsiveness to the DEX/CRH test are elevated during a depressed state. However, these responses tend to normalize after successful treatment and remission of disease. In Chapter 5, the authors also examined the

Sympathetic-Adrenal Medullary (SAM) system as another mediator of the stress response, and have found alterations in this system related to depression and anxiety disorders. Electric stimulation stress and Trier Social Stress Tests were employed in addition to salivary amylase assays as biological markers of stress. As a result, the SAM system was found to react to stressors related to these disorders alongside the HPA system. Although differences exist between the two systems, it is clear that both HPA and SAM systems are involved in depression and anxiety disorders.

Chapter 6 discusses the location, possible mechanisms, interaction and therapeutic possibilities and possible psychiatric influences of the serotonergic receptors 5-HT1A – 5-HT7. It concludes that, although some of the mechanisms of these receptors are widely accepted, their involvements in diseases and their roles in therapeutics are still elusive. Even with their locations, it was only recently perceived that 5-HT1A and 5-HT2A had different localizations in the brainstem, thus making functional correlations possible in due course. In order that a clearer picture or these receptors can emerge, further studies are much needed.

As discussed in Chapter 7, as the "baby boomers" head toward their later years, a social and economic crisis looms: the incidence of Alzheimer's disease is steadily increasing: in 2009, 5.3 million individuals had the diagnosis of Alzheimer's and the incidence of the disease is projected to increase up to 50% in the next 25 years. All the while the age bracket of 85 years and older is the largest growing population in the world. This means that resources of all kinds are being poured into a solution for this calamity: a neuropsychological breakthrough in this arena is not only looming, but necessary.

The study of the neurological system is defined as neurology and is an important branch of medicine. When talking about brain function, the fundamental relating topic is the mental status. The direct branch of medicine dealing with mental status is psychiatry. Hence, a close relationship between neurology and psychiatry can be expected, and this is the starting point for a new specific branch of medical science namely neuropsychiatry. In addition, several disorders in medicine have been shown to have their root cause in the genetic dimension. In Chapter 8, the author focuses on the complex interrelationship among neurology, psychiatry and genetics.

Many acknowledge this to be the year of "bioinformatics". Bioinformatics has several advantages for both physical and biological sciences. In medicine, a branch of biological science, bioinformatics can be applied in all fields including neuropsychiatry. The fundamental functions of bioinformatics, including structural and functional manipulation, can be useful for studies in neuropsychiatry. In Chapter 9, the author will discuss the usefulness of bioinformatics in the study of neuropsychiatry. Brief examples are also available in this specific short paper.

With the increasing anatomical resolution of the neuroimaging methods, clinicians are challenged nowadays, more than ever before, with the problem of detecting and interpreting statistically significant changes on neuroimages that are often distributed and involve simultaneously several structures of the human brain. In Chapter 10, the authors describe a general multivariate linear framework that analyses all the data simultaneously rather than segmented versions separately or feature-by-feature. This approach has been specially designed for extracting discriminative information from high dimensional data, dealing with the problem of small sample sizes, and it has been successfully applied in MR imaging analysis of the human brain. The multivariate linear framework is not restricted to any particular set of features and describes a simple and straightforward way of explaining multivariate changes of the whole brain on the original MR image domain, giving results that are statistically relevant to be further validated and interpreted by clinicians.

In: Handbook of Neuropsychiatry Research
Editor: Rebecca S. Davies, pp. 1-38

ISBN: 978-1-61668-138-8
© 2010 Nova Science Publishers, Inc.

Chapter 1

PROLACTINOMAS, PRL & WEIGHT GAIN

Erika C.O. Naliato
Serra dos Órgãos University Center – Teresópolis/RJ - Brazil

Abstract

Prolactinomas, tumors that produce prolactin (PRL), are one of the most frequent pituitary tumors and the main cause of pathological hyperprolactinemia. These tumors are more frequently diagnosed in women and usually affect the reproductive axis, leading to secondary hypogonadism. The diagnosis of prolactinoma is based on the presence of clinical features – such as menstrual irregularity, erectile dysfunction, galactorrhea, and infertility – and the detection of elevated serum PRL levels and confirmed by the existence of a pituitary tumor on magnetic resonance imaging.

As a consequence of secondary hypogonadism, hyperprolactinemia can affect body composition by reducing bone density. Moreover, data have suggested that lean mass reduction might not be the only way in which hyperprolactinemia may interfere with body composition. Clinical studies have reported that patients with prolactinoma may present with weight gain, indicating that PRL could also alter body fat content. In obese women without prolactinoma, PRL secretion is enhanced in proportion to their body mass index and particularly associated with the size of visceral fat, considered more metabolically active than subcutaneous fat. A few studies have also concluded that normalization of PRL levels in patients with prolactinoma has beneficial effects on body fat distribution. The presence of four PRL receptor (PRLR) isoforms in the human abdominal adipose tissue reinforces the potential role of PRL on fat tissue metabolism and the expression of PRLR has been reported to influence adipocyte differentiation and fat tissue development. Additionally, PRL might interfere with adipose tissue metabolism in an indirect form through the regulation of affinity and concentration of the insulin receptor. Studies of seasonally obese animals have brought up another mechanism for the increase in adipose tissue content in subjects with hyperprolactinemia. In these animals, increased PRL levels lead to hyperphagia and consequent weight gain. PRL has also been reported to interfere with body weight control through the regulation of leptin and adiponectin synthesis and secretion. Interestingly, the prolactin-leptin interaction is reciprocal, since other studies have demonstrated that leptin is capable of inducing PRL secretion.

However, in studying the effects of hyperprolactinemia on body composition, the role of type D2 dopamine receptors (D2R) must be taken into account. It is well known that dopamine exerts the main inhibitory control of PRL secretion, which provides the basis for dopamine agonist treatment in patients with prolactinoma. Furthermore, the D2R gene has also been reported to play a major role in the regulation of appetite, weight, and energy expenditure. Consequently, some studies have suggested that hyperprolactinemia *per se* is not a cause of obesity but only reflects the reduction in D2R activity, which is supposedly the real source of metabolic dysfunction and weight gain in patients with prolactinoma.

Abbreviations

AGRP:	Agouti-related peptide
CCAAT:	Cytidine-cytidine-adenosine-adenosine-thymidine
C/EBP:	Cytidine-cytidine-adenosine-adenosine-thymidine enhancer-binding-protein(s)
D2R:	Dopamine receptor(s) – type D2
FAS:	Fatty acid synthase
GALP:	Galanin-like peptide
IRS-1:	Insulin receptor substrate-1
JAK:	Janus kinase(s)
MAPK:	Mitogen-activated protein kinase
mRNA:	Messenger ribonucleic acid
PDK:	Pyruvate dehydrogenase kinase(s)
PPAR gamma:	Peroxisome proliferator-activated receptor gamma
PRL:	Prolactin
PRLR:	Prolactin receptor(s)
STAT:	Signal transducer and activator of transcription
TNF:	Tumor necrosis factor
UCP1:	Uncoupling protein or thermogenin

Introduction

Prolactin (PRL) is a peptide hormone (199 amino acids) produced essentially in the anterior pituitary gland by the lactotrophs, which correspond to 40% of the hormone-producing cells in this portion of the gland [1]-[4]. PRL is also synthesized and secreted in a lesser scale in extrapituitary sites such as brain, decidua, myometrium, mammary and lachrymal glands, lymphocytes, lymphoid cells of the bone marrow, thymus, spleen, and fibroblasts [3]. The primary structure of PRL is similar to that of growth hormone and its main function consists in inducing milk secretion in mammals [2], [5]. However, it is more than likely that PRL has other biological functions besides the induction of lactation, considering that the secretion of this hormone is also observed in non-mammal vertebrates such as fishes, amphibians, and birds [3]. In fact, additional actions of PRL have been identified in different vertebrate species. In mammals, disturbances of PRL activity have been linked to infertility and defective preimplantation embryonic development [6]. In fishes, it has been demonstrated that PRL can influence osmoregulation [7]. PRL has also been shown to induce growth and cellular proliferation [8]-[11]. Furthermore, PRL seems to be involved in the parental behavior of fishes, birds and mammals [3].

The actions of PRL depend on its binding to a specific membrane receptor denominated the PRL receptor (PRLR) [3], [12]. It is only during the neonatal period that PRL becomes the major ligand to PRLR, since placental lactogen remains the most important activator of PRLR throughout gestation [13]-[16]. Although different species have been reported to share part of the structure of the PRL molecule, *in vitro* studies have shown that non-human PRL is not as potent as the corresponding human molecule in stimulating human PRLR, which implies the establishment of a species-specific response in PRLR activation [17].

PRLR is a member of the class 1 cytokine receptor superfamily and presents three domains: extracellular, which contains the ligand-binding interface, transmembrane, and intracellular [3]. Cytokine receptors do not present enzymatic activity and, in order to transmit signals inside the cells, must work together with one or more Janus kinases (JAK), activating the JAK/STAT (Signal transducer and activator of transcription) MAPK (Mitogen-activated protein kinase) pathway [3], [18]-[21]. The activation of this pathway leads to a cascade of events that initiates specific patterns of gene transcription depending on the cell type. Some authors have suggested that PRL's actions may as well depend on the type of PRLR that is stimulated. To date four isoforms of PRLR have been identified: long, intermediate, short 1a and short 1b. The available data indicate that the long form PRLR is the one more likely to be involved in the control of cell proliferation and the stimulation of tyrosine phosphorylase activity [21], [22].

PRLR are widely distributed throughout vertebrates. Central nervous system, pituitary, adrenal cortex, skin, sebaceous glands, bone, lung, heart, skeletal muscle, liver, pancreas (islet beta-cells), gastrointestinal tract, kidney, bladder, lymphoid tissue, and reproductive system express PRLR [3], [11]. Human fetuses express PRLR early in the first trimester of pregnancy in several tissues such as kidney, adrenal, lungs, duodenum, muscles, bone marrow, cartilages, and bones [23]. The broad distribution of PRLR throughout the human body favors the hypothesis that, besides inducing lactation and interfering with gonadal function, PRL may also have additional effects in humans.

In men and nonlactating women, PRL secretion is maintained predominantly in an inhibited status by dopamine, a neurotransmitter that belongs to the class of catecholamines [20]. Dopaminergic inhibition of PRL synthesis and secretion is mediated by type D2 dopamine receptors (D2R) located in the membrane of lactotrophs [20]. D2R belong to the family of G protein-coupled receptors and are characterized by a single polypeptide chain containing seven hydrophobic transmembrane domains [20], [24]. The activation of D2R results in inhibition of adenylyl cyclase activity, which reduces PRL gene expression and subsequently blocks hormonal production and release. Two dopaminergic systems regulate PRL synthesis and secretion: the tuberoinfundibular and the tuberohypophysial systems [20]. PRL itself has been reported to establish a feedback mechanism and influence the control of tuberoinfundibular dopaminergic activity [20], [25]. Interestingly, while normal serum PRL concentrations exert a positive feedback stimulus to dopamine synthesis, long-term hyperprolactinemia leads to a reduction in the dopaminergic tone and a further increase in PRL secretion [20].

Prolactinomas are pituitary adenomas that produce PRL. Approximately 40% of all functioning pituitary tumors secrete PRL and prolactinomas represent the main cause of pathological hyperprolactinemia [26], [27]. These essentially benign tumors may be divided according to their maximum dimensions: those below 1 cm are classified as microprolactinomas and those equal or above 1 cm, as macroprolactinomas [2].

Two hypotheses were put forward to explain the pathogenesis of prolactinomas: dopamine dysregulation and local somatic mutation [3]. It has been argued that specific environmental changes could predispose some individuals to the development of hyperprolactinemia and prolactinomas, especially through the disruption of the hypothalamic dopaminergic tone [28]. *Nunes et al.* (1980) [29] concluded that the exposure to an environment characterized by an absent, alcoholic or violent father during childhood conditioned some women to develop hyperprolactinemia. In addition, paternal deprivation has also been connected to the advent of prolactinomas [30].

The most important clinical features that characterize prolactinomas result from hyperprolactinemia itself or tumoral compression of the surrounding healthy pituitary tissue. One of the most frequent consequences of the elevation of PRL levels is secondary hypogonadism, since hyperprolactinemia inhibits the secretion of gonadotropin-releasing hormone [31]. This leads to oligomenorrhea or amenorrhea, which are very frequently reported by patients with prolactinomas [2], [27], [32]. Galactorrhea may be another consequence of the elevated PRL levels and affect both women and men [2], [27]. Another important feature of prolactinomas is the reduction of bone mass. Most studies associate the adverse effects of hyperprolactinemia on the bone tissue with the secondary hypogonadism [33]-[37]. Tumoral mass effects such as headaches, visual disturbances (especially temporal hemianopsia), and rhinorrhea are characteristic of larger tumors, usually macroprolactinomas [2].

Due to the occurrence of menstrual irregularity, women are more frequently diagnosed with prolactinomas then men and represent the major part of subjects who receive treatment for hyperprolactinemia [2], [38], [39]. Noteworthy, controversy still surrounds the issue of prolactinomas in men. Male patients with prolactinoma are often diagnosed after the development of tumoral mass effects [2], [27], [40]. Some authors have ascribed this to the fact that men have prolactinomas of larger dimensions and with more invasiveness potential [40], [41]. On the other hand, others have argued that men tend to relate clinical features of hypogonadism (erectile dysfunction and decreased libido) to other causes or minimize the importance of these findings until the appearance of tumoral mass effects [2], [38], [42]. Nevertheless, whether the higher frequency of tumoral mass effects in men is due to delayed diagnosis or more invasive tumoral forms remains a matter of debate.

Administration of dopamine agonists is currently the treatment of choice for prolactinomas [2], [3], [27], [38], [43]. These drugs act through the stimulation of the D2R located in the lactotroph membrane [44], [45]. They initially reduce PRL release and later suppress its production through the inhibition of gene transcription [46]. Dopamine agonist treatment also results in reduction of tumoral volume, since these drugs induce local necrosis, fibrosis, and a decrease in cellular size [47]. Dopamine agonist administration is able to normalize PRL levels and correct secondary hypogonadism in 70 to 95% of patients [32], [44], [48]-[52].

Besides bone loss, hyperprolactinemia has been linked to other disturbances of body composition and metabolism. *Berlanga et al.* (1997) [53] observed that, along with the JAK/STAT pathway, PRL's coupling with PRLR leads to the activation of IRS-1 (insulin receptor substrate-1) and 3-phosphatidylinositol kinase phosphorilation. The activation of this pathway could promote insulin-like effects. Additionally, PRL has been reported to directly stimulate insulin secretion and reduce the threshold for glucose-induced insulin release, actions that could contribute to the development of insulin resistance [54]-[60]. Either through direct effects on glucose metabolism or induction of weight gain, hyperprolactinemia could predispose patients with prolactinomas towards insulin resistance and obesity with consequent increase in cardiovascular risk. Since 1980, the involvement of PRL in the pathogenesis of obesity has been object of research. Women who develop overweight and obesity have been shown to have higher serum PRL levels than normal weight peers [28], [61]. On the other hand, weight gain is one of the clinical signs of hyperprolactinemia [29], [32], [62]-[65]. Moreover, there have been a few reports on the beneficial effects of disease control (i.e. PRL normalization) on body fat distribution in patients with prolactinoma [32], [63].

When not adequately treated, patients with prolactinoma may remain in hyperprolactinemia for long periods of time. If the causative relationship between PRL and weight gain is proven to be consistent, these patients can be at risk for the development of obesity and consequent increased cardiovascular risk. The present review will focus on data regarding the relationship between prolactinoma and obesity and analyze possible mechanisms through which PRL might induce weight gain in such patients. The influence of dopamine on both PRL secretion and body weight control will also be object of concern.

Prolactinomas and Weight Gain

PRL is one of the hormones responsible for the control of seasonal fat deposition in vertebrates. The infusion of PRL has been shown to promote appetite enhancement and weight gain [66]-[73].

Some authors have reported that patients with prolactinoma have an increased prevalence of overweight and obesity when compared with the general population and subjects with other types of pituitary adenomas [63], [64], [74], [75]. In addition, weight gain has been shown to be a frequent complaint of patients with hyperprolactinemia [29], [32], [63], [64], [74]. Some authors have reported a gender difference on body weight increase in hyperprolactinemia, since men with prolactinomas seem to be more affected than women [2], [32], [63]. In a cross-sectional study developed with male subjects with prolactinoma, newly-diagnosed patients with hyperprolactinemia presented higher body fat content than healthy controls and normoprolactinemic dopamine agonist-treated patients [65]. Moreover, the same study has demonstrated that patients with normal levels of PRL had a mean body fat content similar to the one obtained in the control group [65]. These results can be reinforced by data from a few reports on the beneficial effects of disease control on body fat distribution in patients with prolactinoma. Weight loss has been recorded in patients with prolactinoma whose PRL levels have been normalized [63], [64], [74].

Several mechanisms have been proposed in order to explain the hyperprolactinemia-induced weight gain: (1) stimulation of lipogenesis, (2) reduction of the dopaminergic tone, and (3) disruption of circadian neuroendocrine hypothalamic activities that regulate dopaminergic tone and consequently body composition [64].

Nevertheless, the association between hyperprolactinemia and body weight in subjects with prolactinoma has not been object of consensus. *Delgrange et al.* (1999) [76] reported that only a minority of their patients with prolactinoma (25%) complained of weight gain. Other authors have not succeeded in detecting weight variations after treatment with dopamine agonists [77]. Furthermore, although dopamine agonist treatment may result in weight loss in patients with prolactinoma, this reduction has been weakly correlated with a concomitant decrease in PRL levels in either men or women [64], [74], [78]. Therefore, some authors have argued that weight loss in patients with prolactinoma treated with dopamine agonists is likely due to adequate activation of the D2R rather than a reduction in PRL levels *per se* [64], [78].

Based on the above mentioned data, studies into the metabolic and body composition alterations induced by hyperprolactinemia are divided among those that ascribe these changes to direct effects of PRL and others that favor the role of dopamine dysregulation. The latter consider the elevation of PRL levels solely a reflex of hypothalamic dysfunction. In a hypothesis that could link both influences, normal levels of PRL could participate in a feedback mechanism, stimulating dopamine synthesis and release, while persistent hyperprolactinemia could alter this mechanism of control, resulting in a decreased dopaminergic tone and further consequences on appetite and adipose tissue metabolism [20].

Prolactin and Adipocytes

The study of null mutations of the PRLR have suggested that the essential physiological role of PRL is the control of mammary gland development, lactation, and reproduction, while other reported target tissues for the action of PRL are in fact modulated rather than strictly dependent on this hormone [79].

Since 1960, studies have been focusing on the potential influence of PRL on the metabolism of lipids. Initially, it has been demonstrated that, in birds, PRL administration resulted in an increased rate of fatty acid accumulation in the liver [80]. More recent data support these initial findings. Hyperprolactinemia elevates hepatic lipids and phospholipids [81]. Furthermore, PRLR expression has been detected in the liver of mice and this expression increases during pregnancy but decreases during lactation [82]. Some reports have indicated that PRLR expression in the liver is regulated by estrogen, progesterone, cortisol, and GH [83]-[86]. It should also be mentioned that the regulation of PRLR expression seems to vary among different tissues, which points to the existence of tissue-specific regulatory events [81], [85]. PRL itself is also an important regulator of PRLR expression [82], [84], [87].

More recently, studies have detected the expression of PRLR in the adipose tissue, which suggested the possibility of a direct influence of PRL on local adipocyte metabolism [12]. The expression of PRLR has been reported to influence adipocyte differentiation and fat tissue development [23], [88], [89]. This section will review the available data on the actions and interactions of PRL in the adipose tissue. The main data on PRL and the adipose tissue are summarized in Table 1.

Brown Adipose Tissue

Brown adipose tissue is typically found in mammals. It has thermogenic properties, which functionally distinguish it from the energy-storing white adipose tissue, and is characterized by the presence of the uncoupling protein (UCP1), also denominated thermogenin [79] [90]. At the end of fetal life, brown adipocytes differentiate based on the expression of a set of lipogenic enzymes resulting in the appearance of multilocular fat droplets [90]. Brown adipose tissue is found in defined but dispersed areas in the body and the functional capacity of this type of tissue decreases with age [90].

In 1998, *Symonds et al.* [85] identified the presence of PRLR in fetal brown adipose tissue of sheep. These authors successfully demonstrated that PRLR gene expression increased during the period of rapid adipose tissue deposition, which indicated that PRL might play a role in prenatal growth and maturation of brown adipose tissue.

Table 1. Prolactin and Adipose Tissue

Data	References
Expression of PRLR in white adipose tissue	[82]
Expression of PRLR in brown adipose tissue	[79] [85] [91]
PRL stimulates UCP1 expression (brown adipose tissue)	[91] [92] [93]
Expression of PRLR in human adipose tissue	[12]
PRL influences adipocyte differentiation	[23] [88] [89] [118] [119]
PRL influences acetyl-CoA carboxylase activity	[95]
PRL influences lipoprotein lipase activity	[12] [96] [97] [98] [99] [100]
PRL regulates concentration and affinity of the insulin receptor	[96] [105]
PRL regulates insulin secretion	[18] [54] [57] [100]
PRL modulates insulin function on the adipose tissue	[106] [107]
PRL has antiadipogenic effects	[116] [117]
PRL influences adipokines	[64] [79] [87] [88] [134] [135] [139] [140]
PRL is secreted by the adipocytes	[141]

PRLR: Prolactin receptors; UCP1: uncoupling protein (thermogenin)

These data have been corroborated by the demonstration that, in this type of adipose tissue, the expression of PRLR is associated with that of UCP1 and accompanies the process of cell differentiation [79], [91]. The observation that PRL activates STAT5 in brown adipocytes confirmed PRLR to be functional in these cells [79]. Moreover, the rate of postnatal loss of UCP1 from brown adipose tissue has been shown to parallel a decrease in the expression of PRLR [91]. Conversely, exogenous PRL administration has been reported to improve thermo-regulation and increase UCP1 in brown adipocytes of sheep [91]. The effect of PRL administration on UCP1 has been confirmed by *in vivo* studies [92] but UCP1 increase seems to be limited to the prenatal period, since the daily injections of PRL have not resulted in UCP1 enhancement in postnatal rats [93].

Metabolic Enzyme Activity

PRL has been shown to interfere with metabolic enzyme activity in the adipose tissue. It should be emphasized that the role of PRL in metabolic homeostasis seems to differ among species; for example, it appears to have gross metabolic effects in rats but not in mice [94]. In addition, reciprocal changes in lipogenesis involving mammary gland and adipose tissue during lactation have been ascribed to tissue-specific regulation of enzymatic activities by PRL [95].

Tissue-specific PRL regulation of activity and gene expression of acetyl-CoA carboxylase, an enzyme involved in the synthesis of fatty acids, has been studied in rats. The increased PRL levels presented during lactation have been shown to inhibit both enzymatic activity and gene transcription in the adipose tissue, but the inverse result has been observed in the mammary gland [95]. Similar results were obtained when the activity of lipoprotein lipase, an enzyme that provides non-esterified fatty acids and 2-monoacylglycerol for tissue utilization, was evaluated in adipose tissue and mammary glands of lactating rats and pigeons [96]-[98]. In human subcutaneous adipose tissue, PRL administration, either isolated or combined with cortisol, has been demonstrated to reduce the activity of lipoprotein lipase. The opposite effect has been obtained in adipocytes located at the mammary glands [12]. Treatment with the dopamine agonist bromocriptine reverses the original results of PRL administration [99]. These changes in lipoprotein lipase activity would be especially beneficial during lactation in order to switch the use of fatty acids to the mammary gland [12]. In severely obese women treated with bariatric surgery, a reduction of lipoprotein lipase expression has been observed one year after significant weight loss [100]. This reduction has been correlated with a decrease in both insulin and spontaneous 24-hour PRL secretion, which led the authors to consider hyperinsulinemia and hyperprolactinemia as potential inductors of severe obesity in these patients [100]. More data on PRL secretion in obese subjects will be provided ahead in the present review.

Indirect Influence

One of the similarities between subjects with obesity and hyperprolactinemia is that both groups present an increase in insulin secretion [54], [57], [58]. Before the expression of PRLR could be successfully demonstrated in adipocytes, studies used to suggest that PRL could influence adipose tissue metabolism in an indirect form, such as through the regulation of the affinity and concentration of insulin receptors [96], [101]. *In vitro*, PRL is able to decrease insulin-receptor binding and glucose uptake in adipocytes from pregnant women and also reduce glucose transport independently of insulin binding [102], [103]. In seasonally obese animals, the number of insulin receptors and the peak amplitude of lipogenic response to insulin have been attributed to the circadian hepatic response to PRL [104], [105]. In addition, PRL is also considered an important regulator of insulin secretion and pancreatic beta-cell proliferation in situations characterized by increased insulin demand and/or the presence of high levels of PRL [18].

PRL is likely to modulate insulin function on the adipose tissue through the activation of STAT5. Pyruvate dehydrogenase kinases (PDK) are enzymes that negatively regulate the activity of the pyruvate dehydrogenase complex in glucose metabolism [106]. Induction of PDK4 leads to decreased glucose oxidation [107]. Interestingly, it has been revealed that PRL can induce the expression of PDK4 in 3T3-L1 adipocytes [107]. Furthermore, a hormone responsive region has been identified in the murine PDK4 promoter and a STAT5 binding site has been characterized in this region [107]. This binding site has been shown to mediate the PRL effects on PDK4 expression [107].

Adipocytes and preadipocytes have been reported to express androgen and estrogen receptors [108], [109]. Data have suggested that gonadal steroids are able to induce coordinate modifications to food intake, metabolism, storage, and expenditure of metabolic fuels [108], [110]-[113]. Likewise, estrogen and androgen deficiencies have been revealed to facilitate body fat increase while bioavailable testosterone levels have been shown to predict fat deposition in subcutaneous adipose tissue [114], [115]. Since PRL is able to inhibit the synthesis of gonadal steroids, this is another indirect mechanism through which this hormone could influence body weight.

Adipocyte Differentiation

In mice, PRLR expression has been detected in the adipose tissue (in both adipocytes and stromal fraction) and data have indicated that this expression increases during lactation [82]. *Ling et al.* (2003) [12] demonstrated the expression of the four PRLR isoforms currently known in human white adipose tissue and suggested that PRL may directly influence adipose tissue development in humans. This study reinforced the results of others that identified both adipogenic and antiadipogenic effects of PRL in adipocytes [87], [99], [116], [117].

The expression of PRLR has been reported to increase during adipocyte differentiation. *McAveney et al.* (1996) [118] studied the expression of PRLR in bone marrow stromal cells. The bone marrow stromal compartment includes fibroblasts, endothelial cells, macrophages, osteoblasts and adipocytes; these cells are known to express PRLR during adipocyte differentiation [118]. The authors verified that the expression of PRLR paralleled that of the lipoprotein lipase gene in the 3T3-L1 preadipocyte cell line during adipocyte differentiation. This finding suggested that PRL and its receptor might play a role in differentiation and metabolism of preadipocytes and adipocytes [118]. These data were supported by the observation that the lipoprotein lipase gene was expressed early in fat cell differentiation and its promoter region contained several elements to which STAT factors could bind and mediate PRL stimulation of lipoprotein lipase gene transcription [118].

NIH-3T3 cells are a multipotential mesenchymal stem cell line that does not readily differentiate into adipocytes [119]. Nevertheless, adipogenic differentiation occurs when transcription factors such as cytidine-cytidine-adenosine-adenosine-thymidine (CCAAT) enhancer-binding-proteins (C/EBP) and peroxisome proliferator-activated receptor gamma (PPAR gamma) are expressed [120], [121]. C/EBP and PPAR gamma have in fact been considered potential regulators of adipocyte differentiation [119]. However, the process seems to be complex, since it has been observed that hormones can up-regulate the expression of C/EBP and PPAR gamma and finally trigger the conversion of NIH-3T3 cells into adipocytes. It has been demonstrated that PRL is among the hormones able to enhance C/EBP and PPAR gamma gene expression and increase the adipogenic conversion of NIH-3T3 cells [119].

Studies of PRLR knockout (gene disrupted) mice have reinforced the influence of PRL in the development of the adipose tissue. Although preadipocytes from these mice have presented normal rates of proliferation and differentiation *in vitro*, indicating the absence of intrinsic cellular modification, PRLR knockout mice have impaired development of internal and subcutaneous adipose tissue due to a decreased number of adipocytes without evidence of reduction in cell volume [88], [89]. This disruption in adipose tissue development could not be explained by a decrease in food intake, since no change was noted during the *in vivo* phase of the study [89]. The authors indicated that the impaired development of the adipose tissue could be ascribed to the absence of PRL stimulation.

Antiadipogenic Effects

Lactogens have been reported to induce lipolysis during pregnancy and lactation [116]. However, some studies have failed in demonstrating the influence of PRL on lipolysis [122], [123].

On the other hand, considering that PRL is a potent activator of STAT5 capable of producing different effects on lipid metabolism depending on the tissue that it stimulates, some authors have suggested that, besides promoting adipogenesis, PRL would also be able to induce antiadipogenic effects. *Hogan & Stephens* (2005) [117] evaluated the influence of PRL on the regulation of fatty acid synthase (FAS) expression. FAS is a key enzyme in *de novo* lipogenesis [124]. These authors succeeded in demonstrating that PRL treatment of 3T3-L1 adipocytes resulted in a decrease in FAS mRNA and protein. The study has also indicated the presence of a region within the FAS promoter that contained a PRL-responsive STAT5 binding site [117].

PRL Influence on Adipokines

PRL has been revealed to interfere with leptin secretion. Leptin is an adipocyte-derived hormone with a key importance on body weight control [79], [125]-[127]. It functions as the afferent signal in a negative feedback loop regulating body weight and appetite [128]-[131]. Leptin has also been suggested to act as a signal triggering puberty and linking nutrition to reproductive function, which has been evidenced by its ability to induce LH surges and accelerate reproduction in mice [132], [133]. On the other hand, some reports have indicated the existence of a reciprocal influence of gonadal steroids on leptin with a stimulative effect of estrogens and a suppressive one of androgens [64]. Hyperprolactinemic rodents have been shown to exhibit enhanced serum leptin levels and PRL administration, to increase serum leptin concentrations and leptin messenger RNA levels in rat white adipose tissue [134]. Mice with PRLR knockout present a significant decrease in leptin levels and fat mass content [88]. However, starvation has been demonstrated to reduce leptin levels despite the presence of hyperprolactinemia, which argues against a major role of PRL in the control of leptin secretion in this setting [134]. In agreement with this data, *Gualillo et al.* (1999) [134] found out that, in rats treated with dopamine agonists, PRL levels below the physiological range were not associated with changes in leptin secretion. The interaction between PRL and leptin seems to be different in lactating women, in whom an inverse relationship between leptin and PRL levels has been reported [135]. To date no correlation between leptin and PRL levels has been detected in men or women with prolactinoma [64].

The regulation of leptin secretion by PRL has been argued to involve a direct stimulation of PRLR located in the adipocytes with consequent activation of the JAK/STAT pathway [79] [87]. In addition, PRL control of leptin secretion in brown adipocytes has been ascribed to a concomitant activation of the insulin signaling pathway while in white adipocytes the dependency on insulin pathway co-activation has not been reported [79], [88], [134], [136]. An indirect mechanism could also be responsible for the regulation and would be based on the induction of serum factors as well as proinflammatory cytokines such as tumor necrosis factor (TNF) alpha or interleukin-1 by PRL [134].

Adiponectin has been referred as another target for PRL influence in the adipose tissue. Adiponectin has been described as an adipokine with anti-inflammatory properties [137], [138]. Its levels are decreased in obesity and insulin resistance [138]. PRL has been reported to suppress adiponectin secretion and influence the expression of adiponectin receptors in human adipocytes [139], [140].

Local Prolactin Secretion by the Adipocytes

In a recent study, the human adipocyte cell line named LS14 was shown to produce and release PRL, which was recognized as an important adipokine [141]. According to the authors' estimative, PRL production by each adipocyte is four to five orders of magnitude lower than that from the pituitary lactotroph and the release is lower in subcutaneous than in visceral adipocytes [141]. The authors speculated that the adipose tissue could be one of the sources of the elevated circulating PRL levels found in individuals with extreme obesity. As opposed to what is observed in the case of pituitary secretion, PRL release from differentiated adipocytes was negatively influenced by insulin in this study [141].

Prolactin and Appetite

Studies of seasonally obese animals have brought up another mechanism for weight gain in hyperprolactinemia [142], [143]. It has been speculated that PRL could influence appetite, contributing to the development of hyperphagia and consequent weight gain. However, studies into the effects of PRL administration on food intake have produced conflicting results.

In rats, PRL administration has been verified to result in increased food intake [68], [70]-[72], [144]-[146]. Moreover, the response to PRL has been suggested to be sex-specific, since only females presented an enhancement in appetite [144], [145]. Nonetheless, the hyperphagic effect of PRL has been shown not to be dependent on the presence of ovarian hormones [70], [71]. *Heil* (1999) [145] investigated the roles of activational and organizational actions of gonadal hormones on the sex differences observed during a study into feeding responses to PRL. She concluded that organizational effects (i.e. actions that take place during a limited time period, usually perinatally) were responsible for the sex-specific response to PRL.

Some reports have indicated that the effects of PRL on food intake were centrally mediated and the response dependent on the hypothalamic site into which PRL was infused [70], [72], [147]-[149]. In addition, PRL effects on appetite also seem to differ among species [150].

Appetite enhancement induced by PRL is probably mediated by the activation of PRLR, since these receptors have been detected in several regions of the brain and the administration of anti-PRL antibodies results in marked reduction of hyperphagia [72], [151], [152]. Nevertheless, it has been suggested that PRL could also activate other peptide receptors in a cross-talk fashion in order to induce hyperphagia [71].

Hyperprolactinemia has been implicated in the weight gain observed during treatment with antipsychotic and antidepressant drugs [110], [153], [154]. It has been hypothesized that elevated PRL levels might stimulate appetite by changing the estrogen-to-testosterone ratio and their consequent modulation of satiety-related hypothalamic neurons [113], [155]-[157].

When centrally infused, PRL antagonizes the leptin-induced decrease in food intake and body weight, creating a leptin-resistance status [130], [148]. Furthermore, PRL-induced leptin-resistance is accompanied by attenuation of the induction of transcription factor Fos and the phosphorilation of STAT3 [148].

Neuropetide-Y is a neurotransmitter expressed in the hypothalamic nuclei that contributes to the regulation of food intake and body weight [127], [129], [158], [159]. Evidence has implicated neuropeptide-Y in the response to leptin and other nutritional signals [128]. Neuropeptide-Y has also been pointed out as a mediator of PRL-induced appetite enhancement, since intracerebroventricular administration of PRL at doses shown to induce hyperphagia has been referred to increase the number of neuropeptide-Y receptors in the infundibular region in ring doves [159].

Agouti-related peptide (AGRP) is an endogenous melanocortin receptor antagonist that confers stimulation of appetite [127], [128]. AGRP has been indicated to play a role in response to absent or low leptin levels [129]. *Strader & Buntin* (2003) [160] reported that intracerebroventricular administration of PRL increases the number of AGRP neurons in the hypothalamus of doves and suggested that the orexigenic effects of PRL could be mediated in part by changes in AGRP activity.

Both galanin and galanin-like peptide (GALP) have been implicated in the regulation of food intake. Galanin is a neuropeptide that is largely distributed among the central and peripheral nervous systems. It is very abundant in the hypothalamus where it serves in the regulation of the anterior pituitary hormones [161], [162]. This neuropeptide is located within the GH and PRL secretory granules and the over-expression of galanin in the somatomammotroph cell lineage has been associated with increased secretion of GH and PRL as well as the development of pituitary hyperplasia and adenomas [161], [162]. Galanin has been indicated as a possible mediator of estrogen effects on the anterior pituitary, including tumorigenesis, and as the main paracrine/autocrine regulator of PRL synthesis and secretion [162]. So far three centrally expressed galanin receptors and one galanin-like receptor have been identified [127]. GALP is another neuropetide that plays an important role in the regulation of appetite, energy balance and reproduction [163]. It is produced in the hypothalamic arcuate nucleus, an area that also contains a population of dopaminergic neurons that suppress PRL production from the anterior pituitary [163]. *Kageyama et al.* (2008) [163] demonstrated that the GALP-containing neurons innervate the dopaminergic ones. These authors speculated that PRL could act as a mediator in the feeding regulation established by GALP.

Interestingly, although studies have identified an increase in appetite induced by PRL administration, not all of them have succeeded in detecting repercussions on body weight [70], [71], [144], [145]. Some hypotheses have been proposed in order to explain the absence of weight gain despite the induction of hyperphagia after PRL infusion: (1) the use of rather small sample sizes in the studies, (2) the possibility that weight gain might result from a peripheral rather than a central action of PRL, since the studies used centrally administrated PRL, and (3) the observation that centrally infused PRL increases dopamine release in the nucleus accumbens, a site that has been associated with enhanced locomotor activity, which could compensate the increase in food intake [71], [164], [165].

Prolactin Secretion in Obesity

Data from the literature support the influence of PRL secretion on body weight control. Elevation of PRL levels has been demonstrated in situations characterized by rapid weight gain [28]. In addition, spontaneous secretion of PRL has been shown to be augmented in obese subjects in proportion to their body mass index [61], [154], [166]. In a study developed by *Baptista et al.* (2001) [154], PRL levels were positively correlated with body mass index and waist-to-

Prolactinomas, PRL & Weight Gain

hip ratio in men, while only a trend towards significance was detected in the female subgroup. Furthermore, *Kok et al.* (2004) [61] observed that PRL release was particularly associated with the size of visceral fat mass. On the other hand, dopamine agonist administration is able to prevent antidepressant-induced food intake enhancement and weight gain, which seems to favor the hypothesis of PRL-induced weight gain in these subjects [167], [168]. Amantadine, a substance that increases dopamine and serotonin overflow in the nucleus accumbens and the lateral hypothalamus, has been beneficial in reversing both hyperprolactinemia and body weight gain in patients treated with typical antipsychotic drugs [169]. More information on weight gain induced by antipsychotic drugs will be provided in the next section.

In normoprolactinemic humans, the circadian rhythm, but not the absolute levels of PRL, have been claimed to be critical to the control of body fat deposition [64]. Moreover, the delay in the nocturnal rise of PRL observed in obese subjects can be reversed by weight loss [170].

Dynamic tests such as PRL response to hypoglycemia, TRH, and arginine stimulation have been employed in the evaluation of PRL secretion in obesity. Two different patterns of PRL response to hypoglycemia may be obtained in obese patients: an absent response and a normal one [171]-[174]. It has been argued that the absent response is in fact a result of a hypothalamic dysfunction rather than a cause of obesity because this kind of defective reaction persists even after significant weight loss and the achievement of normal weight [172], [175], [176]. Interestingly, PRL response to hypoglycemia has been inversely associated with insulin resistance, suggesting that hyperinsulinemia may be linked to hypothalamic dysfunction as well [174]. Additionally, PRL response to hypoglycemia has been shown to be negatively associated with upper body segment obesity, which contributes to the development of insulin resistance [177].

Nonetheless, some authors have stated that anterior pituitary reserves are present in obese subjects without PRL response to hypoglycemia, since normal PRL response to TRH has been obtained in these individuals [73], [176]. However, this concept is not unanimous, considering that other studies have obtained subnormal PRL responses to TRH and indicated the presence of a broader hypothalamic dysfunction [171], [178].

Serotonin is known to stimulate PRL release [178]. It has been suggested that a central deficiency of serotonin is in some cases responsible for the impaired PRL response to secretagogues [73], [179], [180]. Furthermore, treatment with fenfluramine, a serotoninergic agent that acts centrally, has been reported to restore PRL responses to TRH and arginine stimulation [181], [182]. In subjects with normal weight, naloxone, an opiate receptor antagonist, has been referred to block the fenfluramine-induced increase in PRL levels [179]. However, in the same study, this drug failed to produce the same effects in obese individuals. These data favor the existence of a physiological relationship between serotoninergic and opiodergic systems in the control of PRL secretion, although this interaction seems not to be adequately maintained in obese subjects [179]. Nevertheless, a low PRL response to 5-hydroxytryptophan, an index of low hypothalamic serotoninergic tone, has not been able to predict weight increase in rodents [183].

On the other hand, it is possible that the increased PRL levels found in obese subjects are not a result of disruption of dopaminergic or serotoninergic pathways but in fact a consequence of obesity. Elevation of leptin levels have been reported in obesity and this adipokine has been demonstrated to directly stimulate PRL secretion and also enhance steroid-induced PRL release [61], [132], [184]. In addition, anti-leptin serum administration results in a delayed onset of PRL surges [184]. However, no association between postpartum leptin and PRL levels has been confirmed in overweight and obese women [133], [185].

Besides hyperprolactinemia, studies have demonstrated the existence of various hormonal abnormalities in obesity: (1) hyperestrogenemia and hypogonadotropic hypogonadism in men, (2) reduction of SHBG levels in both sexes, (3) elevated free estradiol and testosterone in women, (4) polycystic ovary syndrome-like gonadotropin and gonadal steroids abnormalities in women, (5) hyperinsulinemia in both sexes, (6) blunted stimulability of PRL, GH, and vasopressin in both sexes, and (7) elevated basal levels as opposed to blunted stimulability and supressibility of beta-endorphin in both sexes. *Zumoff & Strain* (1994) [186] claimed that the reversibility of nearly all hormonal abnormalities of obesity, with the exception of hyperendorphinemia, by weight loss suggests that none of those is causative of obesity.

Disruption to the Dopamine Control Pathway and Weight Gain

Some authors have stated that environmental changes might lead to the activation of a number of neuroendocrine responses that result in increased PRL secretion and obesity [28], [62], [167], [176]. Since dopamine is the main inhibitor of PRL secretion, disruption to the central dopaminergic pathways could be responsible for the altered PRL secretion detected in obesity [20], [28], [61], [73], [176].

In seasonally obese animals, reduced dopaminergic tone has been implicated in driving noradrenaline and neuropeptide Y-mediated neurotransmissions towards the induction of weight gain at the appropriate time of the year [187]. Dopaminergic pathways have been associated with the regulation of appetite and the etiology of addictive-compulsive behavior with consequences on food ingestion and weight gain [188]-[191]. The disruption to the dopaminergic tone has also been pointed out as the cause of weight gain in patients with prolactinoma [64], [75], [78]. And even in normoprolactinemic subjects, dopamine agonist administration has been linked with appetite reduction [188]. It should be mentioned that dopamine also plays a role in the control of opioid secretion and endogenous opioids have been shown to be increased in obesity [190], [192].

To date variants of the D2R have been found to associate with alcoholism, drug dependency, obesity, smoking, pathological gambling, attention-deficit-hyperactivity disorder, as well as other related compulsive behaviors [155], [190], [191]. Moreover, the presence of a variation of the D2R named Taq A1 has been linked with increases in body mass index [193]. Among the polymorphisms of D2R, haplotype 4 has been indicated to be in linkage disequilibrium with allelic variants which play a major role in appetite, obesity and height [194]. Therefore, a decrease in D2R number or activity could result in disruption to the inhibitory dopaminergic control of PRL secretion and concomitantly increase appetite and induce weight gain through independent mechanisms [75], [155], [187].

Studies into weight gain induced by atypical antipsychotics favor the role of dopamine tone disruption in the pathogenesis of obesity. Until the introduction of the first atypical antipsychotic, clozapine, hyperprolactinemia was considered an inevitable consequence of the treatment with any antipsychotic drug [195]. However, the current use of more modern antipsychotics is no longer associated with significant increases in PRL secretion [195]. These newer agents seem to spare dopamine blockade within the tuberoinfundibular tract, a dopamine pathway that also controls PRL secretion [195]. Nevertheless, increased appetite and body weight gain are still observed during the administration of these atypical antipsychotic drugs [196]-[198]. Most of these agents interact with serotonin, dopamine, histamine, and adrenergic receptors and affect the regulation of hypothalamus-pituitary-adrenal and -gonadal axes [197]. Receptor activation, blockade and disruption to adrenal and gonadal hormone production have been proposed as mechanisms through which antipsychotics could induce increased food intake and body weight gain [197]. Consequently, the effects of these drugs on body fat deposition seem to be dissociated from their ability to elevate PRL levels [198]. These data argue against the importance of PRL in the pathogenesis of antipsychotic-induced obesity.

Other data support the preponderant role of dopamine over PRL in the pathogenesis of obesity. The concomitant use of amantadine has been demonstrated to prevent sulpiride-induced weight gain [199]. Nevertheless, the effects of amantadine on obesity prevention have been shown to be independent of the control of sulpiride-induced hyperprolactinemia, since PRL levels remain elevated during amantadine administration [199]. Similar results were obtained when sulpiride was associated with tamoxifen [168]. In addition, amantadine has also been able to induce weight reduction in patients treated with olanzapine, an antipsychotic drug referred to have small effects on PRL levels [200].

Dopamine Agonists

It has been suggested that dopamine agonists can regulate body weight, glucose, lipids and protein metabolism despite the absence of hyperprolactinemia [69], [143], [201]. Fat mass reduction, lean mass increase and improvement in glucose and lipid metabolism have been successfully induced by dopamine agonist treatment of normoprolactinemic subjects [69], [202]-[206].

Dopamine agonist treatment is capable of inhibiting lipogenesis. The following mechanisms have been implicated in the regulation of lipogenesis by dopamine agonists: (1) a blockage of PRL stimulation on insulin-induced hepatic lipogenesis, (2) a PRL-independent reduction in insulin secretion, and (3) a hypothalamic effect of a reduction of fatty acids [104], [142], [143], [207], [208]. Dopamine agonist administration promotes energy expenditure, by shifting the energy balance from lipids synthesis towards an increase in protein turnover, modulates circadian activities in the hypothalamus and modifies the ratio of dopamine-to-noradrenaline activity in the hypothalamic and peripheral centers [104], [143], [201], [204], [206]. Data has also indicated that dopamine agonists may regulate leptin secretion [64].

In rats and mice, treatment with the dopamine agonist bromocriptine results in a decrease in body fat, glucose, cholesterol, and triglycerides levels [101], [203], [209]. Dopamine agonist treatment is also able to induce appetite reduction [188], [206]. In women with prolactinoma, regular treatment with dopamine agonists has been correlated with lower body fat content independently of PRL levels [78].

Based on such data, it is reasonable to consider the enhanced PRL levels obtained in situations characterized by disruption to the dopaminergic pathways and reduction in D2R activity, such as prolactinomas, a mere marker of abnormal hypothalamic dopaminergic control without considering them determinants of weight gain *per se* [61], [64], [75], [78].

Conclusion

The increased prevalence of overweight and obesity detected in patients with prolactinoma calls the attention for the existence of a causative relationship between hyperprolactinemia and the development of weight gain and obesity in subjects with prolactinomas. The presence of PRLR in the adipocytes suggests a direct mechanism through which PRL could interfere with the adipose tissue metabolism. In fact, the demonstration of the influence of PRL on adipocyte differentiation and metabolic enzyme activity in the adipose tissue, the interaction between PRL and insulin, and the relationship between PRL and adipokines such as leptin and adiponectin favor this hypothesis. In addition to the peripheral effects, PRL could act centrally through the induction of hyperphagia and lead to an increase in food intake and consequent weight gain. Evidence of the enhancement in PRL secretion in prolactinomas and other situations characterized by weight gain and the beneficial effects of disease control on body fat distribution in patients with prolactinoma contributes to the notion that PRL is involved in the pathogenesis of obesity in these patients.

However, the following data argue against a pivotal role of hyperprolactinemia on weight gain in patients with prolactinoma. First, conflicting clinical data is available on the association between PRL levels and weight gain in patients with prolactinoma. Moreover, variable weight loss response to dopamine agonist treatment has been described in these patients and only a weak correlation between PRL levels and weight loss has been detected during treatment with these agents. In addition, the consequence of the orexigenic effect of PRL on body fat deposition can be disputed based on the absence of weight gain in face of PRL-induced hyperphagia. An important role of dopamine and D2R on the process of weight gain in patients with prolactinoma can be assumed based on the identification of variants of the D2R in obese subjects and the demonstration that dopaminergic, serotoninergic and opiodergic pathways could independently influence PRL secretion and weight regulation. These arguments can be reinforced by the observation of a PRL-independent increase in appetite and body weight with the administration of atypical antipsychotic drugs. Finally, the reversibility of nearly all hormonal abnormalities of obesity with the exception of hyperendorphinemia leads to the conclusion that hyperprolactinemia is not causative of obesity. These data suggest that hyperprolactinemia only reflects the reduction in D2R activity as well as a disruption of the serotoninergic and opiodergic pathways, which are supposedly the real sources of metabolic dysfunction and weight gain in patients with prolactinoma.

Although the causative relationship between PRL and weight gain has not been unequivocally proven to be consistent, patients with prolactinoma do present a disruption to the dopaminergic tone and, based on the data available at the moment, could be actually at risk for the development of obesity and consequent increased cardiovascular risk. Fortunately, regular dopamine agonist treatment is able to normalize PRL levels and regulate D2R activity.

References

[1] Li C. H., Dixon J. S., Schmidt K. D., Pankov Y. A., and Lo T. B. Amino and carboxi-terminal sequences of ovine lactogenic hormone. *Nature*,1969, 222:1268-1269.

[2] Faglia G. Prolactinomas and hyperprolactinemic syndrome. In: Leslie Degroot, J. Larry Jameson, ed. *Endocrinology*. Philadelphia, USA: W. B. Saunders Company; 2001:329-342.

[3] Bole-Feysot C., Goffin V., Edery M., Binart N., Kelly P. Prolactin (PRL) and its receptor: Actions, signal transduction pathways and phenotypes observed in PRL receptor knockout mice. *Endocr. Rev.*, 1998, 19:225-268.

[4] Asa S. L., Kovacs K., Laszlo F. A., Domokos I., Ezrin C. Human fetal adenohypophysis: Histologic and immunocytochemical analysis. *Neuroendocrinology*, 1986, 43:308-316.

[5] Nicoll C. S., Mayer G. L., Russell S. M. Structural features of prolactins and growth hormones that can be related to their biological properties. *Endocr. Rev.*, 1986, 7:169-203.

[6] Ormandy C. J., Camus A., Barra J. et al. Null mutation of the prolactin receptor gene produces multiple reproductive defects in the mouse. *Genes Dev.*, 1997, 11:167-178.

[7] Richardson B. P. Evidence for a physiological role of prolactin in osmoregulation in the rat after its inhibition by 2-bromoergokryptine. *BrJ Pharmacol.*, 1973, 47:623P-624P.

[8] Ryníková A., Koppel J., Kuchár S., Cikos S., Mozes S. Effects of ovine prolactin in infant rats. *Exp Clin Endocrinol.*, 1988, 92:241-244.

[9] Pérez-Villamil B., Bordiú E., Puente-Cueva M. Involvement of physiological prolactin levels in growth and prolactin receptor content of prostate glands and testes in developing male rats. *J Endocrinol.*, 1992, 132:449-459.

Prolactinomas, PRL & Weight Gain 23

[10] Piccoletti R., Maroni P., Bendinelli P., Bernelli-Zazzera A. Rapid stimulation of mitogen-activated protein kinase of rat liver by prolactin. *Biochem J.*, 1994, 303:429-433.

[11] Craven A. J., Ormandy C. J., Robertson F. G. et al. Prolactin signaling influences the timing mechanism of the hair follicle: Analysis of hair growth cycles in prolactin receptor knockout mice. *Endocrinology*, 2001, 142:2533-2539.

[12] Ling C., Svensson L., Odén B. et al. Identification of functional prolactin (PRL) receptor gene expression: PRL inhibits lipoprotein lipase activity in human white adipose tissue. *J. Clin. Endocrinol. Metab.*, 2003, 88:1804-1808.

[13] Brelje T. C., Scharp D. W., Lacy P. E. et al. Effect of homologous placental lactogens, prolactins, and growth hormones on islet B-cell division and insulin secretion in rat, mouse, and human islets: Implication for placental lactogen regulation of islet function during pregnancy. *Endocrinology*, 1993, 132:879-887.

[14] Hill D. J., Freemark M., Strain A. J., Handwerger S., Milner R. D. Placental lactogen and growth hormone receptors in human fetal tissues: Relationship to fetal plasma human placental lactogen concentrations and fetal growth. *J. Clin. Endocrinol. Metab.*, 1988, 66:1283-1290.

[15] De Zegher F., Devlieger H., Veldhuis J. D. Properties of growth hormone and prolactin hypersecretion by the human infant on the day of birth. *J. Clin. Endocrinol. Metab.*, 1993, 76:1177-1181.

[16] Debieve F., Beerlandt S., Hubinont C. Thomas K., Gonadotropins, prolactin, inhibin A, inhibin B, and activin A in human fetal serum from midpregnancy and term pregnancy. *J. Clin. Endocrinol. Metab.*, 2000, 85:270-274.

[17] Utama F. E., Tran T. H., Ryder A., LeBaron M. J., Parlow A. F., Hallgeir R. Insensitivity of human prolactin receptors to nonhuman prolactins: Relevance for experimental modeling of prolactin receptor-expressing human cells. *Endocrinology*, 2009, 150:1782-1790.

[18] Sorenson R. L., Stout L. E. Prolactin receptors and JAK2 in islets of Langerhans: An immunohistochemical analysis. *Endocrinology*, 1995, 136:4092-4098.

[19] Pezet A., Favre H., Kelly P. A., Edery M. Inhibition and restoration of prolactin signal transduction by suppressors of cytokine signaling. *J. Biol. Chem.*, 1999, 274:24497-24502.

[20] Ben-Jonathan N., Hnasko R. Dopamine as a prolactin (PRL) inhibitor. *Endocr. Rev.*, 2001, 22:724-763.

[21] Schuler L. A., Nagel R. J., Gao J., Horseman N. D., Kessler M. A. Prolactin receptor heterogeneity in bovine fetal and maternal tissues. *Endocrinology*, 1997, 138:3187-3194.

[22] Goffin V., Kelly P. A. Prolactin and growth hormone receptors. *Clin Endocrinol (Oxf.)*, 1996, 45:247-255.

[23] Freemark M., Driscoll P., Maaskant R., Petryk A., Kelly P. A. Ontogenesis of prolactin receptors in the human fetus in early gestation - Implications for tissue differentiation and development. *J. Clin. Invest.*, 1997, 99:1107-1117.

[24] Kebabian J. W., Calne D. B. Multiple receptors for dopamine. *Nature*, 1979, 277:93-96.

[25] Grosvenor C. E., Shyr S. W., Crowley W. R. Effect of neonatal prolactin deficiency on prepubertal tuberoinfundibular and tuberohypophyseal dopaminergic neuronal activity. *Endocrinol Exp.*, 1986, 20:223-228.

[26] Mah P., Webster J. Hyperprolactinemia: Etiology, diagnosis, and management. *Semin. Reprod. Med.*, 2002, 20:365-374.

[27] Casanueva F. F., Molitch M. E., Schlechte J. A. et al. Guidelines of the Pituitary Society for the diagnosis and management of prolactinomas. *Clin. Endocrinol.*, 2006, 65:265-273.

[28] Ferreira M. F., Sobrinho L. G., Santos M. A., Sousa M. F., Uvnäs-Moberg K. Rapid weight gain, at least in some women, is an expression of a neuroendocrine state characterized by reduced hypothalamic dopaminergic tone. *Psychoneuroendocrinology*, 1998, 23:1005-1013.

[29] Nunes M. C. P., Sobrinho L. G., Calhaz-Jorge C., Santos M. A., Mauricio J. C., Sousa M. F. F. Psychosomatic factors in patients with hyperprolactinemia and/or galactorrhea. *Obstet. Gynecol.*, 1980, 55:591-595.

[30] Assies J., Vingerhoets A. J., Poppelaars K. Psychosocial aspects of hyper-prolactinemia. *Psychoneuroendocrinology*, 1992, 17:673-679.

[31] Lachelin G. C. L., Abu-Fadil S., Yen S. S. C. Functional delineation of hyperprolactinemic-amenorrhea. *J. Clin. Endocrinol. Metab.*, 1977, 44:1163-1174.

[32] Colao A., Di Sarno A., Cappabianca P. et al. Gender differences in the prevalence, clinical features and response to cabergoline in hyperprolactinemia. *Eur. J. Endocrinol*, 2003, 148:325-331.

[33] Klibanski A., Greenspan S. Increase in bone mass after treatment of hyper-prolactinemic amenorrhea. *N. Engl. J. Med.*, 1986, 315:542-546.

[34] Klibanski A., Biller B. M. K., Rosenthal D. I., Schoenfeld D. A., Saxe V. Effects of prolactin and estrogen deficiency in amenorrheic bone loss. *J. Clin. Endocrinol. Metab.*, 1988, 67:124-130.

[35] Biller B. M. K., Baum H. B., Rosenthal D. I., Saxe V. C., Charpie P. M., Klibanski A. Progressive trabecular osteopenia in women with hyperprolactinemia amenorrhea. *J. Clin. Endocrinol. Metab.*, 1992, 75:692-697.

[36] Naliato E. C. O., Farias M. L. F., Braucks G. R., Costa F. S. R., Zylberberg D., Violante A. H. D. Prevalence of osteopenia in men with prolactinoma. *J. Endocrinol. Invest.*, 2005, 28:12-17.

[37] Naliato E. C. O., Violante A. H. D, Caldas D. et al. Bone density in women with prolactinoma treated with dopamine agonists. *Pituitary*, 2008, 11:21-28.

[38] Gillam M. P., Molitch M. E., Lombardi G., Colao A. Advances in the treatment of prolactinomas. *Endocr. Rev.*, 2006, 27:485-534.

[39] Kars M., Souverein P. C., Herings R. M. C. et al. Estimated age- and sex-specific incidence and prevalence of dopamine agonist-treated hyperprolactinemia. *J. Clin. Endocrinol. Metab.*, 2009, 94:2729-2734.

[40] Delgrange E., Trouillas J., Maiter D., Donckier J., Tourniaire J. Sex-related difference in the growth of prolactinomas: A clinical and proliferation marker study. *J. Clin. Endocrinol. Metab.*, 1997, 82:2102-2107.

[41] Molitch M. E. Prolactinoma. In: Shlomo Melmed, ed. *The Pituitary*. Malden, Massachusetts: Blackwell Science, Inc., 2002:455-495.

[42] Spark R. Hyperprolactinemia in males with and without pituitary macroadenomas. *Lancet*, 1982, 2:129-132.

[43] Colao A., Di Sarno A., Cappabianca P., Di Somma C., Pivonello R., Lombardi G. Withdrawal of long-term cabergoline therapy for tumoral and non-tumoral hyperprolactinemia. *N. Engl. J. Med.*, 2003, 349:2023-2033.

[44] Molitch M. E., Elton R. L., Blackwell R. E. et al. Bromocriptine as primary therapy for prolactin-secreting macroadenomas: Results of a prospective multicenter study. *J. Clin. Endocrinol. Metab.*, 1985, 60:698-705.

[45] Gruszka A., Kunert-Radek J., Pawlikowski M. The effect of octreotide and bromocriptine on expression of a pro-apoptotic bax protein in rat prolactinoma. *Folia Histochem. Cytobiol.*, 2004, 42:35-39.

[46] Missale C., Nash S. R., Robinson S. W., Jaber M., Caron M. G. Dopamine receptors: From structure to function. *Physiol. Rev.*, 1998, 78:189-225.

[47] Bevan J. S., Webster J., Burke C. W., Scanlon M. F. Dopamine agonists and pituitary tumor shrinkage. *Endocr. Rev.*, 1992, 13:220-240.

[48] Webster J., Piscitelli G., Polli A., Ferrari C. I., Ismail I., Scanlon M. F. A comparison of cabergoline and bromocriptine in the treatment of hyperprolactinemic amenorrhea. *N. Engl. J. Med.*, 1994, 331:904-909.

26 Erika C.O. Naliato

[49] Verhelst J., Abs R., Maiter D. et al. Cabergoline in the treatment of hyperprolactinemia: A study in 455 patients. *J. Clin. Endocrinol. Metab.*, 1999, 84:2518-2522.

[50] Pinzone J. J., Katznelson L., Danila D. C., Pauler D. K., Miller C. S., Klibanski A. Primary medical therapy of micro- and macroprolactinomas in men. *J. Clin. Endocrinol. Metab.*, 2000, 85:3053-3057.

[51] Essais O., Bouguerra R., Hamzaoui J. et al. Efficacy and safety of bromocriptine in the treatment of macroprolactinomas. *Ann. Endocrinol. (Paris)*, 2002, 63:524-531.

[52] Colao A., Vitale G., Cappabianca P. et al. Outcome of cabergoline treatment in men with prolactinoma: Effects of a 24-month treatment on prolactin levels, tumor mass, recovery of pituitary function, and semen analysis. *J. Clin. Endocrinol. Metab.*, 2004, 89:1704-1711.

[53] Berlanga J. J., Gualillo O., Buteau H., Applanat M., Kelly P. A., Edery M. Prolactin activates tyrosyl phosphorylation of insulin receptor substrate 1 and phosphatidylinositol-3-OH kinase. *J. Biol. Chem.*, 1997, 252:2050-2052.

[54] Landgraf R., Leurs-Landgraf M. M. C., Weissmann A., Hörl R., Von Werder K., Scriba P. C. Prolactin: A diabetogenic hormone. *Diabetologia*, 1977, 13:99-104.

[55] Gustafson A. B., Banasiak M. F., Kalkhoff R. K., Hagen T. C., Kim H. J. Correlation of hyperprolactinemia with altered insulin and glucagon: Similarity to effects of late human pregnancy. *J. Clin. Endocrinol. Metab.*, 1980, 51:242-246.

[56] Brelje T. C., Sorenson R. L. Role of prolactin versus growth hormone on islet B-cell proliferation in vitro: Implications for pregnancy. *Endocrinology*, 1991, 128:45-57.

[57] Foss M. C., Paula F. J., Paccola G. M., Piccinato C. E. Peripheral glucose metabolism in human hyperprolactinemia. *Clin. Endocrinol. (Oxf.)*, 1995, 43:721-726.

[58] Maccario M., Grottoli S., Razzore P. et al. Effects of glucose load and/or arginine on insulin and growth hormone secretion in hyperprolactinemia and obesity. *Eur. J. Endocrinol.*, 1996, 135:205-210.

[59] Matsuda M., Mori T., Sassa S., Sakamoto P. M. K., Kawashima S. Chronic effect of hyperprolactinemia on blood glucose and lipid levels in mice. *Life Sci.*, 1996, 58:1171-1177.

[60] Weinhaus A. J., Stout L. E., Sorenson R. L. Glucokinase, hexokinase, glucose transporter 2, and glucose metabolism in islets during pregnancy

and prolactin-treated islets *in vitro:* Mechanisms for long term up-regulation of islets. *Endocrinology*, 1996, 137:1640-1649.

[61] Kok P., Roelfsema F., Frölich M., Meinders A. E., Pijl H. Prolactin release is enhanced in proportion to excess visceral fat in obese women. *J. Clin. Endocrinol. Metab.*, 2004, 89:4445-4449.

[62] Ferreira M. F., Sobrinho L. G., Pires J. S., Silva M. E., Santos M. A., Sousa M. F. Endocrine and psychological evaluation of women with recent weight gain. *Psychoneuroendocrinology*, 1995, 20:53-63.

[63] Greenman Y., Tordjman K., Stern N. Increased body weight associated with prolactin secreting pituitary adenomas: Weight loss with normalization of prolactin levels. *Clin. Endocrinol.*, 1998, 48:547-553.

[64] Doknic M., Pekik S., Zarkovic M. et al. Dopaminergic tone and obesity: An insight from prolactinomas treated with bromocriptine. *Eur. J. Endocrinol.*, 2002, 147:77-84.

[65] Naliato E. C. O., Violante A. H. D., Gaccione M. et al. Body fat in men with prolactinoma. *J. Endocrinol. Invest.*, 2008, 31:985-990.

[66] Gerardo-Gettens T., Moore B. J., Stern J. S., Horwitz B. A. Prolactin stimulates food intake in a dose-dependent manner. *Am. J. Physiol.*, 1989, 256:R276-R280.

[67] Gerardo-Gettens T., Moore B. J., Stern J. S., Horwitz B. A. Prolactin stimulates food intake in the absence of ovarian progesterone. *Am. J. Physiol.*, 1989, 256:R701-R706.

[68] Byatt J. C., Staten N. R., Salsgiver W. J., Kostelc J. G., Collier R. J. Stimulation of food intake and weight gain in mature female rats by bovine prolactin and bovine growth hormone. *Am. J. Physiol.*, 1993, 264:E986-E992.

[69] Cincotta A. H., MacEachern T. A., Meier A. H. Bromocriptine redirects metabolism and prevents seasonal onset of obese hyperinsulinemic state in Syrian hamsters. *Am. J. Physiol.*, 1993, 264:E285-E293.

[70] Noel M. B., Woodside B. Effects of systemic and central prolactin injections on food in weight gain, and estrous cyclicity in female rats. *Physiol. Behav.*, 1993, 54:151-154.

[71] Sauvé D., Woodside B. The effect of central administration of prolactin on food intake in virgin female rats is dose-dependent, occurs in the absence of ovarian hormones and the latency to onset varies with feeding regimen. *Brain. Res.*, 1996, 729:75-81.

[72] Buntin J. D., Hnasko R. M., Zuzick P. H. Role of ventromedial hypothalamus in prolactin-induced hyperphagia in ring doves. *Physiol. Behav.*, 1999, 66:255-261.

[73] Kopelman P. G. Physiopathology of prolactin secretion in obesity. *Int. J. Obes. Relat. Metab. Disord.*, 2000, 24 (suppl 2):S104-S108.

[74] Creemers L. B., Zelissen P. M., Van't Verlaat J. W., Koppeschaar H. P. Prolactinoma and body weight: A retrospective study. *Acta Endocrinol. (Copenh.)*, 1991, 125:392-396.

[75] Schmid C., Goede D. L., Hauser R. S., Brändle M. Increased prevalence of high body mass index in patients presenting with pituitary tumors: Severe obesity in patients with macroprolactinoma. *Swiss. Med. Wkly.*, 2006, 136:254-258.

[76] Delgrange E., Donckier J., Maiter D. Hyperprolactinemia as a reversible cause of weight gain in male patients? *Clin. Endocrinol. (Oxf.)*, 1999, 50:271-271.

[77] Serri O., Li L., Mamputu J., Beauchamp M., Maingrette F., Renier G. The influences of hyperprolactinemia and obesity on cardiovascular risk markers: Effects of cabergoline therapy. *Clin. Endocrinol. (Oxf.*, 2006, 64:366-370.

[78] Naliato E. C. O., Violante A. H. D., Caldas D. et al. Body fat in non-obese women with prolactinoma treated with dopamine agonists. *Clin. Endocrinol.*, 2007, 67:845-862.

[79] Viengchareun S., Bouzinba-Segard H., Laigneau J. et al. Prolactin potentiates insulin-stimulated leptin expression and release from differentiated brown adipocytes. *J. Mol. Endocrinol.*, 2004, 33:679-691.

[80] Goodridge A. G., Ball E. G. The effect of prolactin on lipogenesis in the pigeon. *Biochemistry*, 1967, 6:1676-1682.

[81] Aruldhas M. M., Thampi L. T., Kumari T. M., Govindarajulu P. Prolactin and bromocriptine induced changes in liver, adipose tissue and blood lipids of mature male bonnet monkeys, Macaca radiata (Geoffroy). *Endocr. J.*, 1994, 41:207-212.

[82] Ling C., Hellgren G., Gebre-Medhin M. et al. Prolactin (PRL) receptor gene expression in mouse adipose tissue: Increases during lactation and in PRL-transgenic mice. *Endocrinology*, 2000, 141:3564-3572.

[83] Hayden T. J., Bonney R. C., Forsyth I. A. Ontogeny and control of prolactin receptors in the mammary gland and liver of virgin, pregnant and lactating rats. *J. Endocrinol.*, 1979, 80:259-269.

[84] Djiane J., Durand P. Prolactin-progesterone antagonism in self regulation of prolactin receptors in the mammary gland. *Nature*, 1977, 266:641-643.

[85] Symonds M. E., Phillips I. D., Anthony R. V., Owens J. A., McMillen I. C. Prolactin receptor gene expression and foetal adipose tissue. *J. Neuroendocrinol.*, 1998, 10:885-890.

[86] Orian J. M., Snibson K., Stevenson J. L., Brandon M. R., Herington A. C. Elevation of growth hormone (GH) and prolactin receptors in transgenic mice expressing ovine GH. *Endocrinology*, 1991, 128:1238-1246.

[87] Brandebourg T. D., Bown J. L., Ben-Jonathan N. Prolactin regulates its receptors and inhibits lipolysis and leptin release in male rat adipose tissue. *Biochem. Biophys. Res. Commun.*, 2007, 357:408-413.

[88] Freemark M., Fleenor D., Driscoll P., Binart N., Kelly P. A. Body weight and fat deposition in prolactin receptor-deficient mice. *Endocrinology*, 2001, 142:582-587.

[89] Flint D. J., Binart N., Boumard S., Kopchick J., Kelly P. Developmental aspects of adipose tissue in GH receptor and prolactin receptor gene disrupted mice: Site-specific effects upon proliferation, differentiation and hormone sensitivity. *J. Endocrinol.*, 2006, 191:101-111.

[90] Cannon B., Nedergaard J. Brown adipose tissue: Function and physiological significance. *Physiol. Rev.*, 2004, 84:277-359.

[91] Pearce S., Budge H., Mostyn A. et al. Prolactin, the prolactin receptor and uncoupling protein abundance and function in adipose tissue during development in young sheep. *J. Endocrinol.*, 2005, 184:351-359.

[92] Budge H., Mostyn A., Wilson V. et al. The effect of maternal prolactin infusion during pregnancy on fetal adipose tissue development. *J. Endocrinol.*, 2002, 174:427-433.

[93] Pearce S., Dieguez C., Gualillo O., Symonds M. E., Stephenson T. Differential effects of age and sex on the postnatal responsiveness of brown adipose tissue to prolactin administration in rats. *Exp. Physiol.*, 2003, 88:527-531.

[94] LaPensee C. R., Horseman N. D., Tso P., Brandebourg T. D., Hugo E. R., Ben-Jonathan N. The prolactin-deficient mouse has an altered metabolic phenotype. *Endocrinology*, 2006, 147:4638-4645.

[95] Barber M. C., Travers M. T., Finley E., Flint D. J., Vernon R. G. Growth-hormone-prolactin interactions in the regulation of mammary and adipose-tissue acetyl-CoA carboxylase activity and gene expression in lactating rats. *Biochem. J.*, 1992, 285:469-475.

[96] Flint D. J., Clegg R. A., Knight C. H. Effects of prolactin, progesterone and ovariectomy on metabolic activities and insulin receptors in the mammary gland and adipose tissue during extended lactation in the rat. *J. Endocrinol.*, 1984, 102:231-236.

[97] Jensen D. R., Gavigan S., Sawicki V., Witsell D. L., Eckel R. H., Neville M. C. Regulation of lipoprotein lipase activity and mRNA in the mammary gland of the lactating mouse. *Biochem. J.*, 1994, 298:321-327.

[98] Garrison M. M., Scow R. O. Effect of prolactin on lipoprotein lipase crop sac and adipose tissue of pigeons. *Am. J. Physiol.*, 1975, 228:1542-1544.

[99] Flint D. J., Clegg R. A., Vernon R. G. Prolactin and the regulation of adipose-tissue during lactation in rats. *Mol. Cell. Endocrinol.*, 1981, 22:265-275.

[100] Mingrone G., Manco M., Iaconelli A. et al. Prolactin and insulin ultradian secretion and adipose tissue lipoprotein lipase expression in severely obese women after bariatric surgery. *Obesity (Silver Spring)*, 2008, 16:1831-1837.

[101] Cincotta A. H., Meier A. H., Southern L. L. Bromocriptine alters hormones rhythms and lipid metabolism in swine. *Ann. Nutr. Metab.*, 1989, 33:305-314.

[102] Jarrett 2nd J. C., Ballejo G., Salemm T. H., Tsibris J. C., Spellacy W. N. The effect of prolactin and relaxin on insulin binding by adipocytes from pregnant women. *Am. J. Obstet. Gynecol.*, 1984, 149:250-5.

[103] Ryan E. A., Enns L. Role of gestational hormones in the induction of insulin resistance. *J. Clin. Endocrinol. Metab.*, 1988, 67:341-347.

[104] Cincotta A. H., Meier A. H. Prolactin permits the expression of a circadian variation in lipogenic responsiveness to insulin in hepatocytes of the golden hamster *(Mesocricetus auratus)*. *J. Endocrinol.*, 1985, 106:173-176.

[105] Cincotta A. H., Meier A. H. Prolactin influences the circadian rhythm of lipogenesis in primary cultured hepatocytes. *Horm. Metab. Res.*, 1989, 21:64-68.

[106] Sugden M. C., Holness M. J. Recent advances in mechanisms regulating glucose oxidation at the level of the pyruvate dehydrogenase complex by PDKs. *Am. J. Physiol. Endocrinol. Metab.*, 2003, 284:E855-E862.

[107] White U. A., Coulter A. A., Miles T. K., Stephens J. M. The STAT5A-mediated induction of pyruvate dehydrogenase kinase 4 expression by prolactin or growth hormone in adipocytes. *Diabetes*, 2007, 56:1623-1629.

[108] Mizutani T., Nishikawa Y., Adachi H. et al. Identification of estrogen receptor in human adipose tissue and adipocytes. *J. Clin. Endocrinol. Metab.*, 1994, 78:950-954.

[109] Dieudonné M. N., Pecquery R., Boumediene A., Leneveu M. C., Giudicelli Y. Androgen receptors in human preadipocytes and adipocytes: Regional specificities and regulation by sex steroids. *Am. J. Physiol.*, 1998, 274:C1645-C1652.

[110] Parada M. A., Hernandez L., Paez X., Baptista T., Puig de Parada M., De Quijada M. Mechanism of the body weight increase induced by systemic sulpiride. *Pharmacol. Biochem. Behav.*, 1989, 33:45-50.

Prolactinomas, PRL & Weight Gain 31

[111] Tikkanen M. J., Nikkilä E. A., Kuusi T., Sipinen S. High density lipoprotein-2 and hepatic lipase: Reciprocal changes produced by estrogen and norgestrel. *J. Clin Endocrinol. Metab.*, 1982, 54:1113-1117.

[112] Bhasin S., Storer T. W., Berman N. et al. Testosterone replacement increases fat-free mass and muscle size in hypogonadal men. *J. Clin. Endocrinol. Metab.*, 1997, 82:407-413.

[113] Wade G. N., Schneider J. E. Metabolic fuels and reproduction in female mammals. *Neurosci. Biobehav. Rev.*, 1992, 16:235-272.

[114] Gambacciani M., Ciaponi M., Cappagli B. et al. Body weight, body fat distribution, and hormonal replacement therapy in early postmenopausal women. *J. Clin. Endocrinol. Metab.*, 1997, 82:414-417.

[115] Smith J. C., Bennett S., Evans L. M. et al. The effects of induced hypogonadism on arterial stiffness, body composition, and metabolic parameters in males with prostate cancer. *J. Clin. Endocrinol. Metab.*, 2001, 86:4261-4267.

[116] Fielder P. J., Talamantes F. The lipolytic effects of mouse placental lactogen II, mouse prolactin, and mouse growth hormone on adipose tissue from virgin and pregnant mice. *Endocrinology*, 1987, 121:493-497.

[117] Hogan J. C., Stephens J. M. The regulation of fatty acid synthase by STAT5A. *Diabetes*, 2005, 54:1968-1975.

[118] McAveney K. M., Gimble J. M., Yu-Lee L. Prolactin receptor expression during adipocyte differentiation of bone marrow stroma. *Endocrinology*, 1996, 137:5723-57.

[119] Nanbu-Wakao R., Fujitani Y., Masuho Y., Muramatu M., Wakao H. Prolactin enhances CCAAT enhancer-binding protein-beta (C/EBP beta) and peroxisome proliferator-activated receptor gamma (PPAR gamma) messenger RNA expression and stimulates adipogenic conversion of NIH-3T3 cells. *Mol. Endocrinol.*, 2000, 14:307-316.

[120] Freytag S. O., Paielli D. L., Glibert J. D. Ectopic expression of the CCAAT/enhancer-binding protein alpha promotes the adipogenic program in a variety of mouse fibroblastic cells. *Genes. Dev.*, 1994, 8:1654-1663.

[121] Tontonoz P., Hu E. Stimulation of adipogenesis in fibroblasts by PPAR gamma2, a lipid-activated transcription factor. *Cell*, 1994, 79:1147-1156.

[122] Iliou J. P., Demarne Y. Evolution of the sensitivity of isolated adipocytes of ewes to the lipolytic effects of different stimuli during pregnancy and lactation. *Int. J. Biochem.*, 1987, 19:253-258.

[123] Houseknecht K. L., Bauman D. E., Vernon R. G., Byatt J. C., Collier R. J. Insulin-like growth factors-I and -II, somatotropin, prolactin, and placental

lactogen are not acute effectors of lipolysis in ruminants. *Domest. Anim. Endocrinol.*, 1996, 13:239-249.

[124] Sul H. S., Wang D. Nutritional and hormonal regulation of enzymes in fat synthesis: Studies of fatty acid synthase and mitochondrial glycerol-3-phosphate acyltransferase gene transcription. *Annu. Rev. Nutr.*, 1998, 18:331-351.

[125] Margetic S., Gazzola C., Pegg C. G., Hill R. A. Leptin: A review of its peripheral actions and interactions. *Int. J. Obes. Relat. Metab. Disord.*, 2002, 26:1407-1433.

[126] Maffei M., Halaas J., Ravussin P. R. E. et al. Leptin levels in human and rodent: Measurement of plasma leptin and ob RNA in obese and weight-reduced subjects. *Nat. Med.*, 1995, 1:1155-1161.

[127] Schiöth H. G protein-coupled receptors in regulation of body weight. *CNS Neurol. Disord. Drug. Targets*, 2006, 5:241-249.

[128] Friedman M. J. Leptin and the neural circuit regulating body weight and metabolism. In: Claude Kordon, Iain Robinson, Jacques Hanoune, Robert Dantzer, Yves Christen, ed. *Brain somatic cross-talk and the central control of metabolism.* Berlin [u.a.]: Springer-Verlag, 2003:15-36.

[129] Friedman M. J. The alphabet of weight control. *Nature*, 1997, 385:119-120.

[130] Mistry A. M., Romsos D. R. Intracerebroventricular leptin administration reduces food intake in pregnant and lactating mice. *Exp. Biol. Med.*, 2002, 227:616-619.

[131] Camastra S., Manco M., Frascerra S., Iaconelli A., Mingrone G., Ferrannini E. Daylong pituitary hormones in morbid obesity: Effects of bariatric surgery. *Int. J. Obes. (Lond.)*, 2009, 33:166-172.

[132] Watanobe H., Suda T., Wikberg J. E., Schïoth H. B. Evidence that physiological levels of circulating leptin exert stimulatory effect on luteinizing hormone and prolactin surges in rats. *Biochem. Biophys. Res. Commun.*, 1999, 263:162-165.

[133] Chehab F. F., Mounzih K., Lu R., Lim M. E. Early onset of reproductive function in normal female mice treated with leptin. *Science*, 1997, 275:88-90.

[134] Gualillo O., Lago F., García M. et al. Prolactin stimulates leptin secretion by rat white adipose tissue. *Endocrinology*, 1999, 140:5149-5153.

[135] Butte N. F., Hopkinson J. M., Nicolson M. A. Leptin in human reproduction: Serum leptin levels in pregnant and lactating women. *J. Clin. Endocrinol. Metab.*, 1997, 82:585-589.

[136] Ling C., Billig H. PRL receptor-mediated effects in female mouse adipocytes: PRL induces suppressors of cytokine signaling expression and

suppresses insulin-induced leptin production in adipocytes *in vitro*. *Endocrinology*, 2001, 142:4880-4890.

[137] Goldstein B. J., Scalia R. Adiponectin: A novel adipokine linking adipocytes and vascular function. *J. Clin. Endocrinol. Metab.*, 2004, 89:2563-2568.

[138] Yang W., Lee W., Funahashi T. et al. Weight reduction increases plasma levels of an adipose-derived anti-inflammatory protein, adiponectin. *J. Clin. Endocrinol. Metab.*, 2001, 86:3815-3819.

[139] Asai-Sato M., Okamoto M., Endo M. et al. Hypoadiponectinemia in lean lactating women: Prolactin inhibits adiponectin secretion from human adipocytes. *Endocr. J.*, 2006, 53:555-562.

[140] Nilsson L., Binart N., Bohlooly Y. M. et al. Prolactin and growth hormone regulate secretion and receptor expression in adipose tissue. *Biochem. Biophys. Res. Commun.*, 2005, 331:1120-1126.

[141] Hugo E. R., Borcherding D. C., Gersin K. S., Loftus J., Ben-Jonathan N. Prolactin release by adipose explants, primary adipocytes, and LS14 adipocytes. *J. Clin. Endocrinol. Metab.*, 2008, 93:4006-4012.

[142] Cincotta A. H., Schiller B. C., Meier A. H. Bromocriptine inhibits the seasonally occurring obesity, hyperinsulinemia, insulin resistance, and impaired glucose tolerance in the Syrian hamster, *Mesocricetus auratus*. *Metabolism*, 1991, 40:639-644.

[143] Cincotta A. H., Meier A. H. Bromocriptine inhibits in vivo free fatty acid oxidation and hepatic glucose output in seasonally obese hamsters (*Mesocricetus auratus*). *Metabolism*, 1995, 44:1349-1355.

[144] Heil S. H. Sex-specific effects of prolactin on food intake by rats. *Horm. Behav.*, 1999, 35:47-54.

[145] Heil S. H. Activational and organizational actions of gonadal hormones and the sex-specific effects of prolactin on food intake by rats. *Dev. Psychobiol.*, 1999, 35:61-67.

[146] Moore B. J., Gerardo-Gettens T., Horwitz B. A., Stern J. S. Hyperprolactinemia stimulates food intake in the female rat. *Brain. Res. Bull.*, 1986, 17:563-569.

[147] Sauvé D., Woodside B. Neuroanatomical specificity of prolactin-induced hyperphagia in virgin female rats. *Brain. Res.*, 2000, 868:306-314.

[148] Naef L, Woodside B. Prolactin/Leptin interactions in the control of food intake in rats. *Endocrinology*. 2007, 148:5977-5983.

[149] Hnasko R. M., Buntin J. D. Functional mapping of neural sites mediating prolactin-induced hyperphagia in doves. *Brain. Res.*, 1993, 623:257-266.

34 Erika C.O. Naliato

[150] Ebenezer I. S., Parrot R. F. Operant food intake in pigs following intracerebroventricular (i.c.v.) administration of prolactin. *Gen. Pharmacol.*, 1991, 22:811-813.

[151] Fechner J. H., Buntin J. D. Localization of prolactin-binding sites in ring dove brain by quantitative autoradiography. *Brain. Res.*, 1989, 487:245-254.

[152] Li C., Kelly P. A., Buntin J. D. Inhibitory effects of anti-prolactin receptor antibodies on prolactin binding in brain and prolactin-induced feeding behavior in ring doves. *Neuroendocrinology*, 1995, 61:125-135.

[153] Baptista T., Alastre T., Contreras Q. et al. Effects of the antipsychotic drug sulpiride on reproductive hormones in healthy men: Relationship with body weight regulation. *Pharmacopsychiatry*, 1997, 30:250-255.

[154] Baptista T., Lacruz A., Meza T. et al. Antipsychotic Drugs and Obesity: Is Prolactin Involved? *Can. J. Psychiatry*, 2001, 46:829-834.

[155] Wang G., Volkow N., Logan J. et al. Brain dopamine and obesity. *Lancet*, 2001, 357:354-357.

[156] Wang C., Lam K. S., Ma J. T., Chan T., Liu M. Y., Yeung R. T. Long-term treatment of hyperprolactinaemia with bromocriptine: Effect of drug withdrawal. *Clin. Endocrinol. (Oxf.)*, 1987, 27:363-371.

[157] McIntyre R. S., McCann S. M., Kennedy SH. Antipsychotic metabolic effects: Weight gain, Diabetes Mellitus, and lipid abnormalities. *Can. J. Psychiatry*, 2001, 46:273-281.

[158] Spiegelman B. M., Flier J. S. Adipogenesis and obesity: rounding out the big picture. *Cell*, 1996, 87:377-389.

[159] Strader A. D., Buntin J. D. Neuropeptide-Y: A possible mediator of prolactin-induced feeding and regulator of energy balance in the ring dove (*Streptopelia risoria*). *J. Neuroendocrinol.*, 2001, 13:386-392.

[160] Strader A. D., Buntin J. D. Changes in agouti-related peptide during the ring dove breeding cycle in relation to prolactin and parental hyperphagia. *J. Neuroendocrinol.*, 2003, 15:1046-1053.

[161] Perumal P., Vrontakis M. E. Transgenic mice over-expressing galanin exhibit pituitary adenomas and increased secretion of galanin, prolactin and growth hormone. *J. Endocrinol.*, 2003, 179:145-154.

[162] Piroli G. G., Pietranera L., Grillo C. A., De Nicola A. F. Gender differences in the expression of galanin and vasoactive intestinal peptide in oestrogen-induced prolactinomas of Fischer 344 rats. *J. Neuroendocrinol*, 2004, 16:64-71.

[163] Kageyama H., Takenoya F., Hori Y., Yoshida T., Shioda S. Morphological interaction between galanin-like peptide- and dopamine-containing neurons in the rat arcuate nucleus. *Regul. Pept.* , 2008, 145:165-168.

Prolactinomas, PRL & Weight Gain 35

[164] Gonzalez-Mora J. L., Guadalupe T., Mas M. In vivo voltammetry study of the modulatory action of prolactin on the mesolimbic dopaminergic system. *Brain. Res. Bull.*, 1990, 25:729-733.

[165] Wise R. A., Carlezon Jr. W. A. Attenuation of the locomotor-sensitizing effects of the D2 dopamine agonist bromocriptine by either the D1 antagonist SCH 23390 or the D2 antagonist raclopride. *Synapse*, 1994, 17:155-159.

[166] Wang D. Y., Stavola B. L., Bulbrook R. D. et al. The relationship between prolactin and risk of breast cancer in premenopausal women. *Eur. J. Cancer. Clin. Oncol.*, 1987, 23:1541-1548.

[167] Baptista T., Parada M., Hernandez L. Long term administration of some antipsychotic drugs increases body weight and feeding in rats. Are D2 dopamine receptors involved? *Pharmacol. Biochem. Behav.*, 1987, 27:399-405.

[168] Baptista T., De Baptista E. A., Hernadez L., Altemus M., Weiss S. R. Tamoxifen prevents sulpiride-induced weight gain in female rats. *Pharmacol. Biochem. Behav.* 1997, 57:215-222.

[169] Correa N., Opler L. A., Kay S. R., Birmaher B. Amantadine in the treatment of neuroendocrine side effects of neuroleptics. *J. Clin. Psychopharmacol.*, 1987, 7:91-95.

[170] Copinschi G., De Laet M. H., Brion J. P. et al. Simultaneous study of cortisol, growth hormone and prolactin nyctohemeral variations in normal and obese subjects. Influence of prolonged fasting in obesity. *Clin. Endocrinol. (Oxf.)*, 1978, 9:15-26.

[171] Kopelman P. G., White N., Pilkington T. R. E., Jeffcoate S. L. Impaired hypothalamic control of prolactin secretion in massive obesity. *Lancet*, 1979, 1:747-750.

[172] Kopelman P. G., Pilkington T. R. E., White N., Jeffcoate S. L. Persistence of defective hypothalamic control of prolactin secretion in some obese women after weight reduction. *Br. Med. J.*, 1980, 281:358-359.

[173] AvRuskin T. W., Pillai S. K. K., Juan C., Kleinberg D. L. Decreased prolactin secretion in childhood obesity. *J. Pediatr.*, 1985, 106:373-378.

[174] Weaver J. U., Noonan K., Kopelman P. G. An association between hypothalamic-pituitary dysfunction and peripheral endocrine function in extreme obesity. *Clin. Endocrinol. (Oxf.)*, 1991, 35:97-102.

[175] Kopelman P. G., Apps M. C. P., Cope T., Empey D. W. Nocturnal hypoxia and prolactin secretion in obese women. *Br. Med. J.*, 1983, 287:859-861.

[176] Röjdmark S., Rössner S. Decreased dopaminergic control of prolactin secretion in male obesity: Normalization by fasting. *Metabolism*, 1991, 40:191-195.

[177] Weaver J. U., Noonan K., Kopelman P. G., Coste M. Impaired prolactin secretion and body fat distribution in obesity. *Clin. Endocrinol. (Oxf.)*, 1990, 32:641-646.

[178] Donders S. H. J., Pieters G. F. F. M., Heevel J. G., Ross H. A., Smals A. G. H., Kloppenborg P. W. C. Disparity of thyrotropin (TSH) and prolactin responses to TSH-releasing hormone in obesity. *J. Clin. Endocrinol. Metab.*, 1985, 61:56-59.

[179] Argenio G. F., Bernini G. P., Vivaldi M. S., Del Corso C., Santorini R., Franchi F. Naloxone does not modify fenfluramine-induced prolactin increase in obese patients. *Clin. Endocrinol. (Oxf.)*, 1991, 35:505-508.

[180] Bernini G. P., Argenio G. F., Vivaldi M. S. et al. Effects of fenfluramine and ritanserin on prolactin response to insulin-induced hypoglycemia in obese patients: Evidence for failure of the serotoninergic system. *Horm. Res.*, 1989, 31:133-137.

[181] Argenio G., Bernini G., Vivaldi M. S. et al. Effect of fenfluramine on prolactin and thyroid-stimulating-hormone response to thyrotropin-releasing-hormone in obese and normal women. *Eur. J. Clin. Pharmacol.*, 1990, 39:13-16.

[182] Altomonte L., Zoli A., Alessi F., Ghirlanda G., Manna R., Greco A. V. Effect of fenfluramine on growth hormone and prolactin secretion in obese subjects. *Horm. Res.*, 1987, 27:190-194.

[183] De Schepper J., Zhou X., Louis O., Velkeniers B., Hooghe-Peters E., Vanhaelst L. The weight gain and ultimate adiposity in cafeteria diet-induced obesity is unrelated to the central serotoninergic tonus. *Eat. Weight Disord.*, 1997, 2:38-43.

[184] Kohsaka A., Watanobe H., Kakizaki Y., Habu S., Suda T. A significant role of leptin in the generation of steroid-induced luteinizing hormone and prolactin surges in female rats. *Biochem. Biophys. Res. Commun.*, 1999, 254:578-581.

[185] Rasmussen K. M., Kjolhede C. L. Prepregnant overweight and obesity diminish the prolactin response to suckling in the first week postpartum. *Pediatrics*, 2004, 113:e465-e471.

[186] Zumoff B., Strain G. W. A perspective on the hormonal abnormalities of obesity: Are they cause or effect? *Obes. Res.*, 1994, 2:56-67.

Prolactinomas, PRL & Weight Gain 37

[187] Pijl H. Reduced dopaminergic tone in hypothalamic neural circuits: Expression of a 'thrifty' genotype underlying the metabolic syndrome? *Eur. J. Pharmacol.*, 2003, 480:125-131.

[188] Carruba M. O., Ricciardi S., Müller E. E., Mantegazza P. Anoretic effect of lisuride and other ergot derivatives in the rat. *Eur. J. Pharmacol.*, 1980, 64:133-141.

[189] Smith G. P., Schneider L. H. Relationships between mesolimbic dopamine function and eating behavior. *Ann. N. Y. Acad. Sci.*, 1988, 537:254-261.

[190] Genazzani A. R., Petraglia F., Facchinetti F. et al. Evidences for a dopamine-regulated peripheral source of circulating beta-endorphin. *J. Clin. Endocrinol. Metab.*, 1988, 66:279-282.

[191] Wise R. A., Rompre P. P. Brain dopamine and reward. *Ann. Rev. Psychol.*, 1989, 40:191-225.

[192] Genazzani A. R., Facchinetti F., Petraglia F., Pintor C., Corda R. Hyperendorphinemia in obese children and adolescents. *J. Clin. Endocrinol. Metab.*, 1986, 62:36-40.

[193] Comings D. E., Gade R., MacMurray J. P., Muhleman D., Peters W. R. Genetic variants of the human obesity (OB) gene: Association with body mass index in young women, psychiatric symptoms, and interaction with the dopamine D2 receptor (DRD2) gene. *Mol. Psychiatry*, 1996, 1:325-335.

[194] Comings D. E., Flanagan S. D., Dietz G., Muhleman D., Knell E., Gysin R. The dopamine D2 receptor (DRD2) as a major gene in obesity and height. *Biochem. Med. Metab. Biol.*, 1993, 50:176-185.

[195] Petty R. G. Prolactin and antipsychotic medications: Mechanism of action. *Schizophr. Res.*, 1999, 35:S67-S73.

[196] Baptista T., Kin N. M., Beaulieu S., De Baptista E. A. Obesity and related metabolic abnormalities during antipsychotic drug administration: Mechanisms, management and research perspectives. *Pharmacopsychiatry*, 2002, 35:205-219.

[197] Baptista T., Zárate J., Joober R. et al. Drug induced weight gain, an impediment to successful pharmacotherapy: Focus on antipsychotics. *Curr. Drug. Targets*, 2004, 2004:279-299.

[198] Cooper G. D., Pickavance L. C., Wilding J. P. H., Halford J. C. G., Goudie A. J. A parametric analysis of olanzapine-induced weight gain in female rats. *Psychopharmacology*, 2005, 181:80-89.

[199] Baptista T., López M. E., Teneud L. et al. Amantadine in the treatment of neuroleptic-induced obesity in rats: Behavioral, endocrine and neurochemical correlates. *Pharmacopsychiatry*, 1997, 30:43-54.

[200] Floris M., Lejeune J., Deberdt W. Effect of amantadine on weight gain during olanzapine treatment. *Eur. Neuropsychopharmacol.*, 2001, 11:181-182.

[201] Carey R. M., Van Loon G. R., Baines A. D., Kaiser D. L. Suppression of basal and stimulated noradrenergic activities by the dopamine agonist bromocriptine in man. *J. Clin. Endocrinol. Metab.*, 1983, 56:595-602.

[202] Meier A. H., Cincotta A. H., Lovell W. C. Timed bromocriptine administration reduces body fat stores in obese subjects and hyperglycemia in type II diabetics. *Experientia*, 1992, 48:248-253.

[203] Cincotta A. H., Meier A. H. Bromocriptine (ergoset) reduces body weight and improves glucose tolerance in obese subjects. *Diabetes Care*, 1996, 19:667-670.

[204] Cincotta A. H., Tozzo E., Scislowski P. W. Bromocriptine/SKF38393 treatment ameliorates obesity and associated metabolic dysfunctions in obese (ob/ob) mice. *Life Sci.* , 1997, 61:951-956.

[205] Kamath V., Jones C. N., Yip J. C. et al. Effects of a Quick-release form of bromocriptine (Ergoset) on fasting and postprandial plasma glucose, insulin, lipid, and lipoprotein concentrations in obese nondiabetic hyperinsulinemic women. *Diabetes Care*, 1997, 20:1697-1701.

[206] Scislowski P. W. D., Tozzo E., Zhang Y., Phaneuf S., Prevelige R., Cincotta A. H. Biochemical mechanisms responsible for the attenuation of diabetic and obese conditions in ob/ob mice treated with dopaminergic agonists. *Int. J. Obes. Relat. Metab. Disord.*, 1999, 23:452-431.

[207] Spooner P., Chernick S. S., Garrison M. M., Scow R. O. Development of lipoprotein lipase activity and accumulation of triacylglycerol in differentiating 3T3-L1 adipocytes. *J. Biol. Chem.* , 1979, 254:1305-1311.

[208] Cincotta A. H., Meier A. H. Prolactin permits the expression of a circadian variation in insulin receptor profile in hepatocytes of the golden hamster (*Mesocricetus auratus*). *J. Endocrinol.*, 1985, 106:177-181.

[209] Cincotta A. H., Meier A. H. Reductions of body fat stores and total plasma cholesterol and triglyceride concentrations in several species by bromocriptine treatment. *Life Sci.*, 1989, 45:2247-2254.

In: Handbook of Neuropsychiatry Research
Editor: Rebecca S. Davies, pp. 39-69

ISBN: 978-1-61668-138-8
© 2010 Nova Science Publishers, Inc.

Chapter 2

CLINICAL AND PATHOLOGICAL CHARACTERISTICS OF PICK'S DISEASE AND FRONTOTEMPORAL LOBAR DEGENERATION WITH TDP-43-POSITIVE INCLUSIONS

Osamu Yokota[1,2,] and Kuniaki Tsuchiya[2,3]*

[1]Department of Neuropsychiatry, Okayama University Graduate School of Medicine, Dentistry and Pharmaceutical Sciences, 2-5-1 Shikata-cho, Kita-ku, Okayama 700-8558, Japan
[2]Department of Neuropathology, Tokyo Institute of Psychiatry, 2-1-8 Kamikitazawa, Setagaya-ku, Tokyo 156-8585, Japan
[3]Department of Laboratory Medicine and Pathology, Tokyo Metropolitan Matsuzawa Hospital, Tokyo, Japan

Abstract

Frontotemporal lobar degeneration (FTLD) is a clinical syndrome of dementia that is composed of three clinical subtypes, frontotemporal dementia (FTD), progressive aphasia (PA), and semantic dementia (SD). The underlying pathologies in FTLD patients are variable, including FTLD with tau-positive Pick bodies (Pick's disease), sporadic and familial FTLD with TDP-43-positive inclusions (FTLD-TDP), FTLD with tau gene mutations, corticobasal degeneration/progressive supranuclear palsy (CBD/PSP), argyrophilic grain

---

* E-mail address: oyokota1@yahoo.co.jp

disease, basophilic inclusion body disease (BIBD), neuronal intermediate filament inclusion disease (NIFID), and Alzheimer's disease with atypical cerebral atrophy. To infer more precisely the underlying pathologies in FTLD patients during life, differences in the clinical characteristics of pathological substrates have been explored, and recent studies support the possibility that the clinical pictures are not necessarily identical between the major pathological substrates. In our autopsy series, early impairment of speech output was more frequent in Pick's disease, and early impairment of semantic memory and auditory comprehension was more frequent in sporadic FTLD-TDP. Asymmetric motor disturbances during the course (e.g., pyramidal signs, parkinsonism, and contracture) were more frequently observed in sporadic FTLD-TDP. The most frequent first syndrome in Pick's disease was FTD followed by PA or speech apraxia, while that in sporadic FTLD-TDP was SD followed by FTD. Interestingly, the most frequent clinical syndrome in familial FTLD-TDP cases with progranulin gene mutations was reported to be FTD followed by PA, which differs from those in sporadic FTLD-TDP. In the present paper, we review recent findings regarding clinical symptoms, biochemical markers, and quantitative radiological findings revealed by MRI in two major pathological substrates of FTLD, FTLD-TDP and Pick's disease.

I. Introduction

The concept of 'Pick's disease' has a long and complicated history with a respect to the pathological base of its diagnosis. The first case of Pick's disease reported was the patient 'H. August' of Arnold Pick in 1892 [Pick, 1892]. This patient showed clinically progressive language disturbance, and pathologically, circumscribed atrophy in the left temporal lobe. Interestingly, it is unclear whether this case had argyrophilic Pick bodies, which are now considered as the sole pathological hallmark of Pick's disease. In 1926, Onari and Spatz first proposed calling cases having circumscribed atrophy in the temporal and frontal lobes 'Pick's disease', regardless of the presence or absence of Pick bodies [Onari and Spatz, 1926]. Thereafter, the pathological base of the diagnosis of 'Pick's disease' was considered to be circumscribed temporofrontal atrophy, but not necessarily Pick bodies. In 1998, the clinical concept of frontotemporal lobar degeneration (FTLD) composed of three clinical subtypes, frontotemporal dementia (FTD) characterized by prominent behavioral abnormalities, progressive aphasia (PA) characterized by non-fluent aphasia, and semantic dementia (SD), was proposed. Although this is a clinical diagnostic criteria, the possibility that there is some difference in the clinical pictures among the underlying pathologies was not supposed.

Clinical and Pathological Characteristics of Pick's Disease...   41

In the most recent pathological classification [Cairns et al., 2007a, Mackenzie et al., 2009], classifications of histologies in FTLD patients are based on the kind of proteins accumulated abnormally in specific inclusions, but not the presence of cerebral atrophy. Major underlying pathologies in FTLD patients are Pick's disease (defined by tau-positive Pick bodies), FTLD with TDP-43-positive inclusions (FTLD-TDP) [Neuman et al., 2006, Arai et al., 2006], neuronal intermediate filament inclusion disease (NIFID; the recently recommended nomenclature is FTLD-IF) [Cairns et al., 2003, Josephs et al., 2003], basophilic inclusion body disease (BIBD; defined by p62-positive, tau-negative, and TDP-43-negative spherical basophilic inclusions) [Munoz-Garcia and Ludwin 1984], corticobasal degeneration (CBD), progressive supranuclear palsy (PSP), argyrophilic grain disease (AGD) [Braak and Braak, 1987], dementia lacking distinctive histologic features (DLDH; now called FTLD-ni), and FTLD with microtubule-associated protein tau gene mutation (FTLD with *MAPT* mutation). Of all FTLD-TDP cases, 5–10% have mutations in the progranulin (*PGRN*) gene [Pickering-Brown, 2007]. Severe frontotemporal atrophy usually develops in all these diseases, except for AGD. Most AGD cases show only mild temporal atrophy without macroscopic frontal atrophy. However, some AGD cases exhibit severe atrophy in the limbic and temporal cortex, and clinically show oral tendency, dietary change, and emotional change like FTLD cases [Ishihara et al., 2005, Tsuchiya et al., 2001]. FTLD-ni was previously considered to be the most frequent among FTLD patients. However, because it was revealed that a large proportion of DLDH (approximately 90%) is actually FTLD with ubiquitin-positive inclusions (FTLD-U) [Mackenzie et al., 2006], the frequency of FTLD-ni is very low. The frequencies of FTLD-ni in several series were 3-10% of FTLD cases [Munoz et al., 2003].

Underlying pathologies in FTLD patients are variable, and at present, it is still difficult to infer the underlying pathologies precisely based on the clinical features of FTLD patients during life. However, considering that the aim is the development of specific pathology–based treatment by clarifying pathogeneses, it is undoubtedly important that clinical, radiological, and laboratory findings that are potentially useful to identify pathologies during the lives of FTLD patients are accumulated. Especially, because sporadic FTLD patients comprise over 50% of all FTLD patients [Snowden et al., 2002, Ikeda et al., 2004], clarifying the clinico-pathological differences between major pathologies in sporadic FTLD patients may be required.

We recently examined the differences between the clinical and pathological features of two major pathological substrates in sporadic FTLD patients, sporadic FTLD-TDP and Pick's disease [Yokota et al., 2009]. In the present paper, we summarize our results and review related clinical and laboratory findings, including biochemical markers and MRI findings in sporadic and familial FTLD-TDP and Pick's disease.

II. FTLD with TDP-43-Positive Inclusions (FTLD-TDP)

II.1. Historical Background

In 1996, Jackson et al. reported nine cases that clinically showed FTD without motor neuron disease and pathologically had ubiquitin-positive tau-negative α-synuclein-negative inclusions in the hippocampal dentate gyrus and frontotemporal cortex [Jackson and Lowe, 1996, Jackson et al., 1996]. These cases lacked Pick bodies. They also noticed that these cases did not show evidence of loss of lower motor neurons, so they were different from amyotrophic lateral sclerosis with dementia characterized by similar ubiquitin-positive inclusions. These cases were considered to represent one distinct pathological entity, and it was called FTLD-U. Thereafter, several epidemiological studies demonstrated that FTLD-U is the most common pathology among FTLD cases: the frequency was reported to be 30% to 40% [Munoz et al., 2003, Josephs et al., 2004, Lipton et al., 2004]. Later, because it was revealed that most FTLD-U cases (about 80%) had TDP-43-positive, tau- and α-synuclein-negative inclusions, and/or neurites, it was renamed FTLD-TDP. Although rare, some FTLD-U cases lack TDP-43 pathology [Mackenzie et al., 2008]. The TDP-43-negative FTLD-U cases were first called atypical FTLD-U, but are now called FTLD-UPS (ubiquitin proteosome system) [Mackenzie et al., 2009]. Currently, FTLD-TDP is considered the most common pathology in FTLD patients.

II.2. Genetic and Histopathological Features

Some cases of familial FTLD-TDP are associated with three causative genes, *PGRN* [Baker et al., 2006], valosin-containing protein (*VCP*), and charged multivesicular body protein 2B (*CHMP2B*) genes [Skibinski et al., 2005, Cairns et al., 2007b]. FTLD with *VCP* mutation, also called inclusion body myopathy, is associated with Paget's disease of bone and frontotemporal dementia (IBMPFD) [Watts et al., 2004]. The *CHMP2B* mutation was found in FTLD linked with chromosome 3 in a Danish pedigree [Skibinski et al., 2005]. A genetic locus on

Clinical and Pathological Characteristics of Pick's Disease...   43

chromosome 9p has been also reported for familial FTLD-MND, and in one family, the presence of a putative disease segregating a stop codon mutation (Q342X) in the intraXagellar transport protein 74 (*IFT74*) gene was revealed [Morita et al., 2006].

TDP-43 pathologies in the frontotemporal cortex are classified into four histologic subtypes based on their morphologic features. Type 1 histology is characterized by many long TDP-43-positive dystrophic neurites predominantly in the superficial cortical layer in the frontotemporal cortex (Figure 1a). TDP-43-positive neuronal cytoplasmic inclusions (NCIs) or neuronal intranuclear inclusions (NIIs) are rare or absent. Type 2 histology is characterized by many TDP-43-positive NCIs with a few or no dystrophic neurites (Figure 1b). NIIs are rare or absent. Type 3 histology is characterized by many NCIs and short dystrophic neurites in the superficial cortical layers with or without NIIs (Figure 1c). Type 4 histology is characterized by many NIIs with few NCIs and dystrophic neurites. Type 1 histology is frequently noted in patients with SD. Type 2 histology is frequently observed in FTLD patients with motor neuron disease (FTLD-MND), which is also called amyotrophic lateral sclerosis with dementia. *PGRN* mutations are exclusively associated with type 3 histology. Type 4 histology is associated with *VCP* mutations.

II.3. Clinical Features in PGRN-Linked FTLD-TDP

The clinical characteristics of FTLD-TDP have been examined mainly in familial cases with *PGRN* mutations. It has been reported that the age at onset in *PGRN*-linked cases ranges 45 to 88 years (mean: 57-64 years) [Van Deerlin et al., 2007, Beck et al., 2008, Pickering-Brown et al., 2008, Le Ber et al., 2008, Kelley et al., 2009]. The onset age in *PGRN*-linked cases tends to be older than that in FTLD cases with tau gene mutation (mean: 49-53 years) [Beck et al., 2008, Pickering-Brown et al., 2008], and similar to that in FTLD-U cases without *PGRN* mutations [Beck et al., 2008].

The clinical phenotypes in *PGRN*-linked cases are reported to be variable. However, the most common clinical syndrome is FTD, not SD or PA. In a French series of 32 *PGRN*-linked cases, the most common clinical diagnosis was FTD (63%), followed by PA (16%), Alzheimer's disease (9%), CBD (6%), and Lewy body disease (6%). Atypical symptoms for FTLD patients, such as visual hallucination (25%), motor apraxia (24%), constructional disturbance (48%), and episodic memory impairment (89%), were also noted in this series. Likewise, in the Manchester series (n = 14), FTD was the most common clinical phenotype (57%), followed by PA (36%) and progressive apraxia (7%).

CBD syndrome and asymmetric parkinsonism were noted in many *PGRN*-linked cases [Masellis et al., 2006, Snowden et al., 2006, Boeve et al., 2006, Spina et al., 2007, Mesulam et al., 2007, Guerreiro et al., 2008, Llado et al., 2008]. Hemineglect [Snowden et al., 2006, Spina et al., 2007], apraxia [Meiner et al., 2005, Masellis et al., 2006, Spina et al., 2007, Rohrer et al., 2008], alien hand sign [Masellis et al., 2006, Spina et al., 2007, Guerreiro et al., 2008], and visuospatial impairment [Meiner et al., 2005, Boeve et al., 2006, Rohrer et al., 2008] were also often noted in *PGRN*-linked cases. These findings led researchers to consider that at least some *PGRN*-linked cases have significant involvement in the parietal cortex. Indeed, parietal atrophy was observed on structural imaging in some *PGRN*-linked cases with parietal symptoms [Masellis et al., 2006, Spina et al., 2007], and FTLD-U cases with *PGRN* mutations tend to show more severe parietal atrophy than FTLD-U cases without it [Whitwell et al., 2007]. It is plausible that the occurrence of asymmetric parkinsonism and parietal involvement leads clinicians to make the clinical diagnosis of CBD, dementia with Lewy bodies, and Alzheimer's disease.

To our knowledge, there is only one histopathological study that semiquantitatively assessed and compared the distributions of degeneration between FTLD-U with and without *PGRN* mutations [Josephs et al., 2007]. In that study, degeneration in the frontal cortex was more severe than that in the temporal cortex in *PGRN*-linked FTLD-U, while temporal degeneration was less severe than frontal degeneration in FTLD-U cases without *PGRN* mutations. In that study, because 55% of FTLD-U cases without *PGRN* mutations had a family history, FTLD-U cases without *PGRN* mutations in that series were not necessarily sporadic cases.

II.4. Clinical Features in Sporadic FTLD-TDP

The frequency of familial cases among FTLD patients is not always high. In clinical FTLD series in Western countries, 6-50% of FTLD patients were reported to have a family history [Stevens et al., 1998, Snowden et al., 2002, Pickering-Brown et al., 2008, Le Ber et al., 2008]. It has been repeatedly reported that familial histories are very rare in Japanese FTLD patients [Ikeda et al., 2000, Hokoishi et al., 2001, Ikeda et al., 2001, Ikeda et al., 2004, Yokota et al., 2005]. Thus, for better understanding of FTLD-TDP patients, clinical information regarding sporadic FTLD-TDP is needed. However, somewhat unexpectedly, the

Clinical and Pathological Characteristics of Pick's Disease...   45

data regarding sporadic FTLD-TDP cases are very limited. Further, because FTLD-TDP was first proposed in 2009, its clinical features are speculated to be actually based on previously reported features of FTLD-U including FTLD-TDP and FTLD-UPS [Mackenzie et al., 2008].

The mean age at onset of sporadic FTLD-U or sporadic FTLD-TDP was reported to be about 55 years, and the mean disease duration about 9-10 years [Godbolt et al., 2005, Yokota et al., 2009]. It has been noticed that some sporadic FTLD-U and FTLD-TDP cases present clinically with SD [Rossor et al., 2000, Yokota et al., 2006]. A clinicopathological study showed that the most frequent pathological base in SD patients (n = 18) was sporadic FTLD-U (n = 9; 50%), followed by familial FTLD-U (n = 4; 22.2%), Pick's disease (n = 3; 16.7%), and Alzheimer's disease (n = 2; 11.1%) [Davies et al., 2005]. Likewise, in a study comparing familial and sporadic FTLD-U cases, only sporadic cases showed SD [Godbolt et al., 2005]. Other rare clinical pictures in sporadic FTLD-TDP were CBD (e.g., asymmetric parkinsonism, pyramidal signs, and/or apraxia) [Grimes et al., 1999] and PSP [Paviour et al., 2004]. Severe memory impairment, which is usually regarded as a symptom of Alzheimer's disease, is also noted in a few sporadic and familial FTLD-TDP cases [Graham et al., 2005].

We recently examined clinical and pathological features in 20 sporadic FTLD-TDP cases [Yokota et al., 2009]. In the study, all of the available clinical information including medical and nursing records was retrospectively reviewed with special attention to the following descriptions: irritability, euphoria, disinhibition, self-centered personality change, stereotypy, oral tendency and pica, language disturbance, semantic memory impairment (impaired comprehension and impaired recognition of common objects, faces, and written words), asymmetric motor symptoms (parkinsonism; pyramidal signs including Babinski sign, clonus, and hypertonia; contracture; and lower motor neuron signs), and other cognitive symptoms (memory impairment, apraxia, and unilateral spatial agnosia). Two FTLD-TDP cases were excluded from examination of clinical symptoms because clinical information was inadequate. The mean age at onset in 20 sporadic FTLD-TDP cases was 54.5 ± 8.2 years, the mean age at death 63.1 ± 9.2 years, and the mean disease duration 9.7 ± 5.4 years. Early symptoms that developed within one year after onset were shown in <u>Figure 2</u>. Frequent early symptoms in these cases were naming difficulty (50%), impaired semantic memory (39%), impaired auditory comprehension (22%), reduced speech output (22%), memory impairment (28%), disinhibition (28%), and apathy (28%). Although rare, gait disturbance, hemiparesis, buccofacial apraxia, persecutory delusion, and dysarthria were also noted. The frequency of semantic memory impairment in sporadic FTLD-TDP cases was significantly higher than that in Pick's disease cases examined simultaneously ($p = 0.008$, χ^2 test). Frequencies of psychiatric, behavioral, and language disturbances during the course were shown in <u>Figures 3 and 4</u>. Frequent psychiatric symptoms during the course were apathy (78%), stereotypy (61%), oral tendency and pica (50%), semantic memory impairment (44%), euphoria (33%), and impaired comprehension (28%). Impairment of speech output was rare (6%). Asymmetric motor disturbances were frequent (<u>Figure 5</u>). Asymmetric rigidity (44%), tremor (6%), pyramidal signs (i.e., Babinski's sign or ankle clonus: 44%), contracture (28%), and hemiparasis or hemiplegia (11%) were noted, and the total frequency of asymmetric motor disturbance was 78%. The mean duration from the disease onset to the development of asymmetric motor disturbances was about 6 years, and the mean duration from the development of asymmetric motor disturbances to death was 2.5 years.

III. FTLD with Tau-Positive Pick Bodies (Pick's Disease)

III.1. Pick Bodies

Although about 100 years have past since Pick bodies were noted by Alois Alzheimer [Alzheimer et al., 1911], the clinical data on Pick's disease is still limited because most of the previous studies collectively examined heterogeneous cases, including Pick's disease with and without Pick bodies. Now it is considered that presence of Pick bodies is a principle pathological hallmark of Pick's disease, and only cases having Pick bodies are diagnosed as having Pick's disease (<u>Figure 1d</u>). Pick bodies are round or oval argyrophilic neuronal intracytoplasmic inclusions. They appear to be less fibrillary than neurofibrillary tangles. Pick bodies are not found in clinically normal elderly people, being different from the neurofibrillary tangles that are often observed in cognitively normal elderly. Several silver stains, such as the Bielschowsky, Bodian, and Campbell methods, visualize this inclusion. In most Pick's disease cases, Pick bodies are not demonstrated with Gallyas-Braak silver stain. Pick bodies are tau-positive and frequently observed in the hippocampal dentate gyrus, CA1, subiculum, entorhinal cortex, and affected cerebral cortex, such as frontal, temporal, cingulated, and insular cortices. In the cerebral cortex, Pick bodies are frequent in layers II and VI.

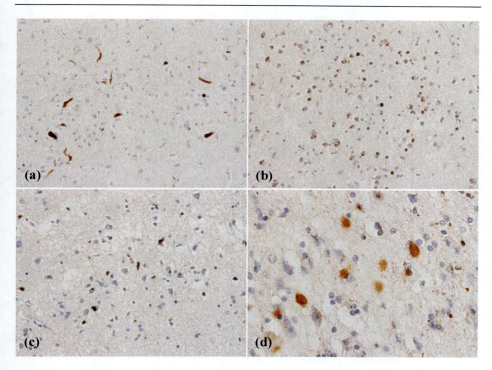

Figure 1. TDP-43 pathology and Pick bodies. (a) Type 1 histology of TDP-43 pathology. (b) Type 2 histology. (c) Type 3 histology. (d) Pick bodies. (a-c) Phosphorylated TDP-43 immunohistochemistry. (d) Tau immunohistochemistry. Scale bars: (a-c) 100 μm, (d) 50 μm.

III.2. Clinical features in Pick's Disease

Pick's disease is the second or third common pathology in FTLD patients, and the frequency is 10% to 30% [Munoz et al., 2003, Josephs et al., 2004, Lipton et al., 2004, Taniguchi et al., 2004, Forman et al., 2006, Kertesz et al., 2005, Shi et al., 2005]. The mean age at onset of Pick's disease is 55-60 years, and the mean disease duration is 8-10 years [Hodges et al., 2004, Kertesz et al., 2005, Forman et al., 2006, Josephs et al., 2004, Yokota et al., 2009]. It is considered that Pick's disease cases lack a family history.

Like FTLD-TDP, Pick's disease cases show several clinical phenotypes; however, several trends different from those in sporadic FTLD-TDP mentioned above are known. The most common clinical phenotype is FTD, and its frequency is reported to be 50–75% [Hodges et al., 2004, Kertesz et al., 2005, Josephs et al.,

2004, Shi et al., 2005]. PA can occur as the first syndrome (7–50%), although it is usually less common than FTD [Hodges et al., 2004, Kertesz et al., 2005, Shi et al., 2005]. SD as the first syndrome is very rare in previously reported FTLD-U cases [Kertesz et al., 2005, Davies et al., 2005, Shi et al., 2005]. A clinical picture of CBD is noted in some Pick's disease cases (8–20%) [Josephs et al., 2006, Shi et al., 2005]. To our knowledge, clinical evidence of motor neuron disease was not noted in any Pick's disease cases reported previously.

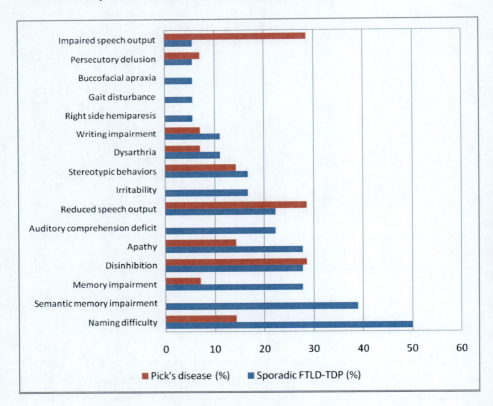

Figure 2. Early symptoms in sporadic FTLD-TDP and Pick's disease.

We recently reported the clinical and pathological features of a large series of Pick's disease (n = 19) [Yokota et al., 2009]. All the available clinical information of these cases was retrospectively examined using the same method as for sporadic FTLD-TDP mentioned above. Because the clinical information was inadequate in five Pick's disease cases, they were included into only pathological examination. Further, one Pick's disease case who suffered from young onset schizophrenia but lacked dementia during the course was also excluded when calculating the frequency of each symptom. The mean age at onset was 55.9 ± 7.5 years, the mean age at death 66.2 ± 8.3 years, and the mean disease duration 8.6 ± 5.0 years. These were not statistically different from those in sporadic FTLD-TDP cases mentioned above. Early symptoms within one year after the onset in Pick's disease cases were obviously different from those in sporadic FTLD-TDP (Figure 2). Frequent early symptoms were reduced speech output (29%), impairments of speech output (29%), and disinhibition (29%). Descriptions of stuttering and a hesitant quality in utterance, paraphasia, and apraxia of speech were counted as an impairment of speech output. Although not statistically significant, impaired speech output in Pick's disease cases was five times as frequent as that in FTLD-TDP cases. Semantic memory impairment, impaired comprehension, memory impairment, and gait disturbance in the early stage were rare or not noted in our Pick's disease cases. Although very rare, some Pick's disease cases showed persecutory delusion or dysarthria in the early stage. Frequencies of psychiatric, behavioral, and language disturbances during the course are shown in Figures 3 and 4.

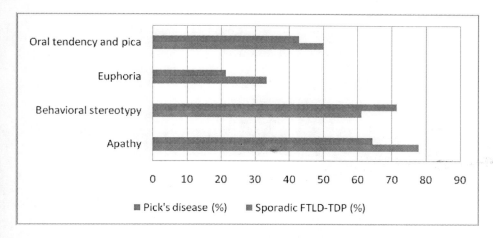

Figure 3. Frequencies of psychiatric and behavioral symptoms during the course in sporadic FTLD-TDP and Pick's disease.

Frequent symptoms were stereotypy (71%), apathy (64%), oral tendency and pica (43%), impaired speech output (29%), and euphoria (21%). Rare symptoms during the course were semantic memory impairment (0%) and impaired comprehension (7%).

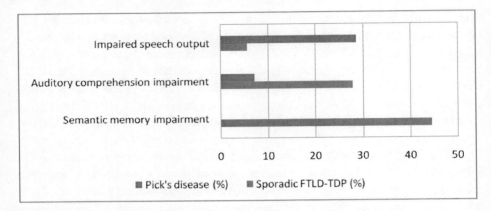

Figure 4. Frequencies of language and semantic memory impairment during the course in sporadic FTLD-TDP and Pick's disease.

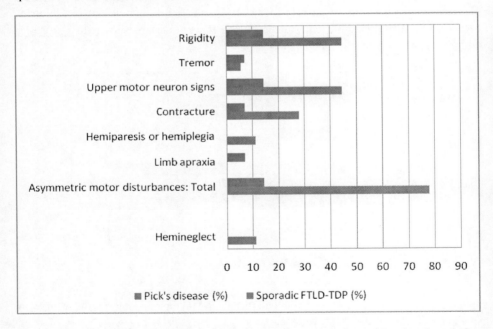

Figure 5. Frequencies of asymmetric motor disturbances, apraxia, and hemineglect during the course in sporadic FTLD-TDP and Pick's disease.

When compared between Pick's disease and sporadic FTLD-TDP, apathy (FTLD-TDP vs. Pick = 78% vs. 64%), euphoria (33% vs. 21%), oral tendency and pica (50% vs. 43%), impaired semantic memory (44% vs. 0%, $p = 0.004$, χ^2 test), and impaired auditory comprehension (28% vs. 7%) were less frequent in Pick's disease cases. In contrast, stereotypy (61% vs. 71%) and impaired speech output (6% vs. 29%) were frequent in Pick's disease. Although most of these differences were not statistically significant, these findings suggest that frontal involvement is more severe in Pick's disease, while temporal involvement is more severe in sporadic FTLD-TDP. Unlike FTLD-TDP, asymmetric motor disturbance was very rare in Pick's disease (Figure 5): it was noted in only 2 of 14 Pick's disease cases. In these two cases, the duration from the disease onset to the development of asymmetric motor disturbances were 4 and 5 years, and the mean durations from the development of asymmetric motor disturbances to death were 15 and 4 years, respectively.

IV. Evolving Patterns of Clinical Syndromes in Sporadic FTLD-TDP and Pick's Disease

The trends of clinical features in sporadic FTLD-TDP and Pick's disease cases led us to speculate the possibility that the temporal cortex is affected in the earlier stage in sporadic FTLD-TDP, while the frontal cortex is affected in the earlier stage in Pick's disease. Unexpectedly, the difference in the times of occurrence of each symptom between our sporadic FTLD-TDP and Pick's disease did not reach statistical significance (data not shown, Mann-Whitney's U-test).

Most of the FTLD patients sequentially developed several key clinical symptoms or syndromes with disease progression. Considering that FTD is characterized by behavioral disturbances mainly due to frontal involvement, SD is characterized by semantic memory impairment due to involvement of the temporal tip, and PA is characterized by progressive non-fluent aphasia due to involvement of the anterior perisylvian region, evolution patterns of clinical syndromes may reflect progression of the degenerative process in FTLD patients. Thus, we examined all evolving patterns of syndromes in all of our sporadic FTLD-TDP and Pick's disease cases. When descriptions of clinical pictures at some stage did not fit these syndromes, the most prominent symptoms at the stage were used (e.g., such as impaired comprehension, memory impairment, delusional state, gait disturbance, asymmetric parkinsonism, or unilateral spatial agnosia). This examination demonstrated clear differences in the clinical courses of the two diseases (Table 1).

Table 1. Evolving Pattern of Clinical Syndromes in Sporadic FTLD-TDP and Pick's Disease

	FTLD-TDP	Pick's disease
1	SD > FTD > AMD(rt)	FTD
2	SD > FTD > AMD(rt)	FTD
3	SD > FTD > AMD(rt)	FTD
4	SD > FTD	FTD
5	SD > FTD	FTD
6	SD	FTD
7	SD > AMD(rt)	FTD
8	FTD > IAC > AMD(rt) >SA(rt)	FTD
9	FTD > IAC > AMD(lt) >SA(lt)	FTD > IAC
10	FTD > SD > AMD(rt)	Delusional state> FTD > AMD(lt)
11	FTD > AMD(lt)	PA > FTD
12	FTD	PA
13	IAC > FTD > AMD(lt)	AOS > AMD(rt)
14	IAC > FTD > AMD(rt)	Schizophrenia (subclinical FTLD)
15	Memory impairment > FTD > AMD(rt)	
16	Memory impairment > FTD > AMD(lt)	
17	Gait disturbance > FTD > AMD(lt)	
18	Delusional state > IAC > FTD > AMD(rt)	

FTD, frontotemporal dementia; SD, semantic dementia; PA, progressive non-fluent aphasia; AOS, apraxia of speech; IAC, impairment of auditory comprehension; AMD(rt), right side-predominant motor disturbance; AMD(lt), left side-predominant motor disturbance; SA, unilateral spatial agnosia.

The most frequent first syndrome in sporadic FTLD-TDP was SD (39%), followed by FTD (28%). Other first clinical symptoms in sporadic FTLD-TDP were impairment of auditory comprehension, memory impairment, gait disturbance, and delusional state. It is possible that 'impaired comprehension' and 'memory impairment' were actually a part of the features of semantic memory impairment. Most patients who first showed SD presented later with FTD (5 of 7 cases). It was also noteworthy that most of the sporadic FTLD-TDP patients showed asymmetric motor disturbances during the course, including pyramidal signs, parkinsonism, and contracture. In contrast to sporadic FTLD-TDP, the most frequent first syndrome in Pick's disease cases was FTD (62%), followed by PA or speech apraxia (21%). Asymmetric motor disturbances were rare in Pick's disease. Therefore, even if patients showed FTD as the first syndrome, the

Clinical and Pathological Characteristics of Pick's Disease...   53

subsequent courses of sporadic FTLD-TDP and Pick's disease were different with respect of the development of asymmetric motor disturbances.

V. Clinicopathological Correlation in FTLD-TDP and Pick's Disease

The different trends in clinical features observed in our sporadic FTLD-TDP and Pick's disease cases led us to consider that the distribution of degeneration is different in these two conditions. Thus, we examined the distribution of neuronal loss in the major anatomical regions in 20 sporadic FTLD-TDP and 19 Pick's disease cases [Yokota et al., 2009]. The disease duration and brain weight in FTLD-TDP cases was not significantly different from those in Pick's disease cases (9.7 ± 5.4 years vs. 8.6 ± 5.0 years, 1049 ± 207 vs. 1012 ± 216 g, Mann-Whitney U-test).

The distribution of neuronal loss was significantly different in the two diseases. Neuronal losses in all regions of the frontal cortex in Pick's disease cases, including the orbital, superior frontal, middle frontal, and superior frontal gyri, were more severe than those in FTLD-TDP cases. The temporal cortex in sporadic FTLD-TDP cases was more severely degenerated than that in FTLD-TDP cases, and neuronal loss in the superior temporal gyrus in sporadic FTLD-TDP cases was significantly more severe than that in Pick's disease cases ($p = 0.022$, Mann-Whitney's U-test). Further, 75% cases of sporadic FTLD-TDP cases showed temporal-predominant neuronal loss, and the frontal and temporal cortices were degenerated almost equally in only 25% cases. In our series, no sporadic FTLD-TDP case showed frontal-predominant neuronal loss. In contrast, only 44% of Pick's disease cases showed temporal-predominant degeneration and 25% frontal-predominant degeneration. In 31% of Pick's disease cases, the frontal and temporal cortices were almost equally degenerated. Figures 6 and 7 show the proportion of cases having each distribution pattern of degeneration in the fronto-temporal cortex by disease duration. Interestingly, our Pick's disease cases with a disease duration of 0–5 years showed either frontal-predominant or temporal-predominant neuronal loss. However, as the duration increased, the proportion of these cases was reduced, and the proportion of cases which frontal and temporal cortices were equally affected was increased. In contrast, in sporadic FTLD-TDP cases, temporal-predominant cases were the most common, and cases in which the frontotemporal cortex was equally affected were less frequent, regardless of the disease duration. These histopathological findings appear to be consistent with the clinical trends that sporadic FTLD-TDP cases frequently show SD, and that

Pick's disease cases frequently show FTD in the early of the course. In addition, the parietal cortex was affected by evident neuronal loss in 20% of our FTLD-TDP and 16% of our Pick's disease cases, and some of these FTLD-TDP cases clinically showed unilateral spatial agnosia. Clinicians should be aware that the parietal cortex can be affected in some cases of sporadic FTLD-TDP and Pick's disease, and parietal symptoms can also develop in the late stage.

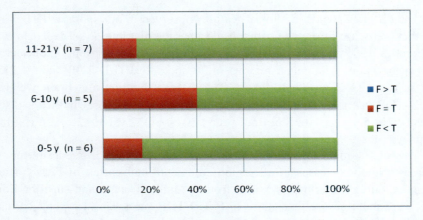

Figure 6. Distribution of neuronal loss in frontal and temporal cortices in sporadic FTLD-TDP by disease duration. F < T, temporal-predominant neuronal loss; F = T, equal degeneration in the frontal and temporal cortices; F > T, frontal-predominant neuronal loss.

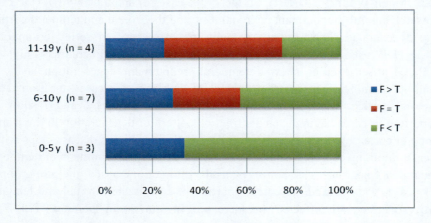

Figure 7. Severity of macroscopic atrophy in frontal and temporal cortices in Pick's disease by disease duration. F < T, temporal-predominant neuronal loss; F = T, equal degeneration in the frontal and temporal cortices; F > T, frontal-predominant neuronal loss.

Both FTLD-TDP and Pick's disease cases frequently showed moderate to severe degeneration in the insular cortex, cingulate gyrus, subiculum, parahippocampal gyrus, and amygdala. The reduction of pyramidal neurons in the hippocampal CA1 was found in about 40% cases of both disease groups, respectively.

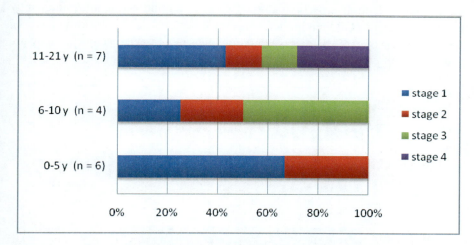

Figure 8. Severity of macroscopic atrophy in basal ganglia in sporadic FTLD-TDP by disease duration. Stage 0, no atrophy noted in the basal ganglia; stage 1, mild atrophy of the basal ganglia, but the structure of the caudate nucleus not flattened; stage 2, the structure of the caudate nucleus flattened, leading to dilation of the lateral ventricle; stage 3, the basal ganglia further degenerated, as evidenced by a concavity of the ventricular surface; and stage 4, the basal ganglia dramatically reduced in volume, and the ventricle consequently concave and grossly dilated.

The distributions of degeneration in the basal ganglia and brain stem were different in sporadic FTLD-TDP and Pick's disease [Yokota et al., 2009]. The caudate nucleus, putamen, and globus pallidus were significantly more severely degenerated in sporadic FTLD-TDP than in Pick's disease cases (p = 0.002, 0.002, 0.004, respectively; Mann-Whitney U-test). Degeneration in the substantia nigra in sporadic FTLD-TDP cases was significantly more severe than that in Pick's disease cases (p = 0.003, Mann-Whitney U-test). These histopathological trends were also noted in a macroscopic assessment of the sections. We semiquantitatively assessed the macroscopic reduction in the volume of the basal ganglia at the level of the temporal pole on the coronal slice using the modified staging system originally reported by Broe et al. [Broe et al., 2003]: stage 0, no atrophy was noted in the basal ganglia; stage 1, there was mild atrophy of the basal ganglia, but the structure of the caudate nucleus was not flattened; stage 2, the structure of the caudate nucleus was flattened, leading to dilation of the lateral ventricle; stage 3, the basal ganglia was further degenerated, as evidenced by a concavity of the ventricular surface; and stage 4, the basal ganglia was dramatically reduced in volume, and the ventricle was consequently concave and grossly dilated. The macroscopic atrophy of stages 3 and 4 was more frequently observed in FTLD-TDP than in Pick's disease cases (30% and 13%, respectively). The proportions of cases by disease duration and stage of macroscopic atrophy are shown in <u>Figures 8 and 9</u>.

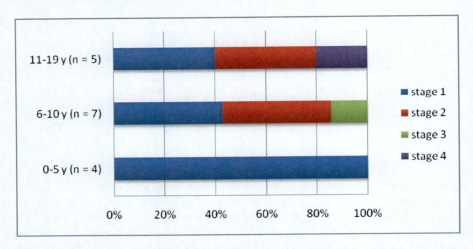

Figure 9. Severity of macroscopic atrophy in basal ganglia in Pick's disease by disease duration. See the definition of each stage in Figure 8.

The basal ganglia tended to shrink more severely in the FTLD-TDP group than the Pick's disease group. Given these findings, clinicians should be aware of the possibility that the atrophy of the basal ganglia on coronal images of MRI in sporadic FTLD-TDP patients tends to be severe than that in Pick's disease patients.

VII. Atrophy Patterns in FTLD Patients: Recent Findings of Volumetric MRI

Several studies have attempted to identify potential differences in the atrophy pattern among underlying pathologies using voxel-based morphometry on MRI.

Clinical and Pathological Characteristics of Pick's Disease...   57

We should direct attention to at least the following three factors potentially associated with an atrophy pattern when interpreting these findings: (i) FTLD-TDP patients have genetic heterogeneity. Namely, sporadic FTLD-TDP cases, *PGRN*-linked cases, and familial cases without *PGRN* mutations may not necessarily show identical distributions of cerebral atrophy, and at least sporadic FTLD-TDP may show a different atrophy pattern from *PGRN*-linked FTLD-TDP; (ii) disease duration may be a factor potentially associated with atrophy patterns in sporadic FTLD-TDP and Pick's disease patients, (iii) especially in studies employing a binary classification of tau- or ubiquitin-positive cases, the proportions of pathological disease entities in each group (e.g., the proportion of CBD/PSP in the tau-positive group) may strongly influence the results regarding atrophy patterns. Probably because of the influence of these issues, previous results were not always consistent.

Whitwell et al. examined nine tau-positive and eight tau-negative FTLD cases [Whitwell et al., 2004]. The tau-positive group included five Pick's disease cases and four FTLD-17, and the tau-negative cases were eight FTLD-U cases. A family history in FTLD-U cases was not noted. The mean age at examination in tau-positive group was 52 years, and that in tau-negative group 62 years. The mean disease duration in both groups was four years, respectively. The data on family history in the eight FTLD-U cases were not provided. In comparison with healthy controls, atrophy was observed in the anterior temporal lobes, frontal opercula and frontal convexities bilaterally in both disease groups. There was no region that was involved exclusively in the tau-positive or tau-negative group; however, atrophy was relatively more severe in the right anterior temporal lobe and bilateral prefrontal regions in the tau-positive group, and relatively more severe in the left posterior temporal lobe in the tau-negative group. A comparison of tau-positive and tau-negative groups yielded no significant differences in the regional gray matter volume.

Kim et al. examined six tau-positive cases (FTLD-T) and eight ubiquitin-positive cases (FTLD-U) [Kim et al., 2007]. Six of eight FTLD-U cases were FTLD-TDP. A family history in FTLD-U or FTLD-TDP cases was not noted. CBD, PSP, or dementia lacking distinctive histology (DLDH) cases were not included in this study. Further detailed data regarding underlying pathologies and a family history in each group were not noted. Compared with controls, both disease groups showed atrophy in the frontal and temporal lobes. When the two disease groups were compared, FTLD-T showed greater atrophy in the striatum that FTLD-U, although not statistically significantly.

Whitwell et al. examined 37 tau-positive cases (FTLD-T group: CBD = 12, PSP = 14, Pick's disease = 4, sporadic multisystem tau pathology = 2, FTLD with tau gene mutations = 5) and 44 FTLD-TDP cases (FTLD-U = 33, FTLD-MND = 11) [Whitwell et al., 2009a]. The family history data were not noted. Both disease groups showed frontal and temporal atrophy but with no statistical significance between the two groups. They suggested that the variability in patterns of atrophy in the variable diseases (e.g., CBD, PSP, Pick's disease, FTLD with tau gene mutations, FTLD-U) may have resulted in an overall absence of any meaningful signature for FTLD-T and FTLD-TDP.

Perreira et al. examined 9 FTLD-U and 6 tau-positive FTLD (FTD-T) cases [Perreira et al., 2009]. The FTLD-U cases included seven FTLD-TDP and two DLDH cases. The FTLD-T cases included three Pick's disease and three CBD cases. Two of seven FTLD-TDP cases had a family history, but did not have any *PGRN* mutations. The mean duration from the onset to MRI examination was 5.0 years in FTLD-U and 4.3 years in FTLD-T. The distribution of atrophy was very similar between FTLD-U and FTLD-T, and the severely affected sites included the temporal poles, medial frontal lobes, and insular cortex. The authors concluded that histologies were not linked with any specific pattern of atrophy, and previous findings, such as that FTLD-TDP was associated with the greater temporal atrophy, may be explained by case selection bias. However, their results may be influenced by the fact that half their FTLD-T cases were CBD, which usually shows severe frontal atrophy, that FTLD-U cases were genetically heterogeneous, and that the mean duration in their subjects was relatively short.

In contrast to the reports using a binary classification, there are a few studies that examined differences between more specific underlying pathologies. Whitwell et al. examined nine FTLD-U (three cases had a family history) and seven Pick's disease cases, and demonstrated that FTLD-U showed left-side predominant temporal atrophy and Pick's disease left-side frontal atrophy [Whitwell et al., 2005]. The disease duration and age at examination were matched between groups. Compared with controls, the FTLD-U group showed left-side predominant frontal and temporal atrophy, and the Pick's disease group showed severe and extensive bifrontal atrophy with milder atrophy in the temporal lobes. Atrophy unique to the FTLD-U group involved the orbitofrontal cortex, posterior superior temporal lobe, and posterior fusiform gyri bilaterally, and the atrophy was more severe in the left side. Atrophy unique to the Pick's disease group involved the dorsolateral frontal regions bilaterally. The bifrontal atrophy in the Pick's disease group was significantly more severe that that in FTLD-U group.

Whether there is a difference between in the pattern of atrophy in FTLD-U with and without *PGRN* mutations was also examined [Whitwell et al., 2007]. The *PGRN*-positive group (n = 8) showed widespread and severe atrophy in the

Clinical and Pathological Characteristics of Pick's Disease... 59

frontal, temporal, and parietal lobes, and the *PGRN*-negative group (n = 8) showed a less severe pattern of atrophy, mainly restricted to the temporal and frontal lobes. On direct comparison, the *PGRN*-positive cases showed more severe atrophy in the frontal and parietal lobes than the *PGRN*-negative cases. Two *PGRN*-negative cases had an autosomal dominant family history.

Atrophy patterns in FTLD cases with *PGRN* mutations were compared with those in FTLD cases with tau gene mutations in one previous study [Whitwell et al., 2009b]. Both disease groups showed atrophy in the frontal, temporal, and parietal lobes compared with controls. The atrophy was more predominant in the posterior temporal and parietal lobes in *PGRN*-linked cases and in the anteromedial temporal lobes in cases with tau gene mutations. Cases with tau gene mutations showed greater atrophy in the medial temporal lobes, insular cortex, and putamen than that in *PGRN*-linked cases.

In sum, taking previous pathological findings into consideration, atrophy patterns should be compared separately by specific pathology, especially with respect to sporadic and familial FTLD-TDP, rather than on a simple binary basis of histological type, so that more reliable and clinically useful data can be acquired.

VIII. Potential Biochemical Markers in FTLD

Use of several biochemical markers to infer underlying pathologies in FTLD patients has been reported. The concentration of PGRN in the plasma is a reliable biochemical marker in FTLD patients. Finch et al. reported that the plasma PGRN level in patients with *PGRN* loss-of-function mutations was significantly reduced to about one third of the levels observed in non-*PGRN* carriers and controls [Finch et al., 2009]. The reduction of PGRN level was also noted in asymptomatic cases with *PGRN* loss-of-function mutations. No overlap in the distributions of PGRN levels was observed between the *PGRN* loss-of-function mutation carriers and non-*PGRN* mutation carriers. Ghidoni et al. also demonstrated the potential usefulness of plasma PGRN levels in the diagnosis of familial FTLD cases [Ghidoni et al., 2008].

Foulds et al. [Foulds et al., 2008] reported that plasma TDP-43 level was elevated in 46% of FTLD patients and 22% of AD patients, compared to 8% of control subjects, although these cases were not pathologically confirmed. The TDP-43 level in the cerebrospinal fluid (CSF) was examined in two recent studies. Kasai et al. reported that the CSF TDP-43 level in patients with amyotrophic lateral sclerosis (ALS) was significantly higher than that in controls

[Kasai et al., 2009]. Steinacker et al. examined CSF TDP-43 levels in FTLD and ALS cases, and demonstrated that ALS patients and FTLD patients had significantly higher TDP-43 levels than controls but with a prominent overlap of values [Steinacker et al., 2008].

IX. Conclusion

Given the data presented in this paper, it is plausible that there are many clinical and pathological differences between the two major pathologies, sporadic FTLD-TDP and Pick's disease. Considering that in vivo Aβ imaging will soon be put to practical use, further clinical differentiation of pathological subtypes of FTLD besides AD will be needed. It is also important that to note that FTLD patients may have variable pathological entities such as CBD, PSP, BIBD, FTLD-IF, or Alzheimer's disease with atypical cerebral atrophy as well. However, given at least the results in our previous study, (i) when sporadic FTLD patients present with early impairment of semantic memory or auditory comprehension and subsequently develop asymmetric motor disturbances such as pyramidal signs, parkinsonism, or contracture, sporadic FTLD-TDP rather than Pick's disease may be a plausible pathology, and (ii) in sporadic FTLD patients who initially show behavioral symptoms or some impairment of speech output but lack subsequent asymmetric motor disturbances, Pick's disease rather than sporadic FTLD-TDP is a plausible pathology. Further, based on previous findings, (iii) the trend of clinical pictures in sporadic FTLD-TDP may be different from that in familial FTLD-TDP with *PGRN* mutations, which is clinically and pathologically characterized by frontal-predominant involvement. For more precise prediction of pathologies, comparative analysis focusing the clinical differences regarding between pathological entities should be done. In particular, data to predict clinical courses may aid clinicians and families in delivering appropriate medical care to FTLD patients.

Acknowledgement

This work was supported in part by a research grant from the Zikei Institute of Psychiatry.

Clinical and Pathological Characteristics of Pick's Disease... 61

References

Alzheimer, A. (1911). Über einenartige Krankheitsfälle des späteren alters. *Z. Gemsamte Neurol Psychiate*, **4**, 356-385.

Arai, T., Hasegawa, M., Akiyama, H., Ikeda, K., Nonaka, T., Mori, H., Mann, D., Tsuchiya, K., Yoshida, M., Hashizume, Y., & Oda, T. (2006). TDP-43 is a component of ubiquitin-positive tau-negative inclusions in frontotemporal lobar degeneration and amyotrophic lateral sclerosis. *Biochem Biophys Res Commun*, **351**, 602-611.

Baker, M., Mackenzie, I. R., Pickering-Brown, S. M., Gass, J., Rademakers, R., Lindholm, C., Snowden, J., Adamson, J., Sadovnick, A. D., Rollinson, S., Cannon, A., Dwosh, E., Neary, D., Melquist, S., Richardson, A., Dickson, D., Berger, Z., Eriksen, J., Robinson, T., Zehr, C., Dickey, C. A., Crook, R., McGowan, E., Mann, D., Boeve, B., Feldman, H., & Hutton, M. (2006). Mutations in progranulin cause tau-negative frontotemporal dementia linked to chromosome 17. *Nature*, **442**, 916-919.

Beck, J., Rohrer, J. D., Campbell, T., Isaacs, A., Morrison, K. E., Goodall, E. F., Warrington, E. K., Stevens, J., Revesz, T., Holton, J., Al-Sarraj, S., King, A., Scahill, R., Warren, J. D., Fox, N. C., Rossor, M. N., Collinge, J., & Mead, S. (2008). A distinct clinical, neuropsychological and radiological phenotype is associated with progranulin gene mutations in a large UK series. *Brain*, **131**, 706-720.

Boeve, B. F., Baker, M., Dickson, D. W., Parisi, J. E., Giannini, C., Josephs, K. A., Hutton, M., Pickering-Brown, S. M., Rademakers, R., Tang-Wai, D., Jack, C. R. Jr., Kantarci, K., Shiung, M. M., Golde, T., Smith, G. E., Geda, Y. E., Knopman, D. S., & Petersen, R. C. (2006). Frontotemporal dementia and parkinsonism associated with the IVS1+1G->A mutation in progranulin: a clinicopathologic study. *Brain*, **129**, 3103-3114.

Braak, H., & Braak, E., (1987). Argyrophilic grains characteristic pathology of cerebral cortex in cases of adult onset dementia without Alzheimer changes. *Neurosci. Lett.*, **76**,124-127.

Broe, M., Hodges, J. R., Schofield, E., Shepherd, C. E., Kril, J. J., & Halliday, G. M. (2003). Staging disease severity in pathologically confirmed cases of frontotemporal dementia. *Neurology*, **60**, 1005-1011.

Cairns, N. J., Bigio, E. H., Mackenzie, I. R., Neumann, M., Lee, V. M., Hatanpaa, K. J., White, C. L. 3rd, Schneider, J. A., Grinberg, L. T., Halliday, G., Duyckaerts, C., Lowe, J. S., Holm, I. E., Tolnay, M., Okamoto, K., Yokoo, H., Murayama, S., Woulfe, J., Munoz, D. G., Dickson, D. W., Ince, P. G., Trojanowski, J. Q., & Mann, D. M. Consortium for Frontotemporal Lobar

Degeneration (2007a). Neuropathologic diagnostic and nosologic criteria for frontotemporal lobar degeneration: consensus of the Consortium for Frontotemporal Lobar Degeneration. *Acta Neuropathol.*, **114**, 5-22.

Cairns, N. J., Neumann, M., Bigio, E. H., Holm, I. E., Troost, D., Hatanpaa, K. J., Foong, C., White, C. L. 3rd, Schneider, J. A., Kretzschmar, H. A., Carter, D., Taylor-Reinwald, L., Paulsmeyer, K., Strider, J., Gitcho, M., Goate, A. M., Morris, J. C., Mishra, M., Kwong, L. K., Stieber, A., Xu, Y., Forman, M. S., Trojanowski, J. Q., Lee, V. M., & Mackenzie, I. R. (2007b) TDP-43 in familial and sporadic frontotemporal lobar degeneration with ubiquitin inclusions. *Am. J. Pathol.*, **171**, 227-140.

Cairns, N. J., Perry, R. H., Jaros, E., Burn, D., McKeith, I. G., Lowe, J. S., Holton, J., Rossor, M. N., Skullerud, K., Duyckaerts, C., Cruz-Sanchez, F. F., & Lantos, P. L. (2003). Patients with a novel neurofilamentopathy: dementia with neurofilament inclusions. *Neurosci. Lett.,* **341**, 177-180.

Davies, R. R., Hodges, J. R., Kril, J. J., Patterson, K., Halliday, G. M., & Xuereb, J. H. (2005). The pathological basis of semantic dementia. *Brain,* **128**, 1984-1995.

Finch, N., Baker, M., Crook, R., Swanson, K., Kuntz, K., Surtees, R., Bisceglio, G., Rovelet-Lecrux, A., Boeve, B., Petersen, R. C., Dickson, D. W., Younkin, S. G., Deramecourt, V., Crook, J., Graff-Radford, N. R., & Rademakers, R. (2009). Plasma progranulin levels predict progranulin mutation status in frontotemporal dementia patients and asymptomatic family members. *Brain,* **132**, 583-591.

Forman, M. S., Farmer, J., Johnson, J. K., Clark, C. M., Arnold, S. E., Coslett, H. B., Chatterjee, A., Hurtig, H. I., Karlawish, J. H., Rosen, H. J., Van Deerlin, V., Lee, V. M., Miller, B. L., Trojanowski, J. Q., & Grossman, M. (2006). Frontotemporal dementia: clinicopathological correlations. *Ann. Neurol.,* **59**, 952-962.

Foulds, P., McAuley, E., Gibbons, L., Davidson, Y., Pickering-Brown, S. M., Neary, D., Snowden, J. S., Allsop, D., & Mann, D. M. (2008). TDP-43 protein in plasma may index TDP-43 brain pathology in Alzheimer's disease and frontotemporal lobar degeneration. *Acta Neuropathol.,* **116**, 141-146.

Ghidoni, R., Benussi, L., Glionna, M., Franzoni, M., & Binetti, G. (2008). Low plasma progranulin levels predict progranulin mutations in frontotemporal lobar degeneration. *Neurology,* **71**, 1235-1239.

Godbolt, A. K., Josephs, K. A., Revesz, T., Warrington, E. K., Lantos, P., King, A., Fox, N. C., Al Sarraj, S., Holton, J., Cipolotti, L., Khan, M. N., & Rossor, M. N. (2005). Sporadic and familial dementia with ubiquitin-positive tau-

Clinical and Pathological Characteristics of Pick's Disease... 63

negative inclusions: clinical features of one histopathological abnormality underlying frontotemporal lobar degeneration. *Arch. Neurol., 62,* 1097-1101.

Graham, A., Davies, R., Xuereb, J., Halliday, G., Kril, J., Creasey, H., Graham, K., Hodges, J. (2005) Pathologically proven frontotemporal dementia presenting with severe amnesia. *Brain, 128,* 597-605.

Grimes, D. A., Bergeron, C. B., & Lang, A. E. (1999). Motor neuron disease-inclusion dementia presenting as cortical-basal ganglionic degeneration. *Mov. Disord., 14,* 674-680.

Guerreiro, R. J., Santana, I., Bras, J. M., Revesz, T., Rebelo, O., Ribeiro, M. H., Santiago, B., Oliveira, C. R., Singleton, A., & Hardy, J. (2008). Novel progranulin mutation: screening for PGRN mutations in a Portuguese series of FTD/CBS cases. *Mov. Disord., 23,* 1269-1273.

Hodges, J. R., Davies, R. R., Xuereb, J. H., Casey, B., Broe, M., Bak, T. H., Kri,l J. J., & Halliday, G. M. (2004). Clinicopathological correlates in frontotemporal dementia. *Ann. Neurol., 56,* 399-406.

Hokoishi, K., Ikeda, M., Maki, N., Nebu, A., Shigenobu, K., Fukuhara, R., Komori, K., & Tanabe, H. (2001). Frontotemporal lobar degeneration: a study in Japan. *Dement Geriatr. Cogn. Disord., 12,* 393-399.

Ikeda, K. (2000). Neuropathological discrepancy between Japanese Pick's disease without Pick bodies and frontal lobe degeneration type of frontotemporal dementia proposed by Lund and Manchester Group. *Neuropathology, 20,* 76-82.

Ikeda, M., Hokoishi, K., Maki, N., Nebu, A., Tachibana, N., Komori, K., Shigenobu, K., Fukuhara, R., & Tanabe, H. (2001). Increased prevalence of vascular dementia in Japan: a community-based epidemiological study. *Neurology, 57,* 839-844.

Ikeda, M., Ishikawa, T., & Tanabe, H. (2004). Epidemiology of frontotemporal lobar degeneration. *Dementia and Geriatric Cognitive Disorders, 17,* 265-268.

Ishihara, K., Araki, S., Ihori, N., Shiota, J., Kawamura, M., Yoshida, M., Hashizume, Y., & Nakano, I. (2005). Argyrophilic grain disease presenting with frontotemporal dementia: a neuropsychological and pathological study of an autopsied case with presenile onset. *Neuropathology, 25,* 165-170.

Jackson, M., & Lowe, J. (1996).The new neuropathology of degenerative frontotemporal dementias. *Acta Neuropathol., 91,*127-134.

Jackson, M., Lennox, G., & Lowe, J. (1996). Motor neuron disease-inclusion dementia. *Neurodegeneration, 5,* 339–350.

Josephs, K. A., Ahmed, Z., Katsuse, O., Parisi, J. F., Boeve, B. F., Knopman, D. S., Petersen, R. C., Davies, P., Duara, R., Graff-Radford, N. R., Uitti, R. J.,

Rademakers, R., Adamson, J., Baker, M., Hutton, M. L., & Dickson, D. W. (2007). Neuropathologic features of frontotemporal lobar degeneration with ubiquitin-positive inclusions with progranulin gene (PGRN) mutations. *J. Neuropathol. Exp. Neurol.,* **66**, 142-151.

Josephs, K. A., Holton, J. L., Rossor, M. N., Braendgaard, H., Ozawa, T., Fox, N. C., Petersen, R. C., Pearl, G. S., Ganguly, M., Rosa, P., Laursen, H., Parisi, J. E., Waldemar, G., Quinn, N. P., Dickson, D. W., & Revesz, T. (2003). Neurofilament inclusion body disease: a new proteinopathy? *Brain,* **126**, 2291-2303.

Josephs, K. A., Holton, J. L., Rossor, M. N., Godbolt, A. K., Ozawa, T., Strand, K., Khan, N., Al-Sarraj, S., & Revesz, T. (2004). Frontotemporal lobar degeneration and ubiquitin immunohistochemistry. *Neuropathol. Appl. Neurobiol.,* **30**, 369-373.

Josephs, K. A., Petersen, R. C., Knopman, D. S., Boeve, B. F., Whitwell, J. L., Duffy, J. R., Parisi, J. E., & Dickson, D. W. (2006). Clinicopathologic analysis of frontotemporal and corticobasal degenerations and PSP. *Neurology,* **66**, 41-48.

Kasai, T., Tokuda, T., Ishigami, N., Sasayama, H., Foulds, P., Mitchell, D. J., Mann, D. M., Allsop, D., & Nakagawa, M. (2009). Increased TDP-43 protein in cerebrospinal fluid of patients with amyotrophic lateral sclerosis. *Acta Neuropathol.,* **117**, 55-62.

Kelley, B. J., Haidar, W., Boeve, B. F., Baker, M., Graff-Radford, N. R., Krefft, T., Frank, A. R., Jack, C. R. Jr., Shiung, M., Knopman, D. S., Josephs, K. A., Parashos, S. A., Rademakers, R., Hutton, M., Pickering-Brown, S., Adamson, J., Kuntz, K. M., Dickson, D. W., Parisi, J. E., Smith, G. E., Ivnik, R. J., & Petersen, R. C. (2009). Prominent phenotypic variability associated with mutations in Progranulin. *Neurobiol. Aging.,* **30**, 739-751.

Kertesz, A., McMonagle, P., Blair, M., Davidson, W., & Munoz, D. G. (2005). The evolution and pathology of frontotemporal dementia. *Brain,* **128**, 1996-2005.

Kim, E. J., Rabinovici, G. D., Seeley, W. W., Halabi, C., Shu, H., Weiner, M. W., DeArmond, S. J., Trojanowski, J. Q., Gorno-Tempini, M. L., Miller, B. L., & Rosen, H. J. (2007). Patterns of MRI atrophy in tau positive and ubiquitin positive frontotemporal lobar degeneration. *J. Neurol. Neurosurg .Psychiatry,* **78**, 1375-1378.

Le Ber, I., Camuzat, A., Hannequin, D., Pasquier, F., Guedj, E., Rovelet-Lecrux, A., Hahn-Barma, V., van der Zee, J., Clot, F., Bakchine, S., Puel, M., Ghanim, M., Lacomblez, L., Mikol, J., Deramecourt, V., Lejeune, P., de la Sayette, V., Belliard, S., Vercelletto, M., Meyrignac, C., Van Broeckhoven,

Clinical and Pathological Characteristics of Pick's Disease... 65

C., Lambert, J. C., Verpillat, P., Campion, D., Habert, M. O., Dubois, B., & Brice, A.: French Research Network on FTD/FTD-MND. (2008). Phenotype variability in progranulin mutation carriers: a clinical, neuropsychological, imaging and genetic study. *Brain,* **131**, 732-746.

Lipton, A. M., White, C. L. 3rd, & Bigio, E. H. (2004). Frontotemporal lobar degeneration with motor neuron disease-type inclusions predominates in 76 cases of frontotemporal degeneration. *Acta Neuropathol.,***108**, 379-385.

Lladó, A., Sánchez-Valle, R., Rey, M. J., Ezquerra, M., Tolosa, E., Ferrer, I., & Molinuevo, J. L., Catalan collaborative Study Group for FTLD. (2008). Clinicopathological and genetic correlates of frontotemporal lobar degeneration and corticobasal degeneration. *J. Neurol.,* **255**, 488-494.

Mackenzie, I. R., Foti, D., Woulfe, J., & Hurwitz, T. A. (2008). Atypical frontotemporal lobar degeneration with ubiquitin-positive, TDP-43-negative neuronal inclusions. *Brain,* **131**, 1282-1293.

Mackenzie, I. R., Neumann, M., Bigio, E. H., Cairns, N. J., Alafuzoff, I., Kril, J., Kovacs, G. G., Ghetti, B., Halliday, G., Holm, I. E., Ince, P. G., Kamphorst, W., Revesz, T., Rozemuller, A. J., Kumar-Singh. S., Akiyama, H., Baborie, A., Spina, S., Dickson, D. W., Trojanowski, J. Q., & Mann, D. M. (2009). Nomenclature for neuropathologic subtypes of frontotemporal lobar degeneration: consensus recommendations. *Acta Neuropathol.,* **117**, 15-18.

Mackenzie, I. R., Shi, J., Shaw, C. L., Duplessis, D., Neary, D., Snowden, J. S., & Mann, D. M. (2006) Dementia lacking distinctive histology (DLDH) revisited. *Acta Neuropathol.,* **112**, 551-559.

Masellis, M., Momeni, P., Meschino, W., Heffner, R. Jr., Elder, J., Sato, C., Liang, Y., St George-Hyslop, P., Hardy, J., Bilbao, J., Black, S., & Rogaeva, E. (2006). Novel splicing mutation in the progranulin gene causing familial corticobasal syndrome. *Brain,* **129**, 3115-3123.

Meiner, Z., Newman, J. P., Rosenman, H., Soffer, D., & Steiner, I. (2005). Frontotemporal dementia with ubiquitinated neuronal inclusions and visuospatial impairment. *Neurology,* **65**, 478-480.

Mesulam, M., Johnson, N., Krefft, T.A., Gass, J. M., Cannon, A.D., Adamson, J.L., Bigio, E. H., Weintraub, S., Dickson, D. W., Hutton, M. L., & Graff-Radford, N. R. (2007). Progranulin mutations in primary progressive aphasia: the PPA1 and PPA3 families. *Arch. Neurol.,* **64**, 43-7.

Morita, M., Al-Chalabi, A., Andersen, P. M., Hosler, B., Sapp, P., Englund, E., Mitchell, J. E., Habgood, J. J., de Belleroche, J., Xi, J., Jongjaroenprasert, W., Horvitz, H. R., Gunnarsson, L. G., & Brown, R. H. Jr. (2006). A locus on chromosome 9p confers susceptibility to ALS and frontotemporal dementia. *Neurology,* **66**, 839-844.

Munoz, D. G., Dickson, D. W., Bergeron, C., Mackenzie, I. R., Delacourte, A., & Zhukareva, V. (2003). The neuropathology and biochemistry of frontotemporal dementia. *Ann. Neurol.,* **54**, Suppl 5, S24-S28.

Munoz-Garcia, D., & Ludwin, S. K. (1984). Classic and generalized variants of Pick's disease: a clinicopathological, ultrastructural, and immunocytochemical comparative study. *Ann. Neurol.,* **16**, 467-480.

Neumann, M., Sampathu, D. M., Kwong, L. K., Truax, A. C., Micsenyi, M. C., Chou, T. T., Bruce, J., Schuck, T., Grossman, M., Clark, C. M., McCluskey, L. F., Miller, B. L., Masliah, E., Mackenzie, I. R., Feldman, H., Feiden, W., Kretzschmar, H. A., Trojanowski, J. Q., & Lee, V. M. (2006). Ubiquitinated TDP-43 in frontotemporal lobar degeneration and amyotrophic lateral sclerosis. *Science,* **314**, 130-133.

Onari, K., & Spatz, H. (1926). Anatomische Beiträge zur Lehre von Pickschen umschriebenen Größhirnrinden Atrophie (Picksche Krankheit). *Z. Ges. Neurol. Psychiatr.,* **101**, 470-511.

Paviour, D. C., Lees, A. J., Josephs, K. A., Ozawa, T., Ganguly, M., Strand, C., Godbolt, A., Howard, R. S., Revesz, T., & Holton, J. L. (2004). Frontotemporal lobar degeneration with ubiquitin-only-immunoreactive neuronal changes: broadening the clinical picture to include progressive supranuclear palsy. *Brain,* **127**, 2441-2451.

Pereira, J. M., Williams, G. B., Acosta-Cabronero, J., Pengas, G., Spillantini, M. G., Xuereb, J. H., Hodges, J. R., & Nestor, P. J. (2009). Atrophy patterns in histologic vs clinical groupings of frontotemporal lobar degeneration. *Neurology,* **72**, 1653-1660.

Pick, A. (1892). Ueber die Beziehungen der senilen Hirnatrophie zur Aphasie. *Prag. Med. Wochenschr.,* **17**, 165-167.

Pickering-Brown, S. M. (2007). Progranulin and frontotemporal lobar degeneration. *Acta Neruopathol.,* **114**, 39-47.

Pickering-Brown, S. M., Rollinson, S., Du Plessis, D., Morrison, K. E., Varma, A., Richardson, A. M., Neary, D., Snowden, J. S., & Mann, D. M. (2008). Frequency and clinical characteristics of progranulin mutation carriers in the Manchester frontotemporal lobar degeneration cohort: comparison with patients with MAPT and no known mutations. *Brain,* **131**, 721-731.

Rohrer, J. D., Warren, J. D., Omar, R., Mead, S., Beck, J., Revesz, T., Holton, J., Stevens, J. M., Al-Sarraj, S., Pickering-Brown, S. M., Hardy, J., Fox, N. C., Collinge, J., Warrington, E. K., & Rossor, M. N. (2008). Parietal lobe deficits in frontotemporal lobar degeneration caused by a mutation in the progranulin gene. *Arch. Neurol.,* **65**, 506-513.

Clinical and Pathological Characteristics of Pick's Disease...   67

Rossor, M. N., Revesz, T., Lantos, P. L., & Warrington, E. K. (2000). Semantic dementia with ubiquitin-positive tau-negative inclusion bodies. *Brain,* **123**, 267-276.

Shi, J., Shaw, C. L., Du Plessis, D., Richardson, A. M., Bailey, K. L., Julien, C., Stopford, C., Thompson, J., Varma, A., Craufurd, D., Tian, J., Pickering-Brown, S., Neary, D., Snowden, J. S., & Mann, D. M. (2005). Histopathological changes underlying frontotemporal lobar degeneration with clinicopathological correlation. *Acta Neuropathol.,* **110**, 501-512.

Skibinski, G., Parkinson, N. J., Brown, J. M., Chakrabarti, L., Lloyd, S. L., Hummerich, H., Nielsen, J. E., Hodges, J. R., Spillantini, M. G., Thusgaard, T., Brandner, S., Brun, A., Rossor, M. N., Gade, A., Johannsen, P., Sørensen, S. A., Gydesen, S., Fisher, E. M., & Collinge, J. (2005). Mutations in the endosomal ESCRTIII-complex subunit CHMP2B in frontotemporal dementia. *Nat. Genet.,* **37**, 806-808.

Snowden, J. S., Neary, D., & Mann, D. M. (2002). Frontotemporal dementia. *Br. J. Psychiatry,* **180**, 140-143.

Snowden, J. S., Pickering-Brown, S. M., Mackenzie, I. R., Richardson, A. M., Varma, A., Neary, D., & Mann, D. M. (2006). Progranulin gene mutations associated with frontotemporal dementia and progressive non-fluent aphasia. *Brain,* **129**, 3091-3102.

Spina, S., Murrell, J. R., Huey, E. D., Wassermann, E. M., Pietrini, P., Grafman, J., & Ghetti, B. (2007). Corticobasal syndrome associated with the A9D progranulin mutation. *J. Neuropathol. Exp. Neurol.,* **66**, 892-900.

Steinacker, P., Hendrich, C., Sperfeld, A. D., Jesse, S., von Arnim, C. A., Lehnert, S., Pabst, A., Uttner, I., Tumani, H., Lee, V. M., Trojanowski, J. Q., Kretzschmar, H. A., Ludolph, A., Neumann, M., & Otto, M. (2008). TDP-43 in cerebrospinal fluid of patients with frontotemporal lobar degeneration and amyotrophic lateral sclerosis. *Arch. Neurol.,* **65**, 1481-1487.

Stevens, M., van Duijn, C. M., Kamphorst, W., de Knijff, P., Heutink, P., van Gool, W. A., Scheltens, P., Ravid, R., Oostra, B. A., Niermeijer, M. F., & van Swieten, J. C. (1998). Familial aggregation in frontotemporal dementia. *Neurology,* **50**, 1541-1545.

Taniguchi, S., McDonagh, A. M., Pickering-Brown, S. M., Umeda, Y., Iwatsubo, T., Hasegawa, M., & Mann, D. M. (2004). The neuropathology of frontotemporal lobar degeneration with respect to the cytological and biochemical characteristics of tau protein. *Neuropathol. Appl. Neurobiol.,* **30**, 1-18.

Tsuchiya, K., Mitani, K., Arai, T., Yamada, S., Komiya, T., Esaki, Y., Haga, C., Yamanouchi, H., & Ikeda, K. (2001). Argyrophilic grain disease mimicking

68 Osamu Yokota and Kuniaki Tsuchiya

temporal Pick's disease: a clinical, radiological, and pathological study of an autopsy case with a clinical course of 15 years. *Acta Neuropathol.,***102**,195-199.

Van Deerlin, V. M., Wood, E. M., Moore, P., Yuan, W., Forman, M. S., Clark, C. M., Neumann, M., Kwong, L. K., Trojanowski, J. Q., Lee, V.M., & Grossman, M. (2007). Clinical, genetic, and pathologic characteristics of patients with frontotemporal dementia and progranulin mutations. *Arch. Neurol.,* **64**, 1148-1153.

Watts, G. D., Wymer, J., Kovach, M. J., Mehta, S. G., Mumm, S., Darvish, D., Pestronk, A., Whyte, M. P., & Kimonis, V. E. (2004). Inclusion body myopathy associated with Paget disease of bone and frontotemporal dementia is caused by mutant valosin-containing protein. *Nat. Genet.,* **36**, 377-381.

Whitwell, J. L., Jack, C. R. Jr., Baker, M., Rademakers, R., Adamson, J., Boeve, B. F., Knopman, D. S., Parisi, J. F., Petersen, R. C., Dickson, D. W., Hutton, M. L., & Josephs, K. A. (2007). Voxel-based morphometry in frontotemporal lobar degeneration with ubiquitin-positive inclusions with and without progranulin mutations. *Arch. Neurol.,* **64**, 371-376.

Whitwell, J. L., Jack, C. R. Jr., Senjem, M. L., Parisi, J. E., Boeve, B. F., Knopman, D. S., Dickson, D. W., Petersen, R. C., & Josephs, K. A. (2009a). MRI correlates of protein deposition and disease severity in postmortem frontotemporal lobar degeneration. *Neurodegener. Dis.,* **6**,106-117.

Whitwell, J. L., Jack, C. R. Jr., Boeve, B. F., Senjem, M. L., Baker, M., Rademakers, R., Ivnik, R. J., Knopman, D. S., Wszolek, Z. K., Petersen, R. C., & Josephs, K. A. (2009b). Voxel-based morphometry patterns of atrophy in FTLD with mutations in MAPT or PGRN. *Neurology,* **72**, 813-820.

Whitwell, J. L., Josephs, K. A., Rossor, M. N., Stevens, J. M., Revesz, T., Holton, J. L., Al-Sarraj, S., Godbolt, A. K., Fox, N. C., & Warren, J. D. (2005). Magnetic resonance imaging signatures of tissue pathology in frontotemporal dementia. *Arch. Neurol.,* **62**, 1402-8.

Whitwell, J. L., Warren, J. D., Josephs, K. A., Godbolt, A. K., Revesz, T., Fox, N. C., & Rossor, M. N. (2004). Voxel-based morphometry in tau-positive and tau-negative frontotemporal lobar degenerations. *Neurodegener. Dis.,* **1**, 225-230.

Yokota, O., Sasaki, K., Fujisawa, Y., Takahashi, J., Terada, S., Ishihara, T., Nakashima, H., Kugo, A., Ata, T., Ishizu, H., & Kuroda, S. (2005). Frequency of early and late-onset dementias in a Japanese memory disorders clinic. *Eur. J. Neurol.,* **12**, 782-790.

Yokota, O., Tsuchiya, K., Arai, T., Yagishita, S., Mochizuki, A., Tamaoka, A., Yoshida, H., Terada, S., Ishizu, H., Kuroda, S., & Akiyama, H. (2009)

Clinicopathological characterization of Pick's disease versus frontotemporal lobar degeneration with ubiquitin/TDP-43-positive inclusions. *Acta Neuropathol., 117*, 429-444.

Yokota, O., Tsuchiya, K., Itoh, Y., Ishizu, H., Akiyama, H., Ikeda, M., Kuzuhara, S., & Otomo, E. (2006). Frontotemporal lobar degeneration with ubiquitin pathology: an autopsy case presenting with semantic dementia and upper motor neuron signs with a clinical course of 19 years. *Acta Neuropathol., 112*, 739-749.

In: Handbook of Neuropsychiatry Research
Editor: Rebecca S. Davies, pp. 71-95

ISBN: 978-1-61668-138-8
© 2010 Nova Science Publishers, Inc.

Chapter 3

INTERVENTIONS FOR AFFECTIVE AND BEHAVIOURAL DISTURBANCES IN ACQUIRED BRAIN INJURY: A CONCEPTUAL FRAMEWORK BASED ON THE STAGES OF CHANGE THEORY

Erin M. Warriner[1,2], Hiten Lad[1] and Diana Velikonja[1,2]

[1] Hamilton Health Sciences
[2] McMaster University, Department of Psychiatry
and Behavioural Neurosciences

Abstract

High rates of psychiatric difficulties and poor psychosocial and emotional adjustment occur in ABI. This review chapter briefly summarizes the prevalence and common presentations of emotional disturbances in ABI and reviews the current literature on treatment interventions. While there is general consensus on the utility of psychological treatment in ABI, the research remains less clear on the effectiveness and timing of different types of interventions for specific symptom presentations. We describe a theoretical framework based on the Stages of Change model that offers a way to conceptualize readiness for change and how specific strategies/approaches may be most beneficial to facilitate change in the ABI population.

Inrtoduction

The Prevalence and Presentation of Affective & Behavioural Disturbances in ABI

High proportions of individuals with acquired brain injuries (ABI) experience clinically significant affective and behavioural disturbances that influence functional recovery and long-term adjustment. Studies have estimated that Axis I (50 to 80%) and Axis II (25 to 65%) disorders are prevalent both immediately after a brain injury and even decades later (e.g., Dikmen, Machamer & Temkin, 1993; Hibbard, Uysal, Kepler, Bogdany & Silver, 1998; Hibbard et al., 2000; Koponen et al., 2002). Major depression, anxiety and substance abuse were the most prevalent Axis I diagnoses and personality disorders with features of emotional lability, impulsivity, disinhibition, apathy, and paranoia were frequently identified across these studies. The identification of emotional disturbance in the ABI population is important because affective distress has been associated with poorer recovery and functional declines that often exceed expectation based upon injury severity indicators. This includes an inability to resume premorbid functioning in employment, domestic roles, and community integration, resulting in significant interpersonal and economic losses over time (e.g., Cicerone et al., 1996; Felmingham, Baguley & Crooks, 2001), which often maintains and exacerbates emotional distress.

Previous work by our group has identified several consistent subtypes with distinct emotional and behavioural profiles in large samples of adult ABI patients based on multi-dimensional reliable instruments (i.e., initially done with the Minnesota Multiphasic Personality Inventory and recently replicated with the Personality Assessment Inventory-PAI) (Warriner, Rourke, Velikonja & Metham, 2003; Velikonja, Warriner & Brum, 2009). In the recent study with the PAI, half of the sample showed elevated profiles with affective and behavioural symptoms characterized by multiple DSM Axis I and/or II features, while the other half had profiles generally within the normal range with only minimal or mild symptom complaints. The most prevalent Axis I features identified included depression, anxiety and somatic complaints with 30-40% displaying clinically significant symptoms. Two subgroups comprising about 27% had predominantly internalized presentations with one group of individuals identifying mainly depressive and somatic features, while another subset showed mild anxiety and complaints about cognitive disturbance. A smaller distinct subgroup (7%) had predominantly an externalized presentation with high substance use and antisocial features. Two other subgroups, comprising about 15%, with more severe psychopathology/distress identified marked pervasive diverse affective symptoms (i.e., high levels of depressive and anxiety symptoms, a heightened focus on somatic concerns, and thinking disturbances) along with elevated borderline personality characteristics consistent with affect and behavioural dysregulation and instability in interpersonal relationships. A subset of the severe psychopathology/distress groups also had antisocial features and elevated substance use (7%). More externalized profiles with antisocial features and substance abuse tended to be comprised of higher proportions of younger single males, whereas profiles with more internalized features tended to be comprised of high proportions of females and married folks.

Our most recent research in this area has looked at the interaction between the manifestation of affective symptoms and different coping response styles/strategies used in handling the stress and lifestyle adjustment post-ABI (Warriner, Velikonja & Lad, 2008). We have found that high levels of affective symptom complaints on the PAI typically have been associated with more avoidant coping styles on the Coping Response Inventory (CRI), especially behavioural attempts to reduce tension by expression of negative feelings (*Emotional Discharge*) but also by cognitive attempts to avoid thinking realistically about the problem or just accept it without efforts toward change (e.g., *Cognitive Avoidance* and *Acceptance*/Resignation). Heightened symptoms of anxiety, somatic concerns and cognitive disturbance were also associated with attempts to ease stress by seeking information, guidance, and support (*Seeking Guidance and Support*). Borderline personality features were associated with the three avoidant coping styles, while individuals with higher antisocial personality features showed more cognitive avoidance than reported emotional release. These findings were most notable in males and single folks. Similarly, other studies have found that use of avoidant and emotion-focused coping strategies, such as ignoring the problem, keeping to oneself, emotional dysregulation, worrying, self-blame and use of alcohol or substances, has been associated with higher levels of depression and anxiety in ABI, whereas proactive problem-solving has been associated with better adjustment and overall psychological well-being (e.g., Curran, Ponsford & Crowe, 2000; Finset & Anderson, 2000; Kortte, Wegener & Chwalisz, 2003). In ABI, some studies suggest that self-awareness also seems to influence coping and emotional adjustment post-injury (e.g., Anson & Ponsford, 2006; Ownsworth, McFarland & Young, 2000). Poor self-awareness often results in an underestimation of symptoms and difficulties in recognizing the extent and impact of impairments accompany one's brain injury, which has been associated with long-term adjustment difficulties. Individuals with higher levels of self-awareness may initially endorse greater levels of emotional distress, but have the potential to recognize the problems and overtime may be more motivated to change, seek treatment and adopt alternative strategies, which for some may ultimately translate toward better long-term adjustment.

These studies have provided a better understanding of the broad affective and behavioural presentations in ABI and some of the coping styles that may influence manifestation and maintenance of persistent symptom presentation. This knowledge, however, now needs to be translated into the development of tailored interventions and used to inform and support the application of various treatment approaches in ABI.

Review of Treatment Approaches for Emotional and Behavioural Difficulties in ABI

Presently, a wide variety of treatment approaches are commonly employed in clinical settings to manage persistent emotional and behavioural symptoms in the ABI population. Well-conducted research on the efficaciousness of treatments in ABI, however, remains quite limited, especially supporting evidence for which treatments may be most beneficial for specific presentations and the best timing for their implementation.

In a survey of professionals treating ABI conducted by Mittenberg and Burton (1994), most providers reported that early education about the effects of a brain injury along with support/reassurance about the recovery process were most useful in reducing persistent symptoms following a brain injury. Encouragement of gradual return to daily activities was also felt to be helpful to optimize success in the context of early symptoms of fatigue and cognitive inefficiency. This clinical report was consistent with other studies that found provision of education and reassurance about symptoms and the expected recovery lead to reduced symptoms at follow-up (e.g., Alves, Macciocchi & Barth, 1993; Gronwall, 1986; Paniak, Toller-Lobe, Durand & Nagy, 1998; Ponsford et al., 2002) and a quicker return to previous home, work or school activities (e.g., Minderhoud, Boelens, Huizenga & Saan, 1980; Relander, Troupp & Bjorkesten, 1972). This early psychoeducational intervention tended to be helpful for those who had sustained an uncomplicated mild traumatic brain injury (TBI)/concussion, particularly when offered to both the patient and their social network (e.g., family members, friends, employers, etc.) in order to validate the patient's concerns and work toward individualized, realistic goals for return to responsibilities/activities in the context of natural recovery (Arciniegas, Anderson, Topkoff, & McAllister, 2005).

Alleviation of some of the reported cognitive changes accompanying ABI can improve productivity, independence and interpersonal relationships, which may in turn have reciprocal benefits on psychological adjustment. Studies have documented that individuals with ABI can greatly benefit from training, particularly in the areas of attention, memory and executive skills (e.g., Prigitano et al., 1984; Niemann, Ruff, & Baser, 1990). Recent comprehensive reviews of the literature on cognitive rehabilitation and remediation programs have clearly supported the clinical utility and efficacy of these interventions for both patients with traumatic and acquired brain injuries (Cicerone et al., 2000; Cicerone et al., 2005; Gordon et al., 2006). Moreover, comprehensive rehabilitation programs that offer cognitive remediation plus identify environmental modifications and compensatory strategies to help individuals develop specific skill sets and achieve functional goals have been effective in improving cognitive and emotional adjustment in ABI (for review see Prigitano, 1999). Psychopharmacological treatments are also sometimes used to manage cognitive and behavioural symptoms. For example, methylphenidate has been used to improve arousal, attentional regulation, efficiency of information processing, and the rate of functional recovery during the post-acute recovery period (Kaelin, Cifu & Matthies, 1996; Plenger et al., 1996; Whyte et al., 1997). Some studies have found that methylphenidate may also reduce mood disturbances and aggression in TBI (Gualtieri & Evans, 1988; Speech, Rao, Osmon & Sperry, 1993). Cholinesterase inhibitors, donepezil being the most studied, has been found helpful in some individuals with TBI in improving attention and memory impairments and possibly addressing emotional lability, agitation and apathy/reduced motivation and thus facilitating engagement in daily activities (e.g., Taverni, Seliger & Lichtman, 1998; Van Reekum et al., 1995; Walker et al., 2004; Zhang, Plotkin, Wang, Sandel, & Lee, 2004). Depression, anxiety and emotional lability may also need to be directly treated with psychopharmacological interventions. Although few randomized, double-blind placebo controlled trials are available specific for ABI, the medications recommended for treatment of emotional disturbances in ABI are generally in line with those used for similar issues in the general population (for review, see Arciniegas et al., 2005)

Many professionals treating individuals with ABI clearly identified that use of psychological interventions, especially the more structured, directive approach of cognitive-behavioural therapy (CBT), can be helpful to develop alternative coping and problem-solving strategies, facilitate awareness/insight and alleviate both somatic and emotional symptoms like anxiety and depression (Mittenberg & Burton, 1994). Mittenberg, Zielinski and Fichera (1993) found that early implementation of brief psychological therapy with cognitive-behavioural and stress reduction approaches lead to fewer symptoms, shorter duration of symptoms, and lower symptom severity at 6-months follow-up than controls who received standard treatment. Improved outcomes at follow-up were similarly seen in another randomized trial of brief early psychological intervention offering education, reassurance and basic coping and stress management techniques (Wade, Crawford, Wenden, King & Moss, 1997). While this early psychoeducation seems to be effective for curtailing the development of symptoms in a subset of individuals with perhaps more mild ABIs, less consistent research is available on the management of those with more severe injuries or persistent symptoms.

Most of the past research with ABI has been based on single case studies or small sample sizes, showing various cognitive-behavioural and behavioural-based programs were effective for reducing symptoms of depression, anxiety and anger or at improving self-esteem and problem-solving skills (e.g., Medd & Tate, 2000; Montgomery, 1995; Scheutzow & Wiercisiewski, 1999). Ferguson and Mittenberg (1996) demonstrated that a 12-week outpatient treatment program designed to teach patients a combination of alternative coping skills, stress management techniques, cognitive restructuring, and activity scheduling skills was effective at reducing symptom frequency and severity as well as days that symptoms were disruptive to their daily life. Ownsworth et al. (2000) found their 16-week CBT support group to be helpful in increasing awareness of impairments, use of coping strategies and improving psychosocial functioning in 21 individuals with ABI. Rath et al. (2003) similarly found a CBT group with focus on problem-solving difficulties in 27 mild-to-severe TBI to have increased self-esteem, problem-solving skills and self-appraised emotional self-regulation following treatment with these gains maintained at a 6-month follow-up. Despite the identified skill development, the intervention was not associated with significant changes in overall measures of the level of anxiety, depression or hostility. Tiersky et al. (2005) were able to show significant reduction in generalized anxiety symptoms in their group of individuals with mild-to-moderate TBI who received CBT and neurorehabilitation ($n = 11$) as compared with a control group ($n = 9$). In a study by Anson and Ponsford (2006), participants were used as their own controls by comparing symptoms during their time prior to treatment while on the waiting list. They examined the effect of participation in a 10 session cognitive-behavioural program focusing on developing adaptive coping skills in an ABI group ($n = 31$). Participants reported better understanding and awareness of their emotional issues and improved ability to implement adaptive coping strategies to manage these issues; however, no significant changes in self-reports of anxiety, depression, self-esteem and overall psychosocial function were attained post-treatment. They noticed that better outcomes were associated with greater self-awareness of injury-related deficits, less severe injury and higher premorbid intellectual function. Bradbury and colleagues (2008) evaluated the efficacy of an 11-session CBT program versus education alone in individuals with ABI experiencing significant emotional distress, many with symptoms persistent several years out from their initial injury. The program was designed to target both coping and the symptoms of psychological distress. Significant reductions in emotional symptoms were noted in both group and telephone formats as compared to the education alone comparison group at the end of the sessions and maintained at 1-month follow-up.

More recent studies have directly involved family members in the therapeutic interventions given that they are often responsible for providing care, supervision and support for the person with an ABI at discharge. Many caregivers report feeling overwhelmed, poorly resourced and experience high rates of psychological distress, namely anxiety and depression (Kreutzer, Rapport et al., 2009), all of which can negatively influence recovery and long-term adjustment. Kreutzer, Stejskal and colleagues (2009) examined the effectiveness of a 10-week intervention where both the ABI survivor and family members participated in sessions reviewing typical effects of brain injury, coping with loss and change, managing stress and intense emotions, effective problem-solving, setting reasonable goals and taking care of one's self. This approach was based on principles derived from CBT and family systems theory and included education, skills building and psychological support components. Although the intervention was beneficial in families feeling a better sense of connectedness and access to services and in having their needs met, there was no significant change in self-reported measures of levels of psychological distress, family functioning, and overall satisfaction with life.

While there seems to be a general consensus that a wide variety of psychological treatments can be helpful in addressing the emotional difficulties in ABI, the discrepancy in methodology and sampling characteristics makes it difficult to directly compare many of these treatment studies. In many of these studies, improvements were identified in awareness and use of the coping and problem-solving skills explicitly taught but this did not always translate into reductions in emotional symptoms or improvements in overall psychological adjustment. An important clinical consideration when designing and implementing various treatment approaches would be to work within the client's framework and thus tailor the intervention at any given time point to the client's identified needs, perspectives and readiness in accepting certain strategies/supports.

Readiness for Change – Review of The Stages of Change Theory

Ongoing clinical evaluation of an individual's readiness to accept and implement various levels of support/intervention is pivotal to the success of any psychological treatment. The Stages of Change model is based on the transtheoretical model of behaviour change in which individuals are seen to progress through a number of stages involving decisions about change. Clinicians need to be aware of how different kinds of support, tools/techniques and interventi-ons may be best implemented at various stages to facilitate this change process.

The model was first proposed by Prochaska and DiClemente in 1982 in efforts to understand how people intentionally change based on the transtheoretical concepts. They were curious to better understand how many studies had demonstrated that people can modify problematic behaviour without the benefit of expert assistance in the form of formal psychotherapy. They focused their attention using the transtheoretical framework on the stages and processes of change in developing the Stages of Change model. Prochaska and DiClemente (1982) suggested that people move through five stages (precontemplation, contemplation, preparation, action, and maintenance) when attempting to make behavioural changes. This model acknowledges that there are many changes that precede and follow a person taking action when changing an unwanted behaviour. McConnaughy, Prochaska, and Velicer (1983) argued that the five stages of change were formulated as a fundamental part of a transtheoretical therapy model which has been developed as an integrative model of change for the fragmented field of psychotherapy. The model was first introduced in understanding the processes of change used by smokers quitting on their own and smokers participating in two therapy programs. Since its development, the stages of change model has been used with many other populations including alcohol and substance abuse, eating disorders and obesity, delinquency, high-fat diets, AIDS prevention, mammography screening, medication compliance, unplanned pregnancy prevention, pregnancy and smoking, radon testing, sedentary lifestyles, sun exposure, pain management, anxiety and panic disorders, and acquired brain injury (e.g., Kerns, Rosenberg, Jamison, Caudill, & Haythornwaite, 1997; Prochaska and Velicer, 1997).

It was argued by DiClemente and Prochaska (1982) that clinicians frequently design excellent action-oriented treatment programs/interventions but then are disappointed or confused about its efficacy. Typically, treatment with individuals can progress most smoothly when both the individual and the therapist are in agreement on what the problem and solution needs to be. Often times, clinicians are focused on implementing action-oriented treatment; however, there are many instances when an individual may not be ready to adopt the therapist's understanding and solution to a problem. At such times, discussions about resistance are often brought up. Prochaska and DiClemente (1986) explained that sometimes a more directive action-oriented therapist would find a client who is struggling to understand their problem to be resistant to therapy. From the client's perspective however, the therapist may be seen as wanting to move too quickly. They further elaborated that a therapist who is interested in helping the client understand the causes of their problems might perceive a client who is ready for action as resistant to the insight aspects of therapy and have possible concerns of impulsivity, while the client in return may find the therapist as moving too slowly. Therefore, it was believed that in order to achieve therapeutic success, it will be important to understand an individual's readiness to make changes. Prochaska, DiClemente, and Norcross (1992) found that the amount of progress a client makes following intervention tends to be a function of their pretreatment stage of change. They have suggested that to treat clients as if they were all at the same stage would be naïve; and yet, that is what professionals have often done.

The first stage in the Stages of Change model is called *Precontemplation*. In this stage, there is no intention by the client to change behaviour in the foreseeable future. Prochaska, DiClemente, and Norcross (1992) explain that many individuals in this stage are unaware or underaware of their problems; however, family members, friends, neighbours, and/or employers are well aware that precomtemplators have problems. Directive interventions at this stage can lead the client to feel misunderstood, devalued, threatened and pressured, impeding the establishment of therapeutic rapport and thus limiting the chance for any success to come from working together in the future.

The second stage, *Contemplation,* describes when people are beginning to become aware that a problem exists and are struggling to understand the problem (i.e., cause and solution), are seriously thinking about overcoming it and seeking information (e.g., weighing the pros and cons of the problem as well as solution), but have not yet made a commitment to take action/make change. According to Prochaska and Velicer (1997), it is not uncommon for some people to remain stuck in the contemplation stage for long periods.

The third stage is called *Preparation* and combines intention and behavioural criteria. People at this stage are intending to take action in the immediate future, usually within the month, and they frequently have also taken some significant action in the past year. At this stage, people typically have a plan of action. Prochaska et al. (1992) explained that while individuals in this stage might have made some changes or reduced problematic behaviours, they have not yet reached a criterion for effective action.

The fourth stage is called *Action* and occurs typically when individuals modify their behaviour, experiences, or environment in order to overcome their problem. It is thought to involve the most overt behavioural changes and requires considerable commitment of time and energy. According to Prochaska et al. (1992), because modification of behaviour in the action stage tends to be most visible and receive the greatest external recognition, people including professionals often erroneously equate action with change. They explained that as a consequence people overlook the requisite work that prepares changers for action and the important efforts necessary to maintain the changes following action. At this stage, successfully altering behaviour or making change means reaching a particular criterion.

The last stage is labeled *Maintenance* and describes when the person has already changed and seeks treatment to consolidate previous gains and to prevent relapse from occurring. Prochaska et al. (1992) explained that maintenance is a continuation of change and not an absence. Prochaska and Velicer (1997) noted that people in the maintenance stage are less tempted to relapse and are increasingly more confident that they can continue their changes in the long-run.

Prochaska et al. (1992) reported that while the Stages of Change model was first conceptualized as a linear progression through the stages, this was later found to be a rare occurrence. Instead, the model is described as a spiral pattern, where people move from precontemplation to contemplation to preparation to action to maintenance but then possibly relapse. Relapse, which is viewed as the return from action or maintenance to an earlier stage, tends to be the rule when action is taken for most health behaviour problems. According to Prochaska et al. (1992), the spiral model does not suggest that most relapsers revolve endlessly in circles and that they regress all the way back to where they started the process. Instead, it is believed that each time relapsers recycle through the stages, they potentially learn from their mistakes or set-backs and can try something different the next time around.

As stated earlier, while initially conceptualized for the addiction population, the Stages of Change model has received great attention by professionals working with many other health behaviours/conditions. The attraction to a stage-based model lies not only in its intuitive and theoretical plausibility, but also in its apparent ability to explain why general interventions are rarely effective. Instead, the model proposes that a more tailored intervention which takes into account the current stage which the individual has reached in the change process will be more effective. As explained by Prochaska and Velicer (1997), the transtheoretical theory uses the Stages of Change model to integrate processes and principles of change from different theories of intervention. In their review of the model researchers have reported that there are over 130-300 theories of psychotherapy available (Prochaska and DiClemente, 1986; Prochaska and Velicer, 1997) and therefore people interested in addressing their psychological difficulties are confronted with the confusion of too many choices with too few data to decide what should be the treatments of choice for their particular situation. A comprehensive model can help to integrate a therapy field that has fragmented into an overwhelming number of alternative and competing treatments. Prochaska and Velicer (1997) argued that the goal of the Stages of Change model was to systematically integrate a field that has fragmented theories. They stated that a comparative analysis identified 10 distinct processes of change, such as con-sciousness raising form the Freudian tradition, contingency management form the Skinnerian tradition, and helping relationships from the Rogerian tradition.

In attempts at identifying an individual's readiness for change clinicians and researchers have modified the original Stages of Change scale proposed by McConnaughy et al. (1983) in order to make it relevant to their studied population. Considering that there are numerous versions of the scale specific to various populations, the current authors thought that it would be more prudent to first examine the original instrument and later on to describe the one version modified specific to ABI. In their original work, McConnaughy et al. (1983) reported on the development of a measure, named the Stages of Change Questionnaire, designed to assess the five stages of change thought to account for the temporal dimension of change processes occurring in psychotherapy. Their study consisted of 155 adults participating in psychological treatment. According to the authors, they initially had a pool of 125 items measuring the fives stages which was finally reduced to 32 items on the basis of principle components analysis. Based on their findings, the researchers concluded that the Stages of Change Questionnaire provided a highly reliable instrument for measuring stages of change in psychotherapy. However, their work yielded four well-defined stages which included *Precontemplation, Contemplation, Action,* and *Maintenance.* It was noted that the *Preparation* stage (or as it was previously called Decision-Making) was eliminated as a separate stage because their findings revealed that the items designed to measure this stage loaded highly on the *Contemplation* and *Action* stages. Later on, Prochaska et al. (1992) explained that they misinterpreted the data from their original work (McConnaughy et al., 1983) by thinking that there were only four stages to the model. They clarified that in their original study on the continuous measures, cluster analyses had identified groups of individuals who were in the *Preparation* stage by scoring high on both the *Contemplation* and *Action* scales. Consequently, the authors reverted back to a five stage conceptualization of the model.

Derisley and Reynolds (2002) had also completed an independent investigation of the psychometric properties of the Stages of Change Questionnaire. They evaluated the methods of interpreting scores as discrete stages or as a continuous measure of readiness to change and explored the theoretical underpinnings of the model by assessing whether adjacent stages of change are more highly correlated than non-adjacent stages. Based on their results, the authors concluded that the Stages of Change Questionnaire had acceptable psychometric properties and high internal consistency similar to those originally reported by McConnaughy et al. (1983). In addition, their findings revealed alternative methods of scoring and interpreting the scales. More specifically, they highlighted the limitations in using the "highest score" methodology of scoring as was originally proposed, as it sometimes separated individuals with nearly identical profiles into different stages. Alternatively, it was recommended that interpretation of the sample mean scores for the scale was a better method of scoring. The results also revealed that the majority of participants had above average scores in more than one stage, which concluded that individuals can simultaneously hold beliefs that correspond to a couple different stages of change. Moreover, their findings were mixed regarding the hypothesis that higher correlations would occur for adjacent scales than non-adjacent scales. They concluded that it remained unclear as to whether the Stages of Change model supported a predictable movement from one stage to the next. It was believed that it may be more appropriate to construe readiness to change as a continuum on which individuals are located at a particular point in time rather than as a series of stages through which individuals progress in an invariant sequence, as was first suggested by Sutton (1996).

Although adopted and reportedly applied to many behavioural-based programs, the Stages of Change model is not without its critics. In their systematic review, Bridle and colleagues (2005) reported that more caution about the success of the model may be needed despite the widespread popularity of the stage-based approach to behaviour change. They argued that the methodological quality of the studies reviewed supporting the model was mixed with a number of common limitations related to randomization, blinding, and data analysis. They also found only limited evidence for the effectiveness of interventions based on the transtheoretical framework. Furthermore, they commented that there was no evidence to support the claim that the effectiveness of transtheoretical intervention influenced the behaviour being targeted. Finally, they noted that there was limited evidence to support the claim that transtheoretical interventions would be more effective in promoting stage progression. Bridle et al. (2005) clarified that despite their study suggesting limited evidence for the effectiveness of stage-based interventions, there were possibly other explanations for their findings. For example, they stated that while the null hypothesis in their study was that there would be no difference in effectiveness between stage and non-stage based interventions, they did find some trials that were statistically significant favoring stage based interventions but none reported in the other direction. Another possible reason that they highlighted for their findings was the lack of model specifications in the studies reviewed. For example, many studies reviewed reported interventions that were tailored only to the stage of change and neglected other important components of the model, such as processes of change. As a result, they argued that partial intervention tailoring may reflect a more general confusion in the way stages of change is conceptualized. They expanded by stating that while stage of change is conceptualized as the central organizing construct of the model, in the context of intervention it is often treated as if it were the theory in and of itself. As a result, many of the studies reviewed only used the single variable of stage in the design, delivery, and assessment of stage-based interventions. However, they felt that the processes of change are equally important to consider in both designing and testing the effectiveness of this model.

Tailoring Treatment Approaches – Application of the Stages of Change Theory to ABI

The application of this "tailored" approach is of interest to this group in the context of working with individuals who have sustained an acquired brain injury (ABI). More specifically, the Stages of Change model with an ABI population is of value because of its underpinnings to the transtheoretical approach, which serves as a synthesis for the diverse and sometimes competing treatment methods that are currently available for ABI (i.e., cognitive rehabilitation, behaviour modification, cognitive-behavioural treatment, grief counseling, psychodynamic psychotherapy, ABI education, neuro-biofeedback, etc.). Considering all of the information presented above, the authors were interested in conceptualizing a model of treatment for ABI that highlights potential interventions that might be most effective to use at the different stages and considerations for progressing through the stages (see Figure 1) by acknowledging the limitation of previous studies and building on the existing framework.

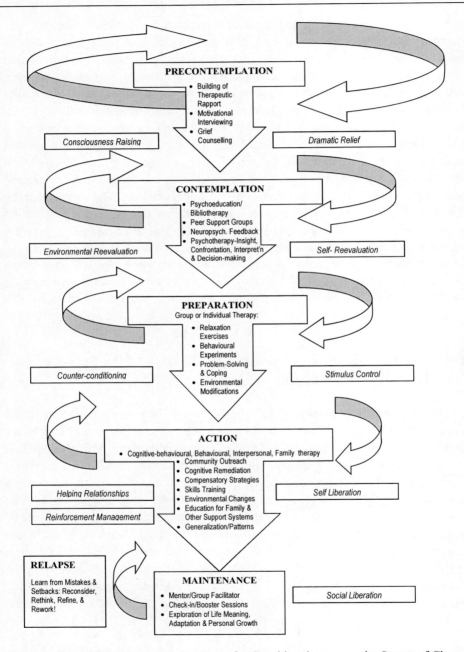

Figure 1. Potential Treatments & Processes for Consideration across the Stages of Change in ABI.

Clinicians would need to have a means to assess an individual's readiness for change for this model to be applicable in clinical contexts. Based on our extensive review of the literature, the only known tool appropriate for an ABI population is the Change Assessment Questionnaire (CAQ) developed by Lam, McMahon, Priddy, and Gehred-Schultz in 1988. This group modified the original Stages of Change Questionnaire and developed the CAQ in efforts to investigate the relation of stages of change to treatment performance in forty-five head-injured clients from a post-acute head injury rehabilitation program. The results obtained were promising for the internal consistency reliability of the CAQ and supported their hypothesis that clients who were aware of their problems and ready to change performed better in treatment than those who were unaware. Lam et al. (1988) concluded based on their findings that the CAQ appeared to be a useful tool in assessing a person with an ABI's stage of change for treatment matching purposes. They also noted that their clusters obtained (Precontemplation cluster – people who scored above average on the *Precontemplation* scale and well below average on the *Contemplation* and *Action* scales; Ambivalent cluster – people who scored above average on the *Precontemplation* scale and about average on the *Contemplation* and *Action* scales; and Participation cluster – people who score below average on the *Precontemplation* scale and above average on the *Contemplation* and *Action* scales) were congruent with the theoretical assumptions of the Stages of Change model.

After identifying what stage an individual is at with respect to their readiness for change, appropriate interventions can be tailored to assist with facilitating change to the next stage. Our group recognizes that identifying the ABI client's stage of change is only one of many factors to consider when selecting appropriate treatment interventions. Given the complexity of factors influencing the manifestation and persistence of emotional and behavioural difficulties in ABI, other neurological, pre-morbid personal, sociodemographic and environmental factors should also be given attention in deciding on the most effective treatment (see Warriner & Velikonja, 2006 for review).

Given the limitations from previous studies looking at only the stages of change, our group believes that consideration of the *processes of change* would be helpful to inform what might likely be an appropriate intervention at each of the five stages. Prochaska and colleagues reportedly first identified ten processes of change in 1979 through a comparative analysis of the leading systems of psychotherapy. These ten processes of change are thought to be activities that people use to progress through the stages. The ten processes are as follows: *Consciousness Raising* which involves increased awareness about the causes, consequences, and solutions for particular problems; *Self-Reevaluation* which assesses how one feels and thinks about oneself with respect to a problem; *Self-Liberation* involves choosing and committing to act or believe in one's ability to make change; *Counter-conditioning* involves substituting alternative strategies for problems; *Stimulus Control* which entails avoiding or countering stimuli that elicit problems and adding prompts for more effective/healthier strategies; *Reinforcement Management* includes rewarding oneself or being rewarded by others for making changes; *Helping Relationships* combines caring, trust, openness, and acceptance as well as support for the healthy/adaptive change; *Dramatic Relief* involves experiencing and expressing feelings about one's problems and solutions; *Environmental Reevaluation* entails assessing how a person's problem affects their physical environment; and *Social Liberation* which requires increasing alternatives for non-problem behaviours available in society.

The literature (Prochaska and DiClemente, 1982 & 1986) suggests that individuals in the *Precontemplation* stage use processes of change less then any of the other stages. Prochaska and DiClemente (1982) stated that people in this stage process less information about their problems, spend less time and energy reevaluating themselves, experience fewer emotional reactions to negative aspects of their problems, are less open with significant others about their problems, and do little to shift their attention or their environment in the direction of overcoming their problems. Considering this information therapists working with ABI clients who are identified to be in the *Precontemplation* stage are likely to find it more frustrating if they were to attempt to apply behavioural or cognitive-behavioural strategies, as typically the application of such strategies works under the basic assumption that the individual is motivated to change and is ready to take action. In fact, directive interventions aimed at attempts to improve awareness about the problem or alter avoidant coping strategies may be viewed as threatening and devaluing and actually result in an increase in certain negative reactions/avoidant coping strategies. Instead, it might be more effective to use motivational interviewing techniques during this phase. This approach is described as a client-centered, semi-directive method for engaging intrinsic motivation to change behaviour by developing discrepancy as well as exploring and resolving ambivalence within the client. Motivational interviewing recognizes and accepts the fact that clients who need to make changes in their lives approach psychotherapy at different levels of readiness to change their behaviour. It is meant to be non-judgmental, non-confrontational and non-adversarial. The approach attempts to increase the client's awareness of the potential problems caused, consequences experienced, and risks faced as a result of the behaviour/problems in question. Alternately, therapists help clients envisage a better future and become increasingly motivated to achieve it. Either way, the strategy seeks to help clients think differently about their behaviour/problem and ultimately to consider what might be gained through change. Motivational interviewing is based upon four general principles: 1) *Express empathy*, guides therapists to share with clients their understanding of the clients' perspective; 2) *Develop discrepancy*, guides therapists to help clients appreciate the value of change by exploring the discrepancy between how clients want their lives to be versus how they currently are (or between their deeply-held values and their day-to-day behaviour); 3) *Roll with resistance*, guides therapists to accept client reluctance to change as natural rather than pathological; and 4) *Support self-efficacy*, guides therapists to explicitly embrace client autonomy (even when clients choose to not change) and help clients move toward change successfully and with confidence. The main goals of motivational interviewing are to establish rapport, elicit change talk, and establish commitment language from the client.

Some individuals who suffer an ABI are unable to appreciate the nature and/or severity of their deficits due to neuropathogenic changes. Such individuals are likely to see no need to make changes in their lives and therefore may be stuck at the *Precontemplation* stage. With such individuals, it might be useful to videotape certain instances or allow for planned failures with teaching "in the moment" to assist with increasing insight into the nature/severity of the problem. ABI clients at this stage might also be experiencing feelings of loss and may be exhibiting denial, anger, depression, etc. Consequently, the therapist might be inclined to consider grief counseling to acknowledge the frustration and upset associated with any life-altering adjustments post-ABI, such as loss of roles/responsibilities at home or work, or for some even bereavement from loss of someone in the accident. Of great importance when working with someone in the *Precontemplation* stage is establishing and maintaining the therapeutic relationship. Prochaska and DiClemente (1986) explained that identification with the therapist is more likely to occur if the client feels that their therapist genuinely cares and is truly trying to understand his/her unique experience, including the client's need to be defensive as well as desire to be open. Identification is also more likely to occur if the client believes that the therapist is committed to helping the client change in ways that are best for the client and not for other people. Although reports from collateral sources are valuable to better understand the issues at hand, it is important at this stage to ensure that the ABI client's voice and perspective is validated and respected despite often discrepant opinions heard from close family and friends.

In the *Contemplation* stage, *Consciousness Raising* was the process of change emphasized the most followed by *Dramatic Relief, Environmental Reevaluation,* and *Self-Reevaluation* (Prochaska & DiClemente, 1982; Prochaska et al., 1992).

Considering these identified processes, strategies aimed at increasing awareness/insight in working with ABI clients may be most beneficial during this stage. Clients with ABI may be more open and find value in education and/or bibliotherapy during this stage. Involvement in ABI peer support groups may also provide clients with opportunities to share and validate their experiences, express their feelings about problems and potential solutions, and start to explore how their behaviour may affect others. Use of the feedback from an objective neuropsychological assessment as a therapeutic intervention may be helpful at this time to individualize the information, facilitate personal insight, and offer education. In the context of a supportive psychotherapeutic relationship, use of perspective-taking techniques as well as strategically-planned confrontation, feedback and interpretation may also be used to bring about increased awareness and insight-oriented techniques may be helpful to assist with exploration of alternatives and decision-making. Ongoing grief counseling may also be needed to deal with the emotions surrounding persistent losses/disability and to assist clients in moving toward more realistic expectations about recovery and thus begin to consider/accept the need to make changes and adjust to their current situation.

During the *Preparation* stage, individuals begin to take small steps toward action, and therefore use of *Counter-conditioning* and *Stimulus Control* processes appear to be the common processes of change identified at this stage (Prochaska & DiClemente, 1982; Prochaska et al., 1992). During this phase, the continued use of support groups and/or individual supportive psychotherapy may be beneficial to come up with alternative problem-solving and coping strategies to handle specific instances that the client wishes to address. Clients may also be amenable to working toward reducing but perhaps not eliminating unhealthy habits, making some simple environmental modifications or trialing basic behavioural experiments to help facilitate this process. Use of relaxation exercises may also be helpful for some clients as a structured, reasonably easily implemented approach to minimize generalized anxiety and stress. Often at this phase, clients may be open to talking about and even trialing new strategies or alternative approaches, but may have difficulty with implementing them consistently and independently outside of therapy or with generalizing them to similar situations not explicitly discussed.

When immersed in the *Action* stage, greater behavioural and cognitive processes are utilized involving *Self-Liberation, Counter-conditioning, Stimulus Control, Helping Relationships, and Reinforcement Management*. It is at this stage that the greatest number of change processes is emphasized (Prochaska & DiClemente, 1982; Prochaska et al., 1992). During this stage, a wide variety of

Interventions for Affective and Behavioural Disturbances... 89

strategies/interventions may be effective if tailored to meet the individual needs of the client and address the issues at hand. Some clients with ABI may benefit from working one-to-one regularly with community outreach workers on attaining individualized goals through use of cognitive remediation, compensatory strategies, specific skills training, as well as environmental modifications. It may be important to utilize social support systems at this phase, including providing adequate education to spouses, family members or coworkers to help them understand the process, including the effort and time devoted and ways for them to best support/reinforce the changes. Individual psychotherapy with focus on use of cognitive-behavioural, behavioural and interpersonal approaches depending on the client's needs would also likely be invaluable for many ABI clients in the action-oriented stage. Setting collaborative plans of action with graduated, realistic steps, clear goals and implementing a variety of strategies can now be used at this stage. Patterns or themes can be explored and work on generalization can be explicitly incorporated into therapy sessions.

During the *Maintenance* stage, *Social Liberation* was the process of change emphasized (Prochaska et al., 1992). At this time, it might be valuable for the client to act as mentors to other ABI clients or to facilitate support groups. ABI clients may also periodically have "check-in" or "booster" sessions with their therapist to assist with any problem solving that they might have encountered which was resulting in increased stress. This would also give them an opportunity to review previously learned strategies in efforts to continue to reinforce the importance of its utilization. At this stage, clients may also be amenable to exploring and reflecting on broader concepts of life meaning, adaptation and personal growth, further reinforcing and sustaining their efforts toward long-term change.

Conclusion

In this review chapter, a theoretical framework based on the Stages of Change model and underlying processes was presented to highlight how a client's individualized needs and readiness for change may influence what strategies/approaches may be most effective at any given time point in addressing the complex cognitive, emotional and behavioural sequelae in ABI (see Figure 1). Additional research in this area is needed to directly test out these hypotheses. We believe that the client's perspective, including self-awareness and underlying change processes, are key to the success of treatments and recommend that these concepts be incorporated into previously identified broader conceptual models of the factors contributing to the differential expression and maintenance of psychiatric and emotional disturbances in ABI. They will likely be clinically valuable in both informing the development and evaluation of tailored ABI interventions.

References

Alves, W., Macciocchi, S. N., & Barth, J. T. (1993). Post concussive symptoms after uncomplicated mild head injury. *Journal of Head Trauma and Rehabilitation*, **8**, 48-59.

Anson, K. & Ponsford, J. (2006). Evaluation of a coping skills group following traumatic brain injury. *Brain Injury*, **20**(2), 167-178.

Arciniegas, D. B., Anderson, C. A., Topkoff, J., & McAllister, T. W. (2005). Mild traumatic brain injury: A neuropsychiatric approach to diagnosis, evaluation and treatment. *Neuropsychiatric Disease and Treatment*, **1**(4), 311-327.

Bradbury, C. L., Christensen, B. K., Lau, M., Ruttan, L. A., Arundine, A. L., & Green, R. E. (2008). The efficacy of cognitive behaviour therapy in the treatment of emotional distress after acquired brain injury. *Archives of Physical Medicine and Rehabilitation*, **89** (S2), S61-S68.

Bridle, C., Riemsma, R. P., Patteden, J., Sowden, A. J., Mather, L., Watt, I. S., & Walker, A. (2005). Systematic review of the effectiveness of health behavior interventions based on the transtheoretical model. *Psychology and Health,* **20** (3), 283-301.

Cicerone, K. D., Dahlberg, C., Kalmar, K., Langenbahn, D. M., Malec, J. F., Bergquist, T. F., Felicetti, T., Giacino, J. T., Harley, J. P., Harrington, D. E., Herzog, J., Kneipp, S., Laatsch, L., & Morse, P. A. (2000). Evidence-based cognitive rehabilitation: Recommendations for clinical practice. *Archives of Physical Medicine and Rehabilitation*, **81**(12), 1596-1615.

Cicerone, K. D., Dahlberg, C., Malec, J. F., Langenbahn, D. M., Felicetti, T., Kneipp, S., Ellmo, W., Kalmar, K., Giacino, J. T., Harley, J. P., Laatsch, L., Morse, P. A., & Catanese, J. (2005). Evidence-based cognitive rehabilitation: Updated review of the literature from 1998 through 2002. *Archives of Physical Medicine and Rehabilitation*, **86**(8), 1681-1692.

Cicerone, K., Smith, L., Ellmo, W., Mangel, H., Nelson, P.l., Chase, R. & Kalmar, K. (1996). Neuropsychological rehabilitation of mild traumatic brain injury. *Brain Injury*, **10**(4), 277-286.

Curran, C. A., Ponsford, J. L., & Crowe, S. (2000). Coping strategies and emotional outcome following traumatic brain injury: A comparison with orthopedic patients. *Journal of Head Trauma Rehabilitation*, **15**, 1256-1274.

Derisley, J., & Reynolds, S. (2002). Evaluation of the stages of change scales to measure client readiness for treatment in a mental health sample. *Behavioural and Cognitive Psychotherapy*, **30**, 217-222.

Dikmen, S., Machamer, J., & Temkin, N. (1993). Psychosocial outcome in patients with moderate to severe head injury: 2-year follow-up. *Brain Injury*, 7(2), 113-124.

Felmingham, K., Baguley, I., & Crooks, J. (2001). A comparison of acute and post-discharge predictors of employment 2 years after traumatic brain injury. *Archives of Physical Medicine and Rehabilitation*, **82**(4), 435-439.

Ferguson, R. J. & Mittenberg, W. (1996, November). *Cognitive behavioural treatment of post-concussion syndrome: Multiple case data from a work in progress*. Paper presented at the 30th Annual convention of the Association for Advancement of Behavior Therapy, New York.

Finset, A. & Anderson, S. (2000). Coping strategies in patients with acquired brain injury: Relationship between coping, apathy, depression and lesion location. *Brain Injury*, **14**, 887-905.

Gordon, W. A., Zafonte, R., Cicerone, K., Cantor, J., Brown, M., Lombard, L., Goldsmith, R., & Chandna, T. (2006). Traumatic brain injury rehabilitation state of the science. *American Journal of Physical Medicine and Rehabilitation*, **85**(4), 343-382.

Gronwall, D. (1986). Rehabilitation programs for patients with mild head injury: Components, problems, and evaluation. *Journal of Head Trauma Rehabilitation*, **1**, 53-63.

Gualtieri, T. & Evans, R.W. (1988). Stimulant treatment for the neurobehavioral sequelae of traumatic brain injury. *Brain Injury*, **2**, 273-290.

Hibbard, M., Bogdany, J., Uysal, S., Kepler, K, Silver, J. M., Gordon, W. A. & Haddad, L. (2000). Axis II psychopathology in individuals with traumatic brain injury. *Brain Injury*, **14**(1), 45-61.

Hibbard, M., Uysal, S., Kepler, K., Bogdany, J., & Silver, J. (1998). Axis I psychopathology in individuals with traumatic brain injury. *Journal of Head Trauma Rehabilitation*, **13**(4), 24-39.

Kaelin, D. L., Cifu, D. X., & Matthies, B. (1996). Methylphenidate effect on attention deficit in the acutely brain-injured adult. *Archives of Physical Medicine and Rehabilitation*, **77**, 6-9.

Kerns, R. D., Rosenberg, R., Jamison, R. N., Caudill, M. A., & Haythornwaite, J. (1997). Readiness to adopt a self-management approach to chronic pain: The pain stages of change questionnaire (PSOCQ). *Pain*, **72**, 227-234.

Koponen, S., Taiminen, T., Portin, R., Himanen, L., Isoniemi, H., Heinonen, H., Hinkka, S. & Tenovuo, O. (2002). Axis I and II psychiatric disorders after traumatic brain injury: A 30-year follow-up study. *American Journal of Psychiatry*, **159**, 1315-1321.

Kortte, K. B., Wegener, S. T., & Chwalisz, K. (2003). Anosognosia and denial: Their relationship to coping and depression in acquired brain injury. *Rehabilitation Psychology*, **48**, 131-136.

Kreutzer, J. S., Rapport, L. J., Marwitz, J. H., Harrison-Felix, C., Hart, T., Glenn, M., & Hammond F. (2009). Caregivers' well-being after traumatic brain injury: A multicenter prospective investigation. *Archives of Physical Medicine and Rehabilitation*, **90**(6), 939-946.

Kreutzer, J. S., Stejskal, T. M., Ketchum, J. M., Marwitz, J. H., Taylor, L. A., & Menzel, J. C. (2009). A preliminary investigation of the brain injury family intervention: Impact on family members. *Brain Injury*, **23**(6), 535-547.

Lam, C. S., McMahon, B. T., Priddy, D. A., & Gehred-Schultz, A. (1988). Deficit awareness and treatment performance among traumatic head injury adults. *Brain Injury*, **2**(3), 235-242.

McConnaughy, E. A., Prochaska, J. O., & Velicer, W. F. (1983). Stages of change in psychotherapy: Measurement and sample profiles. *Psychotherapy: Theory, Research and Practice*, **20**(3), 368-375.

Medd, J. & Tate, R. (2000). Evaluation of an anger management therapy programme following acquired brain injury: A preliminary study. *Neuropsychological Rehabilitation*, **10**, 185-201.

Minderhoud, J. M., Boelens, M. E., Huizenga, J., & Saan, R. J. (1980). Treatment of minor head injuries. *Clinical Neurology and Neurosurgery*, **82**(2), 127-140.

Mittenberg, W. & Burton, D. B. (1994). A survey of treatments for post-concussion syndrome. *Brain Injury*, **8**(5), 429-437.

Mittenberg, W., Zielinski, R. E., & Fichera, S. (1993). Recovery from mild head injury: A treatment manual for patients. *Psychotherapy in Private Practice*, **12**, 37-52.

Montgomery, G. K. (1995). A multi-factor account of disability after brain injury: Implications for neuropsychological counseling. *Brain Injury*, **9**, 453-469.

Niemann, H., Ruff, R. M., & Baser, C. A. (1990). Computer-assisted attention retraining in head-injured individuals: A controlled efficacy study of an outpatient program. *Journal of Consulting and Clinical Psychology*, **58**(6), 811-817.

Ownsworth, T., McFarland, K., & Young, R. (2000). Self-awareness and psychosocial functioning following acquired brain injury: An evaluation of a group support programme. *Neuropsychological Rehabilitation*, **10**, 465-484.

Paniak, C., Toller-Lobe, G., Durand, A., & Nagy, J. (1998). A randomized trial of two treatments for mild brain injury. *Brain Injury*, **12**(12), 1011-1023.

Plenger, P. M., Dixon, C. E., Castillo, R. M., Frankowski, R. F., Yablon, S. A., & Levin, H. S. (1996). Subacute methylphenidate treatment for moderate to moderately to severe traumatic brain injury: A preliminary double-blind placebo-controlled study. *Archives of Physical Medicine and Rehabilitation*, **77**(6), 536-540.

Ponsford, J., Willmott, C., Rothwell, A., Cameron, P., Kelly, A.M., Nelms, R., & Curran, C. (2002). Impact of early intervention on outcome following mild head injury in adults. *Journal of Neurology, Neurosurgery and Psychiatry*, **73**(3), 330-332.

Prigitano, G. P. (1999). *Principles of neuropsychological rehabilitation*. New York: Oxford University Press.

Prigitano, G. P., Fordyce, D. J., Zeiner, H. K., Roueche, J. R., Pepping, M., & Wood, B. C. (1984). Neuropsychological rehabilitation after closed head injury in young adults. *Journal of Neurology, Neurosurgery and Psychiatry*, **47**(5), 505-513.

Prochaska, J. O. & DiClemente, C. C. (1982). Transtheoretical therapy: Toward a more integrative model of change. *Psychotherapy: Theory, Research and Practice*, **19**, 276-288.

Prochaska, J. O. & DiClemente, C. C. (1986). *Treating addictive behaviours: Toward a comprehensive model of change*. (Edited by Miller, W. R., & Heather, N.). Plenum Publishing Corporation, New York, 3-27.

Prochaska, J. O., DiClemente, C. C., & Norcross, J. C. (1992). In search of how people change: Applications to addictive behaviors. *American Psychologist*, **47**(9), 1102-1114.

Prochaska, J. O. & Velicer, W.F. (1997). The transtheoretical model of health behavior change. *American Journal of Health Promotion*, **12**(1), 38-48.

Rath, J. F., Simon, D., Langenbahn, D. M., Sherr, R. L., & Diller, L. (2003). Group treatment of problem-solving deficits in outpatients with traumatic brain injury: A randomized outcome study. *Neuropsychological Rehabilitation*, **13**, 461-488.

Relander, M., Troupp, H., & Bjorkesten, G. (1972). Controlled trial of treatment for cerebral concussion. *British Medical Journal*, **4**(5843), 777-779.

Scheutzow, M. H. & Wiercisiewski, D. R. (1999). Panic disorder in a patient with traumatic brain injury: A case report and discussion. *Brain Injury*, **13**(9), 705-714.

Speech, T. J., Rao, S. M., Osmon, D. C., & Sperry, L. T. (1993). A double-blind controlled study of methylphenidate treatment in closed head injury. *Brain Injury*, **7**(4), 333-338.

Sutton, S. (1996). *Can "stages of change" provide guidance in the treatments of addictions? A critical example of Prochaska and DiClemente's model.* In G. Edwards & C. Dare (Eds.). Psychotherapy, psychological treatments and the addictions. Cambridge: Cambridge University Press.

Taverni, J. P., Seliger, G., & Lichtman, S. W. (1998). Donepezil mediated memory improvement in traumatic brain injury during post acute rehabilitation. *Brain Injury*, **12**(1), 77-80.

Tiersky, L. A., Anselmi, V., Johnston, M. V., Kurtyka, J., Roosen, E., Schwartz, T. & Deluca, J. (2005). A trial of neuropsychologic rehabilitation in mild-spectrum traumatic brain injury. *Archives of Physical Medicine and Rehabilitation*, **86**(8), 1565-1574.

Van Reekum, R., Bayley, M., Garner, S. Burke, I. M., Fawcett, S., Hart, A. & Thompson, W. (1995). N of 1 study: amantadine for the amotivational syndrome in a patient with traumatic brain injury. *Brain Injury*, **9**(1), 49-53.

Velikonja, D., Warriner, E. M., & Brum, C. (2009). Profiles of emotional and behavioural sequelae following Acquired Brain Injury: Cluster analysis of the Personality Assessment Inventory. *Journal of Clinical and Experimental Neuropsychology,* **21**,1-12.

Wade, D. T., Crawford, S., Wenden, F. J., King, N. S., & Moss, N. E. (1997). Does routine follow-up after head injury help? A randomised controlled trial. *Journal of Neurology, Neurosurgery & Psychiatry*, **62**(5), 478-484.

Walker, W., Seel, R., Gibellato, M., Lew, H., Cornis-Pop, M., Jena, T, & Silver, T. (2004). The effects of donepezil on traumatic brain injury acute rehabilitation outcomes. *Brain Injury*, **18**(8), 739-750.

Warriner, E. M., Rourke, B. P., Velikonja, D., & Metham, L. (2003). Subtypes of emotional and behavioural sequelae in patients with Traumatic Brain Injury. *Journal of Clinical and Experimental Neuropsychology*, **25**(7), 904-917.

Warriner, E. M. & Velikonja, D. (2006). Psychiatric disturbances after traumatic brain injury: Neurobehavioural and personality changes. *Current Psychiatry Reports*, **8**(1), 73-80.

Warriner, E. M., Velikonja, D., & Lad, H. (2008). *The influence of coping styles on the manifestation of affective and behavioural disturbance following acquired brain injury*. In Personality Disorders - New Research: Nova Sciences Publishers Inc, Hauppauge, NY.

Whyte, J., Hart, T., Schuster, K, Fleming, M., Polansky, M., & Coslett, H. B. (1997). Effects of methylphenidate on attentional function after traumatic brain injury. A randomized, placebo-controlled trial. *American Journal of Physical Medicine and Rehabilitation*, **76**(6), 440-450.

Zhang, L., Plotkin, R. C., Wang, G., Sandel, M. E., & Lee, S. (2004). Cholinergic augmentation with donepezil enhances recovery in short-term memory and sustained attention after traumatic brain injury. *Archives of Physical Medicine and Rehabilitation*, **85**(7), 1050-1055.

In: Handbook of Neuropsychiatry Research
Editor: Rebecca S. Davies, pp. 97-112

ISBN: 978-1-61668-138-8
© 2010 Nova Science Publishers, Inc.

Chapter 4

SEQUENTIAL EXPRESSION OF IMPAIRED PSYCHOMOTOR AND SENSORIMOTOR ACTIVITIES IN RODENTS DURING AMPHETAMINE WITHDRAWAL

Junichi Kitanaka[*], Nobue Kitanaka and Motohiko Takemura
Department of Pharmacology,
Hyogo College of Medicine, Nishinomiya,
Hyogo 663-8501, Japan

Abstract

Abusers of amphetamines and related drugs need to be treated effectively for any withdrawal symptoms (i.e. depression, anxiety, anhedonia, severe fatigue, and apathy) observed after drug abstinence in order to start pharmacotherapy for drug abuse. However, no effective treatment for amphetamine abuse has been established. The withdrawal symptoms are thought to be strongly associated with decreased motor activity and impaired sensorimotor accuracy observed in animal models. In this chapter, we will review some of the evidence for specific behavioral alterations in rodents chronically treated with amphetamines followed by a drug abstinence period in order to consider which treatment schedule

---

[*] E-mail address: kitanaka-hyg@umin.net

(especially postdrug period) could lead to better understanding of the molecular basis of amphetamine withdrawal in humans.

Keywords: Amphetamine, withdrawal, psychomotor activity, sensorimotor activity, chronic fatigue, postdrug period, animal model.

Introduction

Chronic use of amphetamine-type drugs (AMPH) followed by drug withdrawal induces AMPH withdrawal symptoms including depression, anxiety, anhedonia, severe fatigue, and apathy [17]-[20], [22]. AMPH abusers may commonly suffer from these severe symptoms because they are required to cease their AMPH use in order to start pharmacotherapy for drug abuse. Therefore, treatment for AMPH withdrawal syndrome is important for drug abusers, although no effective treatment for AMPH withdrawal has been established. The AMPH withdrawal symptoms are thought to be strongly associated with decreased motor activity and impaired sensorimotor accuracy observed in animal models. It is clear that investigators need to use an animal model of AMPH withdrawal symptoms to determine an effective treatment for AMPH withdrawal. This review is intended to assess the behavioral consequences of AMPH withdrawal in rodents. As described below, there are a variety of drug treatment schedules. However, there is variability in the results regarding AMPH withdrawal syndrome as indexed by various behavioral measures. We focus on the results that were similar in animal experiments to those observed in AMPH abusers and also discuss the inconsistent data in comparison with the positive observations in order to discuss the molecular basis of AMPH withdrawal syndrome.

Behavioral Consequences of AMPH Withdrawal in Rodents

The significant changes in behavioral parameters that occur during the AMPH withdrawal period are summarized in Table 1. The term "withdrawal" refers to the absence of AMPH or methamphetamine (METH) throughout this review.

Table 1. Significant changes in the behavioral parameters during withdrawal from chronic amphetamine/methamphetamine administration in rodents

Measure	Species[a] and drug treatment schedule	Postdrug period	Effect		Reference
Behavior after drug abstinence period without challenge					
Locomotion	Rat, d,l-AMPH, 3 mg/kg, p.o., 9 mo	2-12 dy	Decrease	(H)	[9]
	Rat, AMPH, 50-200 mg/l, p.o., 3 wk	2-6 dy	Decrease	(N)	[21]
	Rat*, AMPH, 1-10 mg/kg x 2/dy, i.p., 6 wk[b]	8-12 dy	Decrease	(H)	[36]
	Rat*, AMPH, 1-10 mg/kg x 2/dy, i.p., 6 wk[b]	2-3 dy	Decrease	(H)	[29]
	Rat, AMPH, 7.5 mg/kg x 2/dy, i.p., 2 wk	24-54 h	Decrease	(N)	[40]
	Rat, AMPH, 1-10 mg/kg x 3/dy, i.p., 4 dy[c]	1 dy	Decrease	(N)	[37]
	Rat, AMPH, 2 and 4 mg/kg x 1/33-h int, i.p., 10 cycles	19-24 h	Decrease	(H)	[45]
Rearing	Rat, AMPH, 50-200 mg/l, p.o., 3 wk	2 dy	Decrease		[21]
Grooming	Rat, AMPH, 50-200 mg/l, p.o., 3 wk	2 dy	Increase		[21]
Immobility in FST	Mouse, AMPH, 5 mg/kg x 2/dy, i.p., 10 dy	1 dy	Increase		[16]
	Rat, AMPH, 7.5 mg/kg x 2/dy, i.p., 2 wk	36-72 h	Decrease		[40]
	Rat, AMPH, 5 and 10 mg/kg/dy, s.c.[d], 6 dy	2-3 dy	Increase		[7]
	Rat, AMPH, 10 mg/kg/day, s.c.[d], 6 dy	1 dy	Decrease		[7]
Immobility in TST	Mouse, AMPH, 5 and 10 mg/kg/dy, s.c.[d], 7 dy	1 dy	Increase		[7]
PPI	Rat, AMPH, 1-10 mg/kg x 3/dy, i.p., 4 dy[c]	4-40 dy	Decrease		[37]
	Rat, AMPH, 1-8 mg/kg x 3/dy, i.p., 6 dy	55 dy	Decrease		[30]
Conditioned fear	Rat, AMPH, 1-5 mg/kg x 3/dy, i.p., 6 dy	4 dy	Increase		[32]
Sexual behavior	Rat, AMPH, 1-12 mg/kg x 3/dy, i.p., 4 dy	12 h	Decrease		[3]

Table 1. Continued

Measure	Species[a] and drug treatment schedule	Postdrug period	Effect	Reference
Behavior after drug abstinence period followed by drug challenge				
AMPH/METH challenge				
Stereotypy	Rat, AMPH, 3-12 mg/kg x 2/dy, s.c., 3 wk	1-4 wk	Increase	[10]
	Rat, METH, 6 mg/kg x 1/dy, i.p., 3-7 dy	44-89 dy	Increase	[27]
	Rat*, AMPH, 1-10 mg/kg x 2/dy, i.p., 6 wk[b]	12 dy	Increase	[36]
Sensitization	Rat, AMPH, 0.5 mg/kg x 1/dy, i.v., 7 dy	10-12 dy	Increase	[28]
	Rat, AMPH, 1-10 mg/kg x 3/dy, i.p., 4 dy[c]	1 mo	Increase	[38]
	Mouse, METH, 1 mg/kg x 1/dy, i.p., 5 dy	5 dy	Increase	[15]
Apomorphine challenge				
Circling	Mouse, AMPH, 2.5-20 mg/kg, p.o., 3 mo	1 mo	Decrease	[11]

This table shows the published amphetamine/methamphetamine withdrawal effects (more than 12 h withdrawal from multiple injections of the drug) on behavioral parameters in rodents. The term "withdrawal" here refers to the absence of amphetamine/methamphetamine. The drug dose ranges indicate that escalating doses within the ranges were injected into the animals.

Abbreviations: alt dy: alternate days; AMPH: *d*-amphetamine unless otherwise indicated; dy: day(s); FST: forced swimming test; H: locomotor activity of habituated subjects; int: interval; i.p.: intraperitoneally; i.v.: intravenously; METH: *d*-methamphetamine; mo: month(s); N: novelty response measure of exploratory behavior in a novel environment; p.o.: orally (in those cases, it is difficult to estimate the exact dose of the drug the animals received since the drug was taken into the animal with the diet or water); PPI: prepulse inhibition; s.c.: subcutaneously; wk: week(s); TST: tail suspension test.

[a]Male subjects used, but the asterisks and dagger indicate females and both sexes used, respectively.

[b]Injections were given each weekday, but not on weekends.

[c]One injection (10 mg/kg AMPH) was given on Day 4, while three injections were given on Days 1-3.

[d]Drug was delivered via osmotic mini-pumps inserted subcutaneously (in the back of the rodent parallel to the spine).

Spontaneous Locomotion and other Behaviors Observed in Open Field

Similar to inactivity in humans, decreased spontaneous locomotion after AMPH abstinence (1-6 days) was reported in rats measured in a novel environment [21], [37], [40]. These observations suggested a decrease in the neuronal activity contributing to motility during AMPH withdrawal, since the activity level of spontaneous locomotion is thought to relate to the degree of neuronal activity contributing to motility in rodents. However, an inconsistent result was reported using mice; even in a novel environment, AMPH withdrawal (one day) had no effect on locomotor activity [16], suggesting that the observed effects on locomotion after AMPH abstinence depend on the species used (rats vs. mice).

It is recognized that locomotor activity is crucially influenced by the environment to which rodents have been habituated as well as by light-dark cycles. Generally, habituated animals hardly show a decrease in locomotor activity during AMPH withdrawal, compared with rats exposed to a novel environment; however, the lower baseline level of activity observed in habituated animals makes it difficult to observe further decreases [40]. Nevertheless, withdrawal from AMPH in rats treated orally with 3 mg/kg daily AMPH for 9 months caused hypoactivity in habituated rats [9]. Similar results were reported from several laboratories under habituated environments with a precisely defined dosage of AMPH (escalating dosing protocol, see Table 1) [29], [36], suggesting that assessment of locomotor activity in rats is a good index for evaluating the expression of the symptoms of AMPH withdrawal.

Spontaneous nocturnal but not diurnal locomotion was significantly decreased in rodents during the withdrawal period after repeated AMPH treatment [15], [36], since overall locomotor activity during the nocturnal period is higher than that of the diurnal period. Recently, White and White [45] showed decreased locomotion in habituated rats during AMPH withdrawal using a 33-h AMPH administration schedule (2 and 4 mg/kg, 10 cycles), which diminished the association of the effect of drug injection with the circadian rhythm. Overall, measurement of locomotor activity is a good index for demonstrating the expression of depressive state in rodents during AMPH withdrawal since several crucial determinants (habituation, circadian rhythm, and drug injection protocol, but not species) hardly affect the evaluation of AMPH withdrawal by locomotor activity.

Rearing and grooming were significantly decreased and increased, respectively, two days after oral AMPH treatment [21]. The decreased rearing behavior lasted six days after chronic AMPH treatment. Treatment of the rats with mianserin, a tetracyclic antidepressant with a weak inhibitory property of norepinephrine (NE) reuptake, for 4 days significantly reversed the withdrawal effect on rearing and grooming, suggesting that alteration in postdrug NE neurotransmission may be associated with a significant change in the expression levels of rearing and grooming.

Forced Swimming Test

The forced swimming test (FST), as well as the tail suspension test described below, is one of the first-choice tests for screening antidepressants [31]. This behavioral paradigm is based on the natural tendency to escape from a potentially dangerous situation (i.e. acrylic glass cylinders filled with water), which is strongly associated with the psychomotor activity against despair. This behavioral paradigm has been applied to animals for evaluating depressive state during AMPH withdrawal. Fixed-dose treatment of mice with i.p. AMPH increased immobility time in the FST after one-day drug abstinence [16], while decreased immobility time was observed in rats treated with a fixed-dose of AMPH after 36-72-h drug abstinence [40]. These inconsistent results may have arisen from the species used. Therefore, the choice of the species is a crucial determinant for mimicking the AMPH withdrawal symptoms observed in humans. Alternatively, it should be noted that the difference of postdrug period between the two studies [16], [40] might impact the results. Chronic fatigue in AMPH abusers may be associated, at least in part, with a decrease in psychomotor activity [19]. In rats, AMPH withdrawal showed a biphasic effect on immobility time in FST, depending on the postdrug period; it decreased after one day of drug abstinence and increased after 2-3-days of drug abstinence [7]. These observations clearly demonstrate that the postdrug period is an important factor determining the expression of depressive state during AMPH withdrawal when animals are subjected to the forced swimming test.

Tail Suspension Test

This method for screening antidepressants is based on the fact that mice subjected to the short-term, inescapable stress of being suspended by their tail, will develop an immobile posture [42]. Cryan et al. [7] reported that depression-like behavior (i.e. increased immobility time) was observed in mice administered with AMPH released from implanted mini-pumps at a rate of 5 and 10 mg/kg/day for 1 week followed by 1 day of AMPH withdrawal in the test. In contrast to this, the immobility time was not affected in mice that received a continuous s.c. infusion of METH (15 or 76 mg/kg of METH for 2 weeks) followed by 5 days of withdrawal (manuscript in preparation). Furthermore, augmented efforts to escape from a severe stressor like tail suspension were induced by a fixed-dose of METH (1.0 or 2.5 mg/kg, i.p., twice daily for 10 consecutive days) (manuscript in preparation). These inconsistent results between laboratories clearly demonstrate that the period of withdrawal (1 vs. 5 days) and/or infusion period (7 vs. 14 days) are crucial factor(s) determining the expression of depression-like behavior in mice because the total amounts of AMPH used were almost identical (35 and 70 vs. 15 and 76 mg/kg animal). In addition, mice administered with a fixed-dose of AMPH (5 mg/kg, i.p., twice daily for 10 consecutive days; total amount of AMPH = 100 mg/kg/animal) followed by 1 day of withdrawal show depression-like behavior in the forced swimming test [16]. These observations also suggest the importance of the withdrawal period in the expression of depression-like behavior. Overall, the changes in psychomotor activity after drug abstinence depend largely on the postdrug period as indexed by immobility time in the tail suspension test.

Prepulse Inhibition

The magnitude of the startled response to an intense noise stimulus can be attenuated by presentation of a weak pre-stimulus before the startle-eliciting stimulus. This phenomenon is termed prepulse inhibition (PPI). Deficient sensorimotor gating as indexed by PPI of the startled response has been reported in patients suffering from schizophrenia. Chronic administration of AMPH culminates in AMPH psychosis with psychiatric sequelae (paranoia, delusions, and hallucinations) and abnormal behavior clinically undistinguishable from that of paranoid schizophrenia [2], [19], [34], [35], [39]. Therefore, animals treated with chronic AMPH have been subjected to the PPI paradigm. Escalating dose injections (1-10 mg/kg, i.p., x 3 injections per day for 4 days, or 1-8 mg/kg, i.p., x 3 injections per day for 6 days) effectively disrupted PPI in rats on days 4-55 of drug withdrawal [30], [37]. Decreases in the PPI index were observed for more than one month in these reports, suggesting a long-lasting dysfunction of sensorimotor activity during AMPH withdrawal.

Conditioned Fear

Chronic stress can influence fear conditioning in experimental animals, and the basolateral amygdala is implicated in the response to stressful stimuli. Neurotransmitters including NE and -aminobutylic acid (GABA) are thought to be involved in the amygdalar response to such stimuli. AMPH withdrawal can affect the tissue levels of GABA and NE (for review see reference [13]). Therefore, AMPH withdrawal may induce increases in psychomotor output in the amygdala area. Pesse et al. [32] reported that AMPH-withdrawn rats showed increases in conditioned freezing compared with control animals 4 days after drug abstinence, suggesting the expression of AMPH withdrawal symptoms. This observation may be closely associated with PPI in terms of the molecular basis of its action.

Sexual Behavior

Decreased sexual functioning has been described in psychostimulant abusers [1]. It is certain that this decreased motivation, an aspect of anhedonic state during psychostimulant withdrawal, is closely related to decreased locomotion in experimental animals. Rats treated with escalating-dose AMPH (1-12 mg/kg, three injections daily for 4 days) exhibited reduced sexual behavior 4 days after drug abstinence [3]. Treatment schedule is similar to that reported by Russig et al. [37], and they observed a significantly decreased locomotor activity in rats.

Sequential Expression of Impaired Psychomotor and Sensorimotor Activities and Related Behaviors

As summarized in Fig. 1, 6 of 8 behavioral paradigms have been tested in rodents treated with chronic AMPH/METH followed by 1-4 days of drug abstinence. These observations clearly demonstrate that the psychomotor aspects of AMPH withdrawal symptoms can be detected within 1-4 days of drug abstinence. Decreases in locomotion have also been observed in rodents treated with chronic AMPH followed by 19 h-12-days of drug abstinence, suggesting that other behavioral paradigms except locomotion are expected to be affected by AMPH withdrawal for up to 12-days of drug abstinence in rodents, although there have been no reports with respect to this. In humans, the psychomotor aspect of

AMPH withdrawal symptoms (i.e. depression, inactivity, fatigue, and anhedonia) can last for 2-7 days of AMPH abstinence and may disappear thereafter [23], [44].

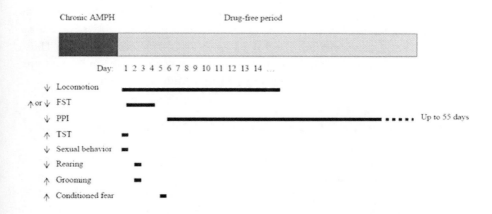

Figure 1. Time-course of decreased psychomotor activity and related behaviors in rodents during AMPH withdrawal. Please note that this figure was summarized based solely on the postdrug period. Up and down arrows mean increase and decrease, respectively. AMPH, amphetamine-type drug(s); FST, forced swimming test; PPI, prepulse inhibition; TST, tail suspension test.

Compared with psychomotor activity, sensorimotor activity is affected by a longer drug withdrawal period; decreases in PPI have been detected in rats treated with chronic AMPH followed by 4-55-days of drug abstinence [30], [37], although there have been some AMPH withdrawal findings of no effect of chronic AMPH (1.5 mg/kg once daily for 5 days) followed by 4-days of drug abstinence on PPI index in rats [25]. The animal models showed a progressive augmentation of locomotor activity called behavioral sensitization and stereotypical behavior when they were challenged with the drug after several days to months of drug abstinence (Table 1; references [10], [15], [27], [28], [36], [38] but not the case of cross-sensitization in mice challenged with apomorphine [11]). This implies that these animals have a susceptibility to AMPH psychosis [39], and may model the prodromal symptoms of schizophrenia in terms of some behavioral paradigms. Impaired sensorimotor gating of the acoustic startled response was found to be already present in subjects with prodromal symptoms of schizophrenia [5], [33]. These two distinct phenomena, decreased PPI in rats treated with chronic AMPH followed by drug withdrawal and impaired PPI in schizophrenic patients are similar in time-course to each other, although there have been some inconsistent findings between the two species with respect to the effect of some drugs (i.e. ketamine and MDMA) on the PPI index [5].

Overall, rodent models can mimic the behavioral aspects of AMPH withdrawal symptoms; the psychomotor aspects of AMPH withdrawal symptoms can be detected within 1-4 days of drug abstinence, and impaired sensorimotor activity can be detected within 4-55-days of drug abstinence (Fig. 1). These animal models are useful for understanding the molecular mechanism of the time-course of impaired motor activities during AMPH withdrawal in humans.

Future Directions and Applications of AMPH Withdrawal

We have reviewed the developments in rodent studies of AMPH withdrawal in various behavioral paradigms. As can be seen in Table 1, a variety of drug treatment schedules exist. Therefore, the variability of the results may not be negligible in terms of the type of behavioral measures and/or drug treatment schedules. Regardless of this, the increasing lines of evidence in rodents and humans have normalized the variability of the results to one possible hypothesis: decreased psychomotor activity and related behaviors can be detected after 1-4 days of drug abstinence as indexed by some behavioral paradigms (locomotion, rearing, grooming, sexual behavior, tail suspension test, and conditioned fear) in rodents treated with chronic AMPH, while sensorimotor accuracy (as indexed by PPI) may be significantly impaired by more than 4 days of AMPH withdrawal (Fig. 1). As mentioned above, use of rodents relevant to the expression of valid behavioral aspects of AMPH withdrawal would be helpful for providing us with reliable and reproducible evidence for the molecular basis of AMPH withdrawal in humans. While AMPH withdrawal has been less studied compared with the vast amounts of research on AMPH dependence and abuse, we and others propose to elucidate the neurochemical consequences of AMPH withdrawal in rodents and determine treatments for AMPH withdrawal to prevent depressive syndromes such as anhedonia, depression, and anxiety as well as subsequent averse outcomes, including impulsive self-injurious behavior or acts that are committed with unconscious or uncontrolled suicidal intentions [4], [13], [14], [26], [46].

Of the neurochemical changes seen in rodents during AMPH withdrawal, alterations in monoaminergic neurotransmission are the most common observation during AMPH withdrawal, which certainly explains the depression-like behavior. Especially, decreases in the tissue levels of serotonin (5-hydroxytryptamine, 5-HT) and NE in specific brain regions such the cerebral cortex and striatum account for the expression of depressive state and related behaviors [41], [43]. For instance, treatment of rats with mianserin, a tetracyclic antidepressant with a weak inhibitory property of NE reuptake, for 4 days significantly reversed the withdrawal effect on rearing and grooming, suggesting that AMPH withdrawal-induced depression may be associated with a significant change in the expression levels of rearing and grooming [21]. Similarly, depression-like behavior in the tail suspension test (i.e. increased immobility time) observed during AMPH withdrawal might be relieved by antidepressants. By using reliable animal models exhibiting altered behavioral measures during AMPH withdrawal, neurochemical approaches can determine the treatment for AMPH withdrawal syndromes.

The chronic fatigue and apathy syndrome observed in AMPH withdrawal needs to be treated to improve individuals' quality of life. However, there is no reliable chronic fatigue treatment, since the neurochemical basis of fatigue remains poorly understood. In animal models, chronic fatigue may certainly impact the motor activity in terms of measures shown in Table 1. Several hypotheses including alterations in dopaminergic and 5-HTergic neurotransmission have been proposed for fatigue [12], [24], and some agents have been studied on the basis of the monoaminergic hypotheses of AMPH withdrawal (for instance, references [6], [8]). Kalinski et al. [12] proposed the involvement of decreases in striatal dopaminergic neurotransmission during exhaustive exercise in fatigue in mice. In their observations, the mice received a relatively high dose of METH (20 mg/kg, i.p., four injections at 2-h intervals within one day). In contrast to this, the tissue levels of dopamine were not altered in mice treated with repeated moderate doses of METH (1 mg/kg, i.p. one injection daily for 5 consecutive days followed by one injection of the same dose of METH after 5-day drug abstinence), although they exhibited a significant reduction in locomotor activity during the nocturnal period [15]. Although fatigue may closely be associated with a reduction in psychomotor activity in rodents, these inconsistent results mean that the process of fatigue involves many factors, and one hypothesis can hardly account for all aspects of fatigue during AMPH withdrawal. Animal models exhibiting a long-lasting decrease in locomotor activity that also is accompanied by disruption of sensorimotor accuracy in expression time-course are useful for studying the management of extreme fatigue and the apathy syndrome induced by drug abstinence.

AMPH abusers most commonly suffered withdrawal symptoms when they are required to cease their drug use before pharmacotherapy. To elucidate the molecular basis of AMPH withdrawal, investigators need to use reliable and valid animal models that mimic human AMPH withdrawal symptoms, although little evidence is available regarding AMPH withdrawal compared with the vast number of studies using rodent models exhibiting positive symptoms such as hyperlocomotion, behavioral sensitization, rewarding effect, and bizarre behavior including stereotypy. This review has attempted to summarize the AMPH withdrawal symptoms in rodents as indexed by alterations in behavioral measures. It is clear that the alterations in behavioral measures were not identical in response to the variety of drug treatment schedules and the postdrug periods used, suggesting that multiple molecular pathways may be responsible for the expression of AMPH withdrawal syndrome. Despite the possible complex mechanisms of AMPH withdrawal, rodents that exhibit behavioral abnormalities that are similar to human symptoms may serve as an appropriate animal model for AMPH withdrawal in humans. Use of these animal models may produce better understanding of the molecular aspects of the expression of AMPH withdrawal symptoms and determine appropriate pharmacotherapy for AMPH abusers.

Acknowledgments

This research was supported, in part, by Grants-in-Aid for Young Scientists from the Ministry of Education, Culture, Sports, Science, and Technology of Japan (No. 21790254 to N.K.) and for Researchers, Hyogo College of Medicine (2009 to J.K.).

References

[1] American Psychiatric Association (1994) *Diagnostic and statistical manual of mental disorders*. 4th ed. American Psychiatric Association, Washington DC.

[2] Angrist, B., Sathananthan, G., Wilk, S., Gershon, S. (1974) Amphetamine psychosis: behavioral and biochemical aspects. *J. Psychiatric Res.*, **11**, 13-23.

[3] Barr, A. M., Fiorino, D. F., Phillips, A. G. (1999) Effects of withdrawal from an escalating dose schedule of *d*-amphetamine on sexual behavior in the male rat. *Pharmacol. Biochem. Behav.*, **64**, 597-604.

[4] Barr, A. M., Markou, A. (2005) Psychostimulant withdrawal as an inducing condition in animal models of depression. *Neurosci. Biobehav. Rev.*, **29**, 675-706.

[5] Braff, D. L., Geyer, M. A., Swerdlow, N. R. (2001) Human studies of prepulse inhibition of startle: normal subjects, patient groups, and pharmacological studies. *Psychopharmacology (Berl.)*, **156**, 234-258.

[6] Chan-Ob, T., Kuntawongse, N., Boonyanaruthee, V. (2001) Bupropion for amphetamine withdrawal syndrome. *J. Med. Assoc. Thai.*, **84**, 1763-1765.

[7] Cryan, J. F., Hoyer, D., Markou, A. (2003) Withdrawal from chronic amphetamine induces depressive-like behavioral effects in rodents. *Biol. Psychiatry*, **54**, 49-58.

[8] Gillin, J. C., Pulvirenti, L., Withers, N., Golshan, S., Koob, G. (1994) The effects of lisuride on mood and sleep during acute withdrawal in stimulant abusers: a preliminary report. *Biol. Psychiatry*, **35**, 843-849.

[9] Herman, Z. S., Trzeciak, H., Chrusciel, T. L., Kmiteciak-Kolada, K., Drybanski, A., Sokola, A. (1971) The influence of prolonged amphetamine treatment and amphetamine withdrawal on brain biogenic amine content and behaviour in the rat. *Psychopharmacologia (Berl.)*, **21**, 74-81.

[10] Hitzemann, R. J., Tseng, L. F., Hitzemann, B. A., Sampath-Khanna, S., Loh, H. H. (1977) Effects of withdrawal from chronic amphetamine intoxication on exploratory and stereotyped behaviors in the rat. *Psychopharmacology (Berl.)*, **54**, 295-302.

[11] Jenner, P., Pycock, C., Marsden, C. D. (1978) The effect of chronic administration and withdrawal of amphetamine on cerebral dopamine receptor sensitivity. *Psychopharmacology (Berl.)*, **58**, 131-136.

[12] Kalinski, M. I., Dluzen, D. E., Stadulis, R. (2001) Methamphetamine produces subsequent reductions in running time to exhaustion in mice. *Brain Res.*, **921**, 160-164.

[13] Kitanaka, J., Kitanaka, N., Takemura, M. (2008) Neurochemical consequences of dysphoric state during amphetamine withdrawal in animal models: a review. *Neurochem. Res.*, **33**, 204-219.

[14] Kitanaka, N., Kitanaka, J., Hall, F. S., Tatsuta, T., Morita, Y., Takemura, M., Wang, X.-B., Uhl, G. R. (2008) Alterations in the levels of heterotrimeric G protein subunits induced by psychostimulants, opiates, barbiturates, and ethanol: implications for drug dependence, tolerance, and withdrawal. *Synapse*, **69**, 689-699.

[15] Kitanaka, N., Kitanaka, J., Takemura, M. (2003) Behavioral sensitization and alteration in monoamine metabolism in mice after single versus repeated methamphetamine administration. *Eur. J. Pharmacol.*, **474**, 63-70.

[16] Kokkinidis, L., Zacharko, R. M., Anisman, H. (1986) Amphetamine withdrawal: a behavioral evaluation. *Life Sci.*, **38**, 1617-1623.

[17] Koob, G. F., Le Moal, M. (1997) Drug abuse: hedonic homeostatic dysregulation. *Science*, **278**, 52-58.

[18] Kosten, T. R., Markou, A., Koob, G.F. (1998) Depression and stimulant dependence: neurobiology and pharmacotherapy. *J. Nerv. Ment. Dis.*, **186**, 737-745.

[19] Kramer, J. C., Fischman, V. S., Littlefield, D. C. (1967) Amphetamine abuse: pattern and effects of high doses taken intravenously. *JAMA*, **201**, 305-309.

[20] Lago, J. A., Kosten, T. R. (1994) Stimulant withdrawal. *Addiction*, **89**, 1477-1481.

[21] Lynch, M. A., Leonard, B. E. (1978) Effect of chronic amphetamine administration on the behaviour of rats in the open field apparatus: reversal of post-withdrawal depression by two antidepressants. *J. Pharm. Pharmacol.*, **30**, 798-799.

[22] Markou, A., Kosten, T. R., Koob, G.F. (1998) Neurobiological similarities in depression and drug dependence: a self-medication hypothesis. *Neuropsychopharmacology*, **18**, 135-174.

[23] McGregor, C., Srisurapanont, M., Jittiwutikarn, J., Laobhripatr, S., Wongtan, T., White, J. M. (2005) The nature, time course and severity of methamphetamine withdrawal. *Addiction*, **100**, 1320-1329.

[24] Meeusen, R., Watson, P., Hasegawa, H., Roelands, B., Piacentini, M. F. (2006) Central fatigue: the serotonin hypothesis and beyond. *Sports Med.*, **36**, 881-909.

[25] Murphy, C. A., Fend, M., Russig, H., Feldon, J. (2001) Latent inhibition, but not prepulse inhibition, is reduced during withdrawal from an escalating dosage schedule of amphetamine. *Behav. Neurosci.*, **6**, 1247-1256.

[26] Nestler, E. J. (2001) Molecular basis of long-term plasticity underlying addiction. *Nature Rev. Neurosci.*, **2**, 119-128.

[27] Nishikawa, T., Mataga, N., Takashima, M., Toru, M. (1983) Behavioral sensitization and relative hyperresponsiveness of striatal and limbic dopaminergic neurons after repeated methamphetamine treatment. *Eur. J. Pharmacol.*, **88**, 195-203.

[28] Ostrander, M. M., Badiani, A., Day, H. E. W., Norton, C. S., Watson, S. J., Akil, H., Robinson, T. E. (2003) Environmental context and drug history modulate amphetamine-induced c-fos mRNA expression in the basal ganglia, central extended amygdala, and associated limbic forebrain. *Neuroscience*, **120**, 551-571.

[29] Paulson, P. E., Camp, D. M., Robinson, T. E. (1991) Time course of transient behavioral depression and persistent behavioral sensitization in

relation to regional brain monoamine concentrations during amphetamine withdrawal in rats. *Psychopharmacology (Berl.)*, **103**, 480-494.

[30] Peleg-Raibstein, D., Sydekum, E., Feldon, J. (2006) Differential effects on prepulse inhibition of withdrawal from two different repeated administration schedules of amphetamine. *Int. J. Neuropsychopharmacol.*, **9**, 737-749.

[31] Petit-Demouliere, B., Chenu, F., Bourin, M. (2005) Forced swimming test in mice: a review of antidepressant activity. *Psychopharmacology (Berl.)*, **177**, 245-255.

[32] Pezze, M. A., Feldon, J., Murphy, C. A. (2002) Increased conditioned fear response and altered balance of dopamine in the shell and core of the nucleus accumbens during amphetamine withdrawal. *Neuropharmacology*, **42**, 633-643.

[33] Quednow, B. B., Frommann, I., Berning, J., Kühn, K. U., Maier, W., Wagner, M. (2008) Impaired sensorimotor gating of the acoustic startle response in the prodrome of schizophrenia. *Biol. Psychiatry*, **64**, 766-773.

[34] Randrup, A., Munkvad, I. (1967) Stereotyped activities produced by amphetamine in several animal species and man. *Psychopharmacologia (Berl.)*, **11**, 300-310.

[35] Robinson, T. E., Becker, J. B. (1986) Enduring changes in brain and behavior produced by chronic amphetamine administration: a review and evaluation of animal models of amphetamine psychosis. *Brain Res. Rev.*, **11**, 157-198.

[36] Robinson, T. E., Camp, D. E. (1987) Long-lasting effects of escalating doses of *d*-amphetamine on brain monoamines, amphetamine-induced stereotyped behavior and spontaneous nocturnal locomotion. *Pharmacol. Biochem. Behav.*, **26**, 821-827.

[37] Russig, H., Murphy, C. A., Feldon, J. (2005) Behavioural consequences of withdrawal from three different administration schedules of amphetamine. *Behav. Brain Res.*, **165**, 26-35.

[38] Russig, H., Pryce, C. R., Feldon, J. (2006) Amphetamine withdrawal leads to behavioral sensitization and reduced HPA axis response following amphetamine challenge. *Brain Res.*, **1084**, 185-195.

[39] Sato, M. (1992) A lasting vulnerability to psychosis in patients with previous methamphetamine psychosis. *Ann. N.Y. Acad. Sci.*, **654**, 160-170.

[40] Schindler, C. W., Persico, A. M., Uhl, G. R., Goldberg, S. R. (1994) Behavioral assessment of high-dose amphetamine withdrawal: importance of training and testing conditions. *Pharmacol. Biochem. Behav.*, **49**, 41-46.

[41] Schmidt, C. J., Sonsalla, P. K., Hanson, G. R., Peat, M. A., Gibb, J. W. (1985) Methamphetamine-induced depression of monoamine synthesis in the rat: Development of tolerance. *J. Neurochem.*, **44**, 852-855.

[42] Steru, L., Chermat, R., Thierry, B., Simon, P. (1985) The tail suspension test: a new method for screening antidepressants in mice. *Psychopharmacology (Berl.)*, **85**, 367-70.

[43] Tonge, S. R. (1974) Noradrenaline and 5-hydroxytryptamine metabolism in six areas of rat brain during post-amphetamine depression. *Psychopharmacologia (Berl.)*, **38**, 181-186.

[44] Watson, R., Hartmann, E., Schildkraut, J. J. (1972) Amphetamine withdrawal: affective state, sleep patterns, and MHPG excretion. *Am. J. Psychiatry*, **129**, 263-269.

[45] White, W., White, I. M. (2006) An activity indicator of acute withdrawal depends on amphetamine dose in rats. *Physiol. Behav.* **87**, 368-376.

[46] Yui, K., Kajii, Y., Nishikawa, T. (2006) Neurobiological and molecular basis of methamphetamine-induced behavioral sensitization and spontaneous recurrence of methamphetamine psychosis and its implication in schizophrenia. *Curr. Psychiatry Rev.*, **2**, 381-393.

In: Handbook of Neuropsychiatry Research ISBN: 978-1-61668-138-8
Editor: Rebecca S. Davies, pp. 113-123 © 2010 Nova Science Publishers, Inc.

Chapter 5

ASSOCIATION BETWEEN SALIVARY AMYLASE, CORTISOL AND STRESS

*Koichi Isogawa[1], Jusen Tsuru[2], Yoshihiro Tanaka[2], Yoshinobu Ishitobi[2], Tomoko Ando[2], Hiroaki Hanada[2], Kensuke Kodama[2] and Jotaro Akiyoshi[*2]*

[1] Center for Neural Science, New York University, 4 Washington Place, Room 809, New York, NY 10003-6621, USA
[2] Department of Neuropsychiatry, Oita University Faculty of Medicine, Hasama-Machi, Oita, 879-5593, Japan

Abstract

The role of the Hypothalamus-Pituitary-Adrenocortical (HPA) system in depression and anxiety disorders has been investigated for decades. Depression is associated with elevated blood cortisol levels. The dexamethasone-suppressed corticotropin-releasing hormone (DEX/CRH) stimulation test is used to demonstrate the failure of negative feedback mechanisms in depression. Both cortisol- and ACTH-responsiveness to the DEX/CRH test are elevated during a depressed state. However, these responses tend to normalize after successful treatment and remission of disease. We also examined the Sympathetic-Adrenal Medullary (SAM) system as another mediator of the stress response, and have found alterations in this system related to depression and anxiety disorders. Electric stimulation stress and Trier Social Stress Tests were employed in addition to salivary amylase assays as biological markers of stress. As a result,

---

[*] E-mail address: akiyoshi@med.oita-u.ac.jp

the SAM system was found to react to stressors related to these disorders alongside the HPA system. Although differences exist between the two systems, it is clear that both HPA and SAM systems are involved in depression and anxiety disorders.

Key words: salivary amylase, salivary cortisol, stress.

Introduction

Stress is an important factor in the development and maintenance of affective and anxiety disorders. Stress also potentiates depression- and anxiety-like responses in animals, but experimental evidence for a similar effect in humans is limited. Grillon et al. (2007) studied the ability of a social stressor (speech presentation plus a counting task) to induce the facilitation of startle in the dark. Measures of individual distress and of hypothalamic–pituitary–adrenal axis and autonomic nervous system activity (e.g., salivary cortisol and amylase levels, blood pressure, and heart rate) were also taken to verify the effectiveness of stress management interventions.

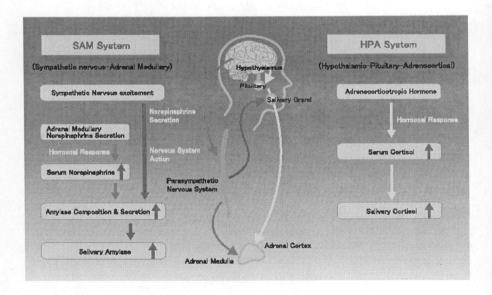

Startle was significantly enhanced in the dark. This effect was further potentiated by previous exposure to a social stressor. The social stressor caused increases in salivary cortisol and salivary amylase as well as increases in blood pressure, heart rate, and subjective distress. These findings indicate that stress potentiates anxiety. Animal studies suggest that such an interaction might be mediated by glucocorticoid effects on corticotropin-releasing hormone regulation within limbic brain structures.

A role for hypothalamic–pituitary–adrenal (HPA) axis activity in mediating stress responses has been intensively investigated for decades. The HPA axis is a complex neuroendocrine stress system involved in bio-behavioral adjustments to confrontational stimuli and change. Cortisol is an essential hormone in the regulation of stress responsiveness. It exists in both free (active) and protein-bound (inactive) forms in serum but only in a free form in saliva. Recently, salivary cortisol has been used as a simple, noninvasive index of free circulating cortisol levels. Stahl and Dorner (1982) showed that cortisol levels increase several fold within a short time period after the onset of psychological stress. This finding has had significant implications for our comprehension of the role of hypothalamic–pituitary–adrenal (HPA) axis dysfunction.

The stress response is regulated by two primary neuroendocrine systems, the hypothalamic-pituitary-adrenocortical (HPA) and sympathetic adrenomedullary (SAM) systems (Figure). Takai et al. (2007) investigated gender differences in the activities of these two systems in response to acute psychological stress. Subjects were categorized according to their score on Spielberger's Trait Anxiety Inventory (STAI), which assesses individual predisposition to anxiety. High (STAI score $\geq$ 55)- and low (STAI score $\leq$ 45)-anxiety groups were selected. A video of corneal surgery served as the stressor over a time course of 15 minutes. Salivary cortisol and amylase levels were used as indices of HPA and SAM activities, respectively. Beta-endorphin was also assayed as an alternative index of HPA activity. There were no differences in baseline (resting) salivary parameters among the groups. As expected, cortisol and amylase levels were significantly increased in all groups after viewing the stressful video. There were no gender differences in amylase levels in either the high- or low-anxiety groups. However, cortisol levels in highly anxious females were significantly lower than those in highly anxious males. These findings demonstrate that highly anxious females exhibited lower cortisol release versus highly anxious males, suggesting that higher trait anxiety in females may be associated with an inability to respond with sufficient activation of the HPA system under acute psychological stress conditions.

Relationship between the SAM System and Stress

Recently, much attention has been given to possible interactions between stress and α-amylase levels. However, significant psychological studies of α-amylase responsiveness are difficult due to the system's complexities. Salivary α-amylase (sAA) is secreted by the parotid gland in response to adrenergic activity and is suppressed by β-adrenoreceptor blockade (van Stegeren et al., 2006). It has also become established as a new biomarker of the psychosocial stress response within the sympathetic nervous system (Granger et al., 2007). While acute investigational stressors induce α-amylase secretion (e.g., Nater et al., 2006; Takai et al., 2007; Yamaguchi and Sakakima, 2007), chronic stress may be associated with reduced α-amylase output (Wolf et al., 2008). Amylase concentration in the saliva is independent of salivary flow rate (Rohleder et al., 2006) and has an endogenous diurnal rhythm (Nater et al., 2007). Therefore, α-amylase activity may most usefully be understood as an autonomic biomarker similar to (but not replacing) catecholamine levels and cardiac activity (DeCaro and Worthman, 2008).

Ehlert et al. (2006) investigated the effects of yohimbine challenge on sAA secretion in humans. Alpha-2-adrenoceptor blockade stimulates not only peripheral norepinephrine (NE) secretion, but also sAA. Because they failed to record meaningful correlations between plasma levels of NE, epinephrine (E), and sAA, sAA secretion may reflect central NE release instead of peripheral NE secretion. This result is similar to animal studies demonstrating that the release of sAA results mainly from NE released from sympathetic nerves acting via the second messenger cAMP in acinar cells. However, NE not only exerts its influence on the salivary glands, it also acts on NE receptors throughout the body. Blood NE levels are derived from both adrenomedullary origins and peripheral leakout. Thus, the weak relationship between sAA and plasma NE levels might be explained by the differences in origin between central and peripheral NE. Noto et al. (2005) reported that a 15-min mental arithmetic task significantly increased both heart rate (HR) and STAI-s score, with a positive correlation between the two measures. HR is increased by sympathetic excitation, and it has been reported that anxiety positively correlates with HR in women (Carrillo et al., 2001). Thus, in the Noto study, an increase in STAI-s score may reflect mental stress-induced sympathetic excitation. Salivary α-amylase levels were also significantly related to STAI-s score. Similarly, Takai et al. (2007) reported a significant correlation between salivary α-amylase and STAI-t score under psychological stress conditions (stressful video viewing). In addition, Chatterton et al. (1996) reported that salivary α-amylase is associated with changes in plasma norepinephrine under both exercise and psychosocial stress conditions. Rohleder et al. (2004) also demonstrated a positive association between increases in α-amylase and plasma norepinephrine under psychosocial stress. Thus, this biomarker may indeed reflect mental stress. Takai et al. (2004) reported the effects of psychological stress on salivary cortisol and amylase levels in healthy young adults. The subjects completed the trait version of STAI to assess their personal predisposition to anxiety. A video of corneal transplant surgery was provided as the stressor. A scenic video was also used as a stress reducer. Amylase levels were significantly increased just after the beginning of the stressful video viewing, and immediately returned to the pre-stress level just after the end of video viewing. Cortisol levels were also increased, but to a lesser extent. The latency to reach peak levels was longer for cortisol than for amylase, and a delayed onset was observed with the cortisol response, but not in amylase levels. Although the correlation between amylase levels and the STAI score was highly significant, this was not true for cortisol levels. In addition, scenic video viewing significantly decreased amylase levels, but did not affect cortisol levels. These results suggest that salivary amylase was increased more robustly and was released more rapidly than cortisol following a psychological stressor, suggesting that it may be a better index of stress responsiveness. Ehlert et al. (2006) reported salivary alpha-amylase levels after yohimbine challenge in healthy men. Yohimbine has high affinity for alpha2A-adrenergic, alpha2B-adrenergic, and alpha2C-adrenergic receptors. They examined cardiovascular effects and sAA and catecholamine secretion after intravenous injection of yohimbine. Yohimbine caused increases in both sAA output and activity. Blood pressure, salivary flow rate, and catecholamine levels were also significantly increased. No significant correlations between alpha-amylase parameters and catecholamines were observed. These results indicate that yohimbine administration activates not only autonomic activity but also sAA via adrenergic mechanisms, suggesting that sAA might be an indirect indicator of central sympathetic system activity.

We compared the levels of sAA and cortisol to electrical stimulation stress responses between patients with major depressive disorder, panic disorder patients, and healthy controls. We predicted a differential stress pattern induction of sAA and cortisol between the groups, and indeed found altered sAA response patterns in patients with major depressive disorder and panic disorder.

Relationship between the HPA Axis and Stress

External information from the five senses (including sight, hearing, smell, taste and touch) is relayed not only to the cerebral cortex but also deep within the limbic system. Activation of the lateral nucleus of the amygdala is required to store emotional memories for future retrieval (LeDoux, 2000). Both innate emotional memories (anxiety at high altitudes, fear of snakes, disgust from bitter tastes, etc.) and acquired emotional memories are stored in the lateral amygdala. This region determines whether the composite information from sensory organs is beneficial or harmful in relation to existing emotional memories, and in turn facilitates the elicitation of a suitable emotional reaction. Anxiety is one of the conditions associated with harmful emotions, and when sensory information is judged to be harmful by the lateral nucleus of the amygdala, the adjacent central nucleus of the amygdala is activated. The outputs of the central amygdala elicit elevated blood pressure (lateral hypothalamic nucleus), freezing behavior (periaqueductal gray matter), arousal (basal forebrain), and hypothalamic-pituitary-adrenocortical (HPA) axis activation (paraventricular nucleus). These outputs serve to evoke anxiety-like behaviors and physical reactions (Davis, 1992).

When humans experience stress and anxiety, the HPA axis is activated. Initially, corticotropin-releasing factor (CRF) is produced in the hypothalamic paraventicular nucleus and released into hypophyseal portal blood vessels (Vale et al., 1981). CRF release is facilitated by acetylcholine (Ach), serotonin (5HT), and neuropeptide Y (NPY), while CRF release is suppressed by gamma-aminobutyric acid (GABA). CRF acts on the anterior pituitary gland to facilitate the secretion of adenocorticotropic hormone (ACTH). The precursor of ACTH is proopiomelanocortin (POMC) (Herman et al., 2002), and the expression of POMC mRNA is facilitated by CRF, vasopressin, catecholamines, and various cytokines, while POMC is suppressed by glucocorticoids (GCs). Secretion of ACTH into the bloodstream acts on the adrenal cortex, which secretes mineralocorticoids (MCs) and GCs. The release of CRF and ACTH in the pituitary gland is suppressed by the negative feedback mechanism of GCs. There are also central MC receptors in the hippocampus, and MCs are known to affect HPA axis function. HPA axis activation and increasing concentrations of cortisol facilitates energy storage while suppressing growth, reproductive system function, and immune responses.

HPA system abnormalities are common in major depressive disorder patients with anxiety as a predominant symptom. In the standard CRF-responsiveness test, ACTH is detected at 30 minute intervals for 2 or 3 hours after intravenous CRF infusion (Hermus et al., 1984). CRF/ACTH responsiveness is blunted in major depressive disorder patients versus healthy controls (Amsterdom et al., 1988). This phenomenon is thought to be caused by chronic over-secretion of CRF in depressed patients, whereby elevated CRF levels desensitize CRF receptor activity, thus decreasing pituitary reaction to CRF.

The combined dexamethasone/CRF test is widely used to diagnose individuals with major depressive disorder. Patients receive oral dexamethasone (1.0 or 1.5 mg at 11 pm), and are injected intravenously with CRF (100μg) the next day (Holsboer et al., 1987). ACTH and cortisol responses to CRF after dexamethasone are markedly increased in major depressive disorder patients compared to healthy subjects (Isogawa 2005). This phenomenon is thought to generally involve a decreased negative feedback of both glucocorticoids and vasopressin (Purba et al., 1996).

Regarding morphological changes, both pituitary gland hypertrophy (Krishman et al., 1991) and adrenal gland hypertrophy (Amsterdom et al., 1987) are reported in major depressive disorder patients. ACTH and cortisol blood concentrations (Carpenter et al., 1971) are also increased in these individuals. These reports reveal an HPA axis hyper-activation at multiple levels in major depression. Importantly, these abnormalities would seem to normalize during remission.

A major determinant of HPA axis function is the early developmental environment (Weinstock, 2001). Perinatal stress and long-term maternal separation in early life facilitates an exaggerated endocrine response and a vulnerability to stress-related diseases (Meaney, 2001). In animal models, individuals that underwent maternal separation immediately after birth showed increased anxiety-like behavior, increased HPA axis responsiveness to acute stressors, increased CRF mRNA in the hypothalamus, and non-suppressed responses in dexamethsone tests (Nemeroff, 1996). There is a possibility that antidepressants at least partially decrease HPA axis activity and thus improve abnormal symptomatology in major depressive disorder patients (Keck, 2001). Antidepressants act not only by increasing glucocorticoid receptor number and binding throughout the central nervous system, but also by decreasing CRF mRNA expression in the hypothalamus.

Following the dexamethasone test in post-traumatic stress disorder (PTSD) patients, cortisol is suppressed. This phenomenon is different from that seen in major depressive disorder patients (Yehuda, 2002). In the CRF test, the responsiveness of ACTH and cortisol to CRF is increased in premenopausal PTSD women, but is blunted in men with military conflict-related PTSD when compared to healthy subjects (Rasmusson, 2001). In the dexamethasone test in panic disorder patients, the rate of non-suppression is the same or higher compared to control subjects, while in the CRF test, the cortisol response is blunted (Charney 2002).

Regarding the relationship between HPA axis function and anxiety, anxiety affects HPA axis activity and in turn chronic HPA axis dysfunction promotes anxiety. Early developmental stress leads to HPA axis abnormalities, and is associated with a greater liability to develop anxiety-related disorders.

Major depressive disorder patients who also report anxiety as a symptom often have HPA axis dysfunction. Antidepressant treatment normalizes HPA axis dysfunction, which may underlie the therapeutic efficacy of this class of drugs. Social support might contribute partially to the TRH and DEX/CRH test results in patients with major depressive disorder (Tsuru et al., 2008). Stressful life events (SLEs) may be negatively associated with the outcome of the DEX/CRH tests in major depressive disorder (Hikichi et al., 2006).

Both SAM and HPA systems are important targets of investigation in psychiatric disorder research. However, we have very little data concerning the relationships between these two systems, and further studies are needed to determine the contribution of both systems in major depression and other stress-related disorders.

References

Amsterdam, J. D., Marinelli, D. L., Arger, P., and Winokur, A. (1987). Assessment of adrenal gland volume by computed tomography in depressed patients and healthy volunteers: a pilot study. *Psychiatry Res., 2*, 189-197.

Amsterdam, J. D., Maislin, G., Winokur, A., Berwish, N., Kling, M., and Gold, P. (1988). The oCRH stimulation test before and after clinical recovery from depression. *J. Affect Disord., 14*, 213-222.

Carpenter, W. T. Jr., and Bunney, W. E. Jr. (1971). Adrenal cortical activity in depressive illness. *Am. J. Psychiatry*, **128**, 31-40.

Carrillo, E., Moya-Albiol, L., González-Bono, E., et al. (2001). Gender differences in cardiovascular and electrodermal responses to public speaking task: the role of anxiety and mood states. *Int. J. Psychophysiol,* **42**, 253-264.

Charney, D. S., and Drevets, W. D. (2002). Neurobiological basis of anxiety disorders, in Neuropsychopharmacology: The Fifth Generation of Progress. Edited by Davis K. L., Charney D., Coyle J. T., et al. Baltimore, M. D., *Lippincott Williams & Wilkins*, 901-930.

Chatterton, R. T. Jr., Vogelsong, K. M., Lu, Y. C., et al. (1996). Salivary alpha-amylase as a measure of endogenous adrenergic activity. *Clin Physiol,* **16**, 433–48.

Davis, M. (1992). The role of the amygdale in conditioned fear. In: Aggleton J. P., ed. The amygdale. *New York: Wiley-Liss*; 255-306.

DeCaro, J. A. and Worthman, C. M. (2008). Culture and the socialization of child cardiovascular regulation at school entry in the US. *Am. J. Hum Biol.,* **20**,572-83.

Ehlert, U., Erni, K., Hebisch, G., and Nater, U. (2006). Salivary alpha-amylase levels after yohimbine challenge in healthy men. *J. Clin Endocrinol Metab.,* **91**, 5130-5133.

Granger, D. A., Kivlighan, K. T., el-Sheikh, M., Gordis, E. B., and Stroud, L. R. (2007). Salivary alpha-α-amylase in biobehavioral research: recent developments and applications. *Ann. NYAcad. Sci.,* **1098**, 122-144.

Grillon, C., Duncko, R., Covington, M. F., Kopperman, L., and Kling, M. A. (2007). Acute stress potentiates anxiety in humans. *Biol. Psychiatry,* **62**, 1183-1186.

Herman, M. A., Majzoub, J. A. (2002). Adrenocorticotropin, in The Pituitary. Edited by Malmed S. *London, Blackwell Scientific*, 45-79.

Hermus, A. R, Pieters, G. F., Smals, A. G., Benraad, T. J., and Kloppenborg, P. W. (1984). Plasma adrenocorticotropin, cortisol, and aldosterone responses to corticotropin-releasing factor: modulatory effect of basal cortisol levels. *J Clin Endocrinol Metab.,* **58**, 187-191.

Hikichi, T., Akiyoshi, J., Ichioka, S., Tanaka, Y., Tsuru, J., Goto, S., Matsushita, H., Hanada, H., Isogawa, K. and Nagayama, H. (2007). Enhanced suppression of adrenocorticotropic hormone and cortisol responses to hypothalamic-pituitary-adrenal function and thyrotropin-releasing hormone tests after stressful life events in patients with major depressive disorder. *Neuropsychobiology,* **55**, 21-27.

Holsboer, F., von Bardeleben, U., Wiedemann, K., Müller, O. A. and Stalla, G. K. (1987). Serial assessment of corticotropin-releasing hormone response after dexamethasone in depression. Implications for pathophysiology of DST nonsuppression. *Biol. Psychiatry,* **22**, 228-234.

Isogawa, K., Nagayama, H., Tsutsumi, T., Kiyota, A., Akiyoshi, J. and Hieda, K. (2005). Simultaneous use of thyrotropin-releasing hormone test and combined dexamethasone/corticotropine-releasing hormone test for severity evaluation and outcome prediction in patients with major depressive disorder. *J. Psychiatr Res.,* **39**,467-473.

Keck, M. E. and Holsboer, F. (2001). Hyperactivity of CRH neuronal circuits as a target for therapeutic interventions in affective disorders. *Peptides,* **22**, 835-844.

Krishnan, K. R., Doraiswamy, P. M., Lurie, S. N., Figiel, G. S., Husain, M. M., Boyko, O. B., Ellinwood, E. H. Jr. and Nemeroff, C. B. (1991). Pituitary size in depression. *J. Clin. Endocrinol Metab.,* **72**, 256-259.

LeDoux, J. E. (2000). Emotion circuits in the brain. *Annu. Rev. Neurosci.,* **23**, 155-184.

Meaney, M. J. (2001). Maternal care, gene expression, and the transmission of individual differences in stress reactivity across generations. *Annu. Rev. Neurosci.,* **24**, 1161-1192.

Nater, U. M., La Marca, R., Florin, L., Moses, A., Langhans, W., Koller, M. M. and Ehlert, U. (2006). Stress-induced changes in human salivary alpha-α-amylase activity –associations with adrenergic activity. *Psychoneuroendocrinology,* **31**, 49-58.

Nater, U. M., Rohleder, N., Schlotz, W., Ehlert, U. and Kirschbaum, C. (2007). Determinants of the diurnal course of salivary alpha-α-amylase. *Psychoneuroendocrinology,* **32**, 392-401.

Nemeroff, C. B. (1996). The corticotropin-releasing factor (CRF) hypothesis of depression: new findings and new directions. *Mol. Psychiatry.* **1**, 336-342.

Noto, Y., Sato, T., Kudo, M., Kurata, K. and Hirota, K. (2005). The relationship between salivary biomarkers and state-trait anxiety inventory score under mental arithmetic stress: a pilot study. *Anesth. Analg.* **101**, 1873-1876.

Purba, J. S., Hoogendijk, W. J., Hofman, M. A. and Swaab, D. F. (1996). Increased number of vasopressin- and oxytocin-expressing neurons in the paraventricular nucleus of the hypothalamus in depression. *Arch. Gen. Psychiatry.,* **53**, 137-143.

Rasmusson, A. M., Lipschitz, D. S., Wang, S., Hu, S., Vojvoda, D., Bremner, J. D., Southwick, S. M. and Charney, D. S. (2001). Increased pituitary and adrenal reactivity in premenopausal women with posttraumatic stress disorder. *Biol. Psychiatry.,* **50**, 965-977.

Rohleder, N., Wolf, J. M., Maldonado, E. F. and Kirschbaum, C. (2006). The psychosocial stress-induced increase in salivary alpha-α-amylase is independent of saliva flow rate. *Psychophysiology,* **43**, 645-652.

Stahl, F. and Dorner, G. (1982). Responses of salivary cortisol levels to stress-situations. *Endokrinologie,* **80**, 158-162, Leibzig.

Rohleder, N., Nater, U. M., Wolf, J. M, et al. (2004). Psychosocial stress-induced activation of salivary alpha-amylase: an indicator of sympathetic activity? *Ann. N. Y. Acad. Sci.,* **1032**, 258-63.

Tsuru, J., Akiyoshi, J., Tanaka, Y., Matsushita, H., Hanada, H., Kodama, K., Hikichi, T., Ohgami, H., Tsutsumi, T., Isogawa, K. and Nagayama, H. (2008). Social support and enhanced suppression of adrenocorticotropic hormone and cortisol responses to hypothalamic-pituitary-adrenal function and thyrotropin-releasing hormone tests in patients with major depressive disorder. *Biol. Psychol.,* **78**, 159-163.

Takai, N., Yamaguchi, M., Aragaki, T., Eto, K., Uchihashi, K., and Nishikawa, Y. Effect of psychological stress on the salivary cortisol and amylase levels in healthy young adults. *Arch. Oral Biol.,* **4912**, 963-968.

Takai, N., Yamaguchi, M., Aragaki, T., Eto, K., Uchihashi, K. and Nishikawa, Y. (2007). Gender-specific differences in salivary biomarker responses to acute psychological stress. *Ann. N. Y. Acad. Sci.,* **1098**, 510-515.

Vale, W., Spiess, J., River, C. and River, J (1981). Characterization of a 41-residue ovine hypothalamic peptide that stimulates secretion of corticotropin and beta-endorphin. *Science,* **213**, 1394-1397.

van Veen, J. F., van Vliet, I. M., de Rijk, R. H., van Pelt, J., Mertens, B., Fekkes, D. and Zitman, F. G. (2009). Tryptophan depletion affects the autonomic stress response in generalized social anxiety disorder. *Psychoneuroendocrinology* (Epub ahead of print).

Weinstock, M. and Weinstock, M. (2001). Alterations induced by gestational stress in brain morphology and behaviour of the offspring. *Prog. Neurobiol.,* **65**, 427-451.

Wolf, J. M., Nicholls, E. and Chen, E. (2008). Chronic stress, salivary cortisol, and alpha-α-amylase in children with asthma and healthy children. *Biol. Psychol.,* **78**, 20-28.

Yamaguchi, M. and Sakakima, J. (2007). Evaluation of driver stress in a motor-vehicle driving simulator using a biochemical marker. *J. Int. Med. Res.* **35**, 91-100.

Yehuda, R. (2002). Current status of cortisol findings in post-traumatic stress disorder. *Psychiatr. Clin. North Am.,* **25**, 341-368.

In: Handbook of Neuropsychiatry Research
Editor: Rebecca S. Davies, pp. 125-135

ISBN: 978-1-61668-138-8
© 2010 Nova Science Publishers, Inc.

Chapter 6

SEROTONERGIC RECEPTORS IN THE CENTRAL NERVOUS SYSTEM – A BRIEF REVIEW

L.Y. Yeung, Ross Y.Y. Lee and D.T. Yew
School of Biomedical Sciences, Faculty of Medicine, The Chinese University of Hong Kong, Shatin, N.T., Hong Kong

Abstract

This review discusses the location, possible mechanisms, interaction and therapeutic possibilities and possible psychiatric influences of the serotonergic receptors 5-HT1A – 5-HT7. It concludes that, although some of the mechanisms of these receptors are widely accepted, their involvements in diseases and their roles in therapeutics are still elusive. Even with their locations, it was only recently perceived that 5-HT1A and 5-HT2A had different localizations in the brainstem, thus making functional correlations possible in due course. In order that a clearer picture or these receptors can emerge, further studies are much needed.

Key words: serotonin receptors – 5-HT1A – 5-HT7 – mechanism – interaction – localization – therapeutics.

Serotonergic receptors in the central nervous system have received much attention in the last 20 years. Receptors 5-HT1A – 5-HT7 were identified and these had intimate connections with the neurotransmitter serotonin. All these receptors, with the exception of 5-HT3, were coupled to G protein. Their localizations in the CNS, their possible mechanisms, their interactions and therapeutic possibilities are all briefly discussed in this minireview.

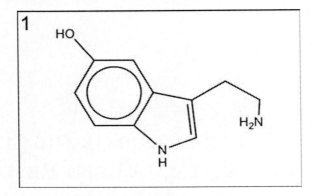

Figure 1. Structure of serotonin.

The transmitter serotonin (Fig. 1) which is involved in modulating hormonal and nervous activities, is found throughout the nervous system (Hoyer et al., 1994; Frazer and Hensler, 1999). While being a transmitter which can affect glutamine, GABA, dopamine and acetylcholine, its action is much more profound and also acts on steroids, central hormones as well as small peptide like substance P. There are at present at least seven receptors (5-HT1 – 5-HT7) identified to this day. With the exception of 5-HT3 which is a ligand gate cation channel, all the other receptors are protein coupled. 5-HT1 and 5-HT5 mediate majorly inhibitory responses while all the others appear to be involved with excitatory cascade and all of them require a group of second messengers. Apart from governing visceral activities, there are important functions and/or malfunctions which can be manipulated by these receptors in the central nervous system. For example, 5-HT1A, 5-HT1B, 5-HT1D, 5-HT2B, 5-HT2C, 5-HT4, 5-HT6 and 5-HT7 are related to anxiety and mood disorders (Kennett et al., 1987, 1996, 1997; Parks et al., 1998; Lin et al., 2002; Amital et al., 2005; Hedlund et al., 2005; Lucas et al., 2007; Wesołowska, 2008). Within this group, 5-HT1A and 5-HT1B are associated with aggression (de Boer and Koolhaas, 2005). Serotonin agonists and antagonists have been discovered for the 5-HT1A, 5-HT2A and 5-HT3 receptors in which they have been reported to be anxiety-related (Delgado et al., 2005). In addition to have played a significant role in the vagal control of the heart (Jordan, 2005), serotonin receptors have also been found to be crucial in regulating the blood pressure homeostasis in the human baroreceptor reflex arc (Raul, 2003; Curran et al., 2007). It has also been documented that abnormalities in serotonergic receptors contributes to the sudden infant death syndrome (Paterson et al., 2006). In a recent study, Freitas et al. (2008) suggested that the 5-HT (2A/2C) receptors are involved critically in the increase of nociceptice thresholds after tonic-clonic seizures.

Learning and memory, an important aspect of the daily life, is regulated by 5-HT1A (Ogren et al., 2008), 5-HT1B (Eriksson et al., 2008), 5-HT3 (Pitsikas et al., 1994), 5-HT4 (Galeotti et al., 1998), 5-HT6 (Perez-García and Meneses, 2005), 5-HT7 (Gasbarri et al., 2008). For cognition, not only was 5-HT2A suggested to be involved, but also was 5-HT6 (Hirst et al., 2006). An equally important part of daily activity is of course the maintenance of sleep and this seemingly is controlled by 5-HT1A (Monti and Jantos, 1992), 5-HT2A (Popa et al., 2005), 5-HT2C (Frank et al., 2002), 5-HT5A (Dietz et al., 2005) and 5-HT7 (Hedlund et al., 2005). In the study by our laboratory on human specimens, we found abundant presence of 5-HT1A positive cells in the dorsal raphé nucleus of the brainstem (Yeung et al., submitted manuscript), with the absence of 5-HT2A positive cells which was reported in other animals. This reflects, of course, a species difference in the location of receptor positive cells in between the nervous system of the human and the rodents (Popa et al., 2005).

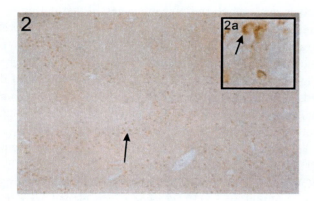

Figure 2. 5-HT1A positive sites in the pontile nuclei of human brainstem (arrow). X50. 2a shows higher magnification of pontile cells having positive sites (arrow) in cytoplasm. X200.

Another very interesting function is locomotion and the 5-HT receptors 5-HT1B, 5-HT5A were found to be associated with locomotion (McCreary et al., 1999; Nelson, 2004). Locomotion undoubtedly concerns the cortex, basal ganglia and the cerebellum. In the latter two regions, research in this laboratory has confirmed the location of 5-HT1A and 5-HT2A receptors (Yeung et al., submitted manuscript; Yew et al., 2009). For many years, the existence of 5-HT and/or its receptors in the cerebellum is controversial, with pros and cons findings (see discussion of Yew et al., 2009).

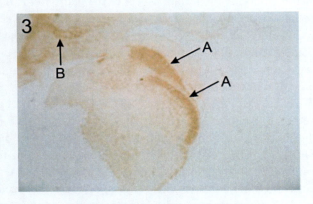

Figure 3. 5-HT2A positive sites in goldfish brain as revealed by immunohistochemistry in "A" (pons brainstem) and "B" fibers to cerebellum. X50.

Recent studies in the mice and human suggested that not only both 5-HT1A and 5-HT2A receptor positive cells were indeed present in the cerebella of both rodents (mice) and human (Yew et al., 2009), but 5-HT1A has also been found in the pontile nuclei of the human brainstem, the area which connects with the cerebellum (Fig. 2). In the Yew et al. (2009) study, specimens of different ages were employed, including mice from 1-12 months and humans from 57-91 years old. A general and nonspecific regional decline of positive labelled cells was observed in both species, suggesting there is perhaps a decline of groups of cells during aging. This kind of cell death could either be specific to groups of neurons in aging or relates to a general decline in all cells during aging (Li et al., 1997; Wai et al., 2009; Yew et al., 2009). During development, interestingly, serotonin receptors (as exemplified by 5-HT2A receptors) developed early, before term in the human. For example, in the region of the insula, 5-HT2A receptors began to appear in the middle third of gestation and increased towards term (Wai et al., 2009). Comparing through species, it is further interesting to find that 5-HT2A receptor immunopositive cells did not only appear in the mammals and human, but were indeed present in the lower vertebrates like the goldfish (Fig. 3, the cerebellum of a goldfish with 5-HT2A incoming fibers). Although the immunostaining was from a polyclonal antibody, the homology of the reaction

Serotonergic Receptors in the Central Nervous System

was high and chances were that 5-HT receptors were indeed present in the lower vertebrates, with the homology extended through the vertebrate scale.

Interaction between hallucinogens and the serotonin pathway requires specific receptors. In this context, the binding can be very specific in the case of DOI and 5-HT2A receptors (Johnson et al., 1987; Krebs-Thomson et al., 1998) while in other cases, e.g. LSD (lysergic acid diethylamide) may involve multiple receptors including 5-HT1A, 5-HT2A, 5-HT6, 5-HT7 with addition of dopamine receptors D1 and D2 (Nichols and Sanders-Bush, 2001). In fact, the interaction sometimes depends on the similarity of the drugs with serotonin. In general, most 5-HT receptors as indicated earlier in this review are bound to G protein which can be dissociated into α and β units to initiate GTP hydrolysis (Wess, 1997). 5-HT2A, for example, is abundant in the cortex and may be associated with cognitive processes. Its presence in the prefrontal pyramidal neurons in animals and human has been affirmed (Apud et al., 1992; Sanders-Bush et al., 1988; Lorke et al., 2006) and initiation of 5-HT2A activates lipase which catalyses the phosphatidylinositol 4, 5-biphosphate to inosital 1, 4, 5-triphosphosphate which can mobilize Ca^{++} to Ca^{++} related kinase in phosphorylation. The production of diacyglycerol in the initiation reaction can induce protein kinase C to produce prostaglandins and prostacyclins (Nichols and Sanders-Bush, 2001). From another angle, Shelton et al. (2009) have just reported that there was an elevation of 5-HT2A receptors in the postmortem prefrontal cortex of depression patients and this is associated with a reduction of protein kinase A activity, while protein kinase C was not affected. 5-HT2A has been also related to attention and motor impulse control (Wingen et al., 2007) while other more direct reactions are feasible in the CNS. For instance, 5-HT2C can modulate incoming synaptic signals (Niswender et al., 1999) while LSD can inhibit firing of the serotonin neurons via the raphé nucleus of the brainstem (Nichols and Sanders-Bush, 2001). The localization of 5-HT1A on the central nervous system of the human are less well known. Although present in the brain (e.g. temporal lobe, orbitofrontal lobe, cingulate, insula and DL prefrontal (Stockmeier, 2003), hippocampus (Fujita et al., 2000)), 5-HT1A are present in many nucleus of the brainstem (Yeung et al., submitted manuscript), much more than those of 5-HT2A. These nuclei, many of which participate in important visceral functions and thus it would be necessary for us to decipher their involvement in homeostasis and even in sensation and movement.

5-HT1A receptors are important for memory as well (Meeter et al., 2006). Many new antipsychotic agents may relate to this receptor (Meltzer et al., 2003). 5-HT1A agonists can enhance dopamine and acetylcholine production in important cognitive areas (Sumiyoshi et al, 2008) and in the schizophrenia, an increase of 5-HT1A sites has been recorded (Sumiyoshi et al., 2008). The increase in these receptors may be 1) to amend for the diminished 5-HT1A receptor stimulation or quite the contrary; 2) to increase as a response to increased 5-HT1A receptor stimulation. The action of this double edge sword needs to be further clarified.

The 5-HTR system as a whole (5-HT1A, 5-HT1B, 5-HT2A and 5-HT2C) has implication in additive related memory, especially in the cocaine addicts (Nic Dhonnchadha and Cunningham, 2008). Many antipsychotic drug appear to associate with one of the receptors of 5-HT. For example, clozapine with 5-HT2A receptors (Kuroki et al., 2008; Meltzer and Huang, 2008), antinicotinic drugs with 5-HT2C receptors (Fletcher et al., 2008). In spite these important findings, controversial results have been obtained, e.g. studies on specimens of frontotemporal dementia and Alzheimer's disease did not yield any decrease of 5-HT1A receptors (Bowen et al., 2008) while another study on the 5-HT receptors and mRNA expression in suicide specimens was inconclusive (Anisman et al., 2008). There is, however, no doubt that 5-HT or its receptors interact with dopaminergic, glutaminergic and cholinergic elements or receptors (Fink and Göthert, 2007; de Almeida et al., 2008; Di Matteo, 2008).

In summary, the importance of serotonin and its receptors in physiological and pathophysiological conditions have attracted much study since the late part of the last century. There is, however, still a huge gap in the picture and further studies are warranted to discover new paths of therapy.

References

Amital D., Fostick L., Sasson Y., Kindler S., Amital H., and Zohar J. (2005) Anxiogenic effects of Sumatriptan in panic disorder: a double-blind, placebo-controlled study. *Eur Neuropsychopharmacol*, **15**(3):279-282.

Anisman H., Du L., Palkovits M., Faludi G., Kovacs G. G., Szontagh-Kishazi P., Merali Z., and Poulter M. O. (2008) Serotonin receptor subtype and p11 mRNA expression in stress-relevant brain regions of suicide and control subjects. *J. Psychiatry Neurosci.*, **33**(2):131-141.

Apud J. A., Grayson D. R., De Erausquin E., and Costa E. (1992) *Pharmacological characterization of regulation of phosphoinositide metabolism by recombinant 5-HT2 receptors of the rat.*, **31**(1):1-8.

Bowen D. M., Procter A. W., Mann D. M., Snowden J. S., Esiri M. M., Neary D., and Francis P. T. (2008) Imbalance of a serotonergic system in

Serotonergic Receptors in the Central Nervous System   131

frontotemporal dementia: implication for pharmacotherapy. *Psychopharmacology (Berl.)*, **196**(4):603-610.

Curran A. K. and Leiter J. C. (2007) Baroreceptor-mediated inhibition of respiration after peripheral and central administration of a 5-HT1A receptor agonist in neonatal piglets. *Exp. Physiol.*, **92**(4):757-767.

de Almeida J., Palacios J. M., and Mengod G. (2008) Distribution of 5-HT and DA receptors in primate prefrontal cortex: implications for pathophysiology and treatment. *Prog. Brain. Res.*, **172**:101-115.

de Boer S. F. and Koolhaas J. M. (2005) 5-HT1A and 5-HT1B receptor agonists and aggression: a pharmacological challenge of the serotonin deficiency hypothesis. *Eur. J. Pharmacol.*, **526**(1-3):125-139.

Delgado M., Caicoya A. G., Greciano V., Benhamú B., López-Rodríguez M. L., Fernández-Alfonso M. S., Pozo M. A., Manzanares J., and Fuentes J. A. (2005) Anxiolytic-like effect of a serotonergic ligand with high affinity for 5-HT1A, 5-HT2A and 5-HT3 receptors. *Eur. J. Pharmacol.*, 511(1):9-19.

Di Matteo V., Di Giovanni G., Pierucci M., and Esposito E. (2008) Serotonin control of central dopaminergic function: focus on in vivo microdialysis studies. *Prog. Brain. Res.*, **172**:7-44.

Dietz B. M., Mahady G. B., Pauli G. F., and Farnsworth N. R. (2005) Valerian extract and valerenic acid are partial agonists of the 5-HT5a receptor in vitro. *Brain. Res. Mol. Brain. Res.*,18, 138(2):191-197.

Eriksson T. M., Madjid N., Elvander-Tottie E., Stiedl O., Svenningsson P., and Ogren S. O. (2008) Blockade of 5-HT 1B receptors facilitates contextual aversive learning in mice by disinhibition of cholinergic and glutamatergic neurotransmission. *Neuropharmacology*, **54**(7):1041-1050.

Fink K. B. and Göthert M. (2007) 5-HT receptor regulation of neurotransmitter release. *Pharmacol. Rev.*, **59**(4):360-417.

Fletcher P. J., Lê A. D., and Higgins G. A. (2008) Serotonin receptors as potential targets for modulation of nicotine use and dependence. *Prog. Brain. Res.*, **172**:361-383.

Frank M. G., Stryker M. P., and Tecott L. H. (2002) Sleep and sleep homeostasis in mice lacking the 5-HT2c receptor. *Neuropsychopharmacology*, **27**(5):869-873.

Frazer A. and Hensler J. G. (1999). "Chapter 13: Serotonin Receptors". in Siegel G. J., Agranoff B. W., Albers R. W., Fisher S. K., Uhler M. D., editors. Basic Neurochemistry: Molecular, Cellular, and Medical Aspects. *Philadelphia: Lippincott-Raven*, pp. 263-292.

Freitas R. L., Bassi G. S., de Oliveira A. M., and Coimbra N. C. (2008) Serotonergic neurotransmission in the dorsal raphe nucleus recruits in situ 5-

HT(2A/2C) receptors to modulate the post-ictal antinociception. *Exp. Neurol.*, **213**(2):410-418.

Fujita M., Charney D. S., and Innis R. B. (2000) Imaging serotonergic neurotransmission in depression: hippocampal pathophysiology may mirror global brain alterations. *Biol. Psychiatry*, **48**(8):801-812.

Galeotti N., Ghelardini C., and Bartolini A. (1998) Role of 5-HT4 receptors in the mouse passive avoidance test. *J. Pharmacol. Exp. Ther.*, **286**(3):1115-1121.

Gasbarri A., Cifariello A., Pompili A., Meneses A. (2008) Effect of 5-HT(7) antagonist SB-269970 in the modulation of working and reference memory in the rat. *Behav. Brain. Res.*, **195**(1):164-170.

Hedlund P. B., Huitron-Resendiz S., Henriksen S. J., and Sutcliffe J. G. (2005) 5-HT7 receptor inhibition and inactivation induce antidepressantlike behavior and sleep pattern. *Biol. Psychiatry*, **58**(10):831-837.

Hirst W. D., Stean T. O., Rogers D. C., Sunter D., Pugh P., Moss S. F., Bromidge S. M., Riley G., Smith D. R., Bartlett S., Heidbreder C. A., Atkins A. R., Lacroix L. P., Dawson L. A., Foley A. G., Regan C. M., and Upton N. (2006) SB-399885 is a potent, selective 5-HT6 receptor antagonist with cognitive enhancing properties in aged rat water maze and novel object recognition models. *Eur. J. Pharmacol.*, **553**(1-3):109-119.

Hoyer D., Clarke D. E., Fozard J. R., Hartig P. R., Martin G. R., Mylecharane E. J., Saxena P. R., and Humphrey P. P. (1994) International Union of Pharmacology classification of receptors for 5-hydroxytryptamine (Serotonin). *Pharmacol. Rev.*, **46**(2), 157-203.

Johnson M. P., Hoffman A. J., Nichols D. E., and Mathis C. A. (2987) Binding to the serotonin 5-HT2 receptor by the enantiomers of 125I-DOI. *Neuropharmacology*, **26**(12):1803-1806.

Jordan D. (2005) Vagal control of the heart: central serotonergic (5-HT) mechanisms. *Exp. Physiol.*, **90**(2):175-181.

Kennett G. A., Dourish C. T., and Curzon G. (1987) Antidepressant-like action of 5-HT1A agonists and conventional antidepressants in an animal model of depression. *Eur. J. Pharmacol.*, **134**(3):265-274

Kennett G. A., Bright F., Trail B., Baxter G. S., and Blackburn T. P. (1996) Effects of the 5-HT2B receptor agonist, BW 723C86, on three rat models of anxiety. *Br. J. Pharmacol.*, **117**(7):1443-1448.

Kennett G. A., Wood M. D., Bright F., Trail B., Riley G., Holland V., Avenell K. Y., Stean T., Upton N., Bromidge S., Forbes I. T., Brown A. M., Middlemiss D. N., and Blackburn T. P. (1997) SB 242084, a selective and brain penetrant 5-HT2C receptor antagonist. *Neuropharmacology*, **36**(4-5):609-620.

Krebs-Thomson K., Paulus M. P., and Geyer M. A. (1998) Effects of hallucinogens on locomotor and investigatory activity and patterns: influence of 5-HT2A and 5-HT2C receptors. *Neuropsychopharmacology*, **18**(5):339-351.

Kuroki T., Nagao N., and Nakahara T. (2008) Neuropharmacology of second-generation antipsychotic drugs: a validity of the serotonin-dopamine hypothesis. *Prog. Brain. Res.*, **172**:199-212.

Li W. P., Chan W. Y., Lai H. W., and Yew D. T. (1997) Terminal dUTP nick end labeling (TUNEL) positive cells in the different regions of the brain in normal aging and Alzheimer patients. *J. Mol. Neurosci.*, **8**(2):75-82.

Lin D. and Parsons L. H. (2002) Anxiogenic-like effect of serotonin(1B) receptor stimulation in the rat elevated plus-maze. *Pharmacol. Biochem. Behav.*, **71**(4):581-587.

Lorke D. E., Lu G., Cho E., and Yew D. T. (2006) Serotonin 5-HT2A and 5-HT6 receptors in the prefrontal cortex of Alzheimer and normal aging patients. *BMC Neurosci.*, **7**:36.

Lucas G., Rymar V. V., Du J., Mnie-Filali O., Bisgaard C., Manta S., Lambas-Senas L., Wiborg O., Haddjeri N., Piñeyro G., Sadikot A. F., and Debonnel G. (2007) Serotonin(4) (5-HT(4)) receptor agonists are putative antidepressants with a rapid onset of action. *Neuron.*, **55**(5):712-725.

McCreary A. C., Bankson M. G., and Cunningham K. A. (1999) Pharmacological studies of the acute and chronic effects of (+)-3, 4-methylenedioxymethamphetamine on locomotor activity: role of 5-hydroxytryptamine(1A) and 5-hydroxytryptamine(1B/1D) receptors. *J. Pharmacol. Exp. Ther.*, **290**(3):965-973.

Meeter M., Talamini L., Schmitt J. A., and Riedel W. J. (2006) Effects of 5-HT on memory and the hippocampus: model and data. *Neuropsychopharmacology*, **31**(4):712-720.

Meltzer H. Y., Li Z., Kaneda Y., and Ichikawa J. (2003) Serotonin receptors: their key role in drugs to treat schizophrenia. *Prog. Neuropsychopharmacol. Biol. Psychiatry*, **27**(7):1159-1172.

Meltzer H. Y. and Huang M. (2008) In vivo actions of atypical antipsychotic drug on serotonergic and dopaminergic systems. *Prog. Brain. Res.*, **172**:177-197.

Monti J. M. and Jantos H. (1992) Dose-dependent effects of the 5-HT1A receptor agonist 8-OH-DPAT on sleep and wakefulness in the rat. *J. Sleep Res.*, **1**(3):169-175.

Nelson D. L. (2004) 5-HT5 receptors. *Curr. Drug. Targets CNS Neurol. Disord.*, **3**(1):53-8.

Nic Dhonnchadha B. A. and Cunningham K. A. (2008) Serotonergic mechanisms in addiction-related memories. *Behav. Brain. Res.*, **195**(1):39-53.

Nichols C. D., Sanders-Bush E. (2001) Serotonin receptor signaling and hallucinogenic drug action. In: *The Heffer Review of Psychedelic Research*, **2**:73-78.

Niswender C. M., Copeland S. C., Herrick-Davis K., Emeson R. B., and Sanders-Bush E. (1999) RNA editing of the human serotonin 5-hydroxytryptamine 2C receptor silences constitutive activity. *J. Biol. Chem.*, **274**(14):9472-9478.

Ogren S. O., Eriksson T. M., Elvander-Tottie E., D'Addario C., Ekström J. C., Svenningsson P., Meister B., Kehr J., and Stiedl O. (2008) The role of 5-HT(1A) receptors in learning and memory. *Behav. Brain. Res.*, **195**(1):54-77.

Parks C. L., Robinson P. S., Sibille E., Shenk T., and Toth M. (1998) Increased anxiety of mice lacking the serotonin1A receptor. *Proc. Natl. Acad. Sci. USA.*, **95**(18):10734-10739.

Paterson D. S., Trachtenberg F. L., Thompson E. G., Belliveau R. A., Beggs A. H., Darnall R., Chadwick A. E., Krous H. F., and Kinney H. C. (2006) Multiple serotonergic brainstem abnormalities in sudden infant death syndrome. *JAMA*, **296**(17):2124-2132.

Perez-García G. and Meneses A. (2005) Oral administration of the 5-HT6 receptor antagonists SB-357134 and SB-399885 improves memory formation in an autoshaping learning task. *Pharmacol. Biochem. Behav.*, **81**(3):673-682.

Pitsikas N., Brambilla A., and Borsini F. (1994) Effect of DAU 6215, a novel 5-HT3 receptor antagonist, on scopolamine-induced amnesia in the rat in a spatial learning task. *Pharmacol. Biochem. Behav.*, **47**(1):95-99.

Popa D., Léna C., Fabre V., Prenat C., Gingrich J., Escourrou P., Hamon M., and Adrien J. (2005) Contribution of 5-HT2 receptor subtypes to sleep-wakefulness and respiratory control, and functional adaptations in knock-out mice lacking 5-HT2A receptors. *J. Neurosci.*, **25**(49):11231-11238.

Raul L. (2003) Serotonin2 receptors in the nucleus tractus solitarius: characterization and role in the baroreceptor reflex arc. *Cell. Mol. Neurobiol.*, **23**(4-5):709-726.

Sanders-Bush E., Burris K. D., and Knoth K. (1988) Lysergic acid diethylamide and 2,5-dimethoxy-4-methylamphetamine are partial agonists at serotonin receptors linked to phosphoinositide hydrolysis. *J. Pharmacol. Exp. Ther.*, **246**(3):924-928.

Shelton R. C., Sanders-Bush E., Manier D. H., and Lewis D. A. Elevated 5-HT 2A receptors in postmortem prefrontal cortex in major depression is associated with reduced activity of protein kinase A. *Neuroscience*, **158**(4):1406-1415.

Stockmeier C. A. (2003) Involvement of serotonin in depression: evidence from postmortem and imaging studies of serotonin receptors and the serotonin transporter. *J. Psychiatr. Res.*, **37**(5):357-373.

Sumiyoshi T., Bubenikova-Valesova V., Horacek J., and Bert B. (2008) Serotonin1A receptors in the pathophysiology of schizophrenia: development of novel cognition-enhancing therapeutics. *Adv. Ther.*, **25**(10):1037-1056.

Wai M. S., Liang Y., Shi C., Cho E. Y., Kung H. F., and Yew D..T. (2009) Co-localization of hyperphosphorylated tau and caspases in the brainstem of Alzheimer's disease patients. *Biogerontology*, **10**(4):457-469.

Wesołowska A. (2008) The anxiolytic-like effect of the selective 5-HT6 receptor antagonist SB-399885: the impact of benzodiazepine receptors. *Eur. J. Pharmacol.*, **580**(3):355-360.

Wess J. (1997) G-protein-coupled receptors: molecular mechanisms involved in receptor activation and selectivity of G-protein recognition. *FASEB J.*, **11**(5):346-354.

Wingen M., Kuypers K. P., and Ramaekers J. G. (2007) The role of 5-HT1a and 5-HT2a receptors in attention and motor control: a mechanistic study in healthy volunteers. *Psychopharmacology (Berl.)*, **190**(3):391-400.

Yeung L. Y., Kung H. F., and Yew D. T. Localization of 5-HT1A and 5-HT2A positive cells in the brainstems of control aged and Alzheimer individuals. (submitted)

Yew D. T, Yeung L. Y., Wai M. S., and Mak Y. T. (2009) 5-HT 1A and 2A receptor positive cells in the cerebella of mice and human and their decline during aging. *Microsc. Res. Tech.* 2009 (E. Pub.)

In: Handbook of Neuropsychiatry Research
Editor: Rebecca S. Davies, pp. 137-143

ISBN: 978-1-61668-138-8
© 2010 Nova Science Publishers, Inc.

Chapter 7

THE NEXT MAJOR NEUROPSYCHOLOGICAL AND NEUROPSYCHIATRICAL BREAKTHROUGH: ALZHEIMER'S DISEASE

Heather Pedersen and F. Richard Ferraro[*]
University of North Dakota, Grand Forks

Abstract

As the "baby boomers" head toward their later years, a social and economic crisis looms: the incidence of Alzheimer's disease is steadily increasing: in 2009, 5.3 million individuals had the diagnosis of Alzheimer's and the incidence of the disease is projected to increase up to 50% in the next 25 years. All the while the age bracket of 85 years and older is the largest growing population in the world. This means that resources of all kinds are being poured into a solution for this calamity: a neuropsychological breakthrough in this arena is not only looming, but necessary.

Key words: neuropsychology, neuropsychiatry, Alzheimer's disease.

---

[*] E-mail address: f_ferraro@und.nodak.edu

The Next Major Neuropsychological Breakthrough: Alzheimer's Disease

The next major breakthrough in the field of neuropsychology will be determining the causal factors of Alzheimer's disease (AD) for the purpose of diagnosis, prevention, and treatment because many resources and attention are being devoted to dealing with this devastating disease. A major national and global crisis is arising: the age bracket of 85 years and older is the largest growing segment of the population, and as the "baby boomers" age this population will only continue to expand. Meanwhile, the incidence of AD is increasing: of those 85 years and older, there is a 50% chance of being diagnosed with this debilitating disease. In 2009, 5.3 million individuals had the diagnosis and there is expected to be up to a 50% increase in incidence over the next 25 years (Alzheimer's Association, 2009). Because of both the rising numbers of individuals with this diagnosis, as well as the sheer amount of resources being poured into research of the disease, breakthroughs with respect to the causal factors and accurate diagnosis are not only pending, but necessary.

Causal (Risk) Factors of AD

Many things have been found to be risk factors for developing AD; however, causal factors are more difficult to come by. Many researchers believe that causal agents are to be found within the risk factors already associated with AD.

Age. One of the largest risk factors associated with being diagnosed with AD is advancing age (Ghanbari, 2000). A difficulty with labeling age as a causal factor is that there are normal "healthy" changes that are also associated with aging,. The normal changes associated with aging can be similar to those associated with AD, although are not as severe as the changes in individuals with AD or affect different systems (e.g. normal aging shows declines in short term memory, while AD is associated with progressive decline in short term memory, working memory, and finally, long term memory; Zillmer, Spiers, & Culbertson, 2008). Differentiating the symptoms of normal "healthy" aging and the symptoms of AD will increase the likelihood of being able to accurately examine the influence of age on AD.

Genetic / family history predictors. The levels of the allele Apolipoprotein E (ApoE) have been linked to an increased probability of early onset AD, as deletion of ApoE lessened neurodegeneration, which is associated with AD and the presence of the allele was associated with the symptoms consistent with AD

(Gallardo, Schluter, & Sudhof, 2008; Grant, Campbell, Itzhaki, & Savory, 2002; Greenwood, Sunderland, Putnam, Levy, & Parasuraman, 2005). Amyloid precursor protein, presenilin 1 and presenilin 2 genes have also been recognized as causal genes for the development of AD (Grazina, et al., 2006). Because of the genetic link to AD, particularly with early onset AD, family history has been identified as a risk factor. However, non-familial (or "sporadic") AD has been found to have a genetic link, also (Ashford & Mortimer, 2002). Genetic and biological research is on the forefront on the search for causes of the disease, and as stem cell research begins to pick up again in the United States, more breakthroughs are on the horizon.

Environmental factors. Diet (particularly a high cholesterol diet), dietary fat, and caloric intake are found to be risk factors in the development of AD. It is thought that an "acid-forming diet" (which is one high in calories and dietary fat) increases the concentration of certain metals, such as aluminum and transition metal ions which may cause neurological damage (Grant, Campbell, Itzhaki, & Savory, 2002; Holden, 1999; Shcherbatykh & Carpenter, 2007).

There appears to be mixed evidence as to whether head injuries are a risk factor for being diagnosed with AD. Some researchers have found support for the link between head injuries and the later development of AD (Kemp, Goulding, Spencer, & Mitchell, 2005; Spear, 1995), others have found a link between head injury and the development of any dementia (not confined to AD; Salib, 2000; Salib & Hillier, 1997), while still others have found no support for the link between the two (Boston, Dennis, & Jagger, 1999).

Heart health has been linked to brain health, particularly AD. Vascular factors have been found to be a risk factor for the development of AD as measured by endothelial function (i.e. the cell lining on the inside of blood vessels; Dede, et al. 2007), heart rate variability and other cardiovascular measures (Zulli, et al., 2005). This indicates that in order to fully understand the causes of AD and therefore the protective factors against AD, the causes and protective factors against heart disease should also be examined thoroughly.

However, the above mentioned environmental risk factors have been found to be *strong* risk factors only in those individuals with a genetic predisposition to developing AD (Ashford & Mortimer, 2002). This indicates that environmental risk factors only increase the likelihood of being diagnosed with AD if the probability was already high for being diagnosed (via genetics).

Diagnosis of AD

Several factors, both biological and neuropsychological, are examined in order to most accurately diagnose AD. On the biological front, the presence of neurofibrillary tangles and senile plaques are used to diagnose AD. Neuropsychologically, memory deficits and overall impaired cognitive functioning are examined for a diagnosis.

Neurofibrillary tangles and senile plaques. There are two hallmarks of AD: neurofibrillary tangles and plaques. Neurofibrillary tangles are proteins ("tau proteins") that accumulate in neurons that eventually die. Senile plaques are clumps of "cellular trash" that collect in synapses, which in turn become inactive (Zillmer, Spiers, & Culbertson, 2008). Amyloid beta peptide 1-42 (AB(1-42)) is a primary constituent of the plaques associated with AD and is considered a definitive marker of the disease (Boyd-Kimball, Sultana, Mohammad-Abdul, & Butterfield, 2004).

However, to definitively establish the presence of either neurofibrillary tangles or senile plaques, a brain tissue biopsy is required, which is such an invasive and uncertain procedure that it is rarely, if ever, done. Typically, only in the autopsy is the presence of tangles and plaques determined for certain. AD is normally diagnosed with various neuropsychological assessments and brain imaging techniques that rule out other possible diagnoses – it is a diagnosis of last resort. As such, many types of evidence are collected and examined prior to diagnosis so as to ensure as much as possible a correct diagnosis.

Neuropsychological assessment markers. Progressive cognitive and memory decline is one of the requirements for an AD diagnosis (Buccione, et al., 2007). Researchers have been clarifying which cognitive and memory systems decline and at what rate they decline as the disease progresses. Certain markers have been found to predict steeper rates of cognitive and memory decline: psychosis, diffuse cognitive impairment in verbal and visuospatial abilities (as opposed to specific problems with either verbal *or* visuospatial abilties), and low performances in visuospatial abilities in particular indicates faster *functional* decline (Buccione, et al., 2007). While these markers indicate faster progression of the disease, many cognitive faculties are affected by the disease and used as markers for diagnosis.

As previously mentioned, one of the major cognitive markers of AD is the onset of memory problems. Short term memory (as measured by the Digit Span subtest of the Wechsler's Adult Intelligence Scale; WAIS), long term memory (as measured by the California Verbal Learning Test and Controlled Oral Word Association Task), and working memory (as measured by the Letter-Number Sequencing subtest of the WAIS) abilities all decline as the disease progresses

(Bondi, et al., 1994). It appears that all aspects of these systems (encoding, storage, and retrieval) are affected by the progression of AD (Zillmer, Spiers, & Culbertson, 2008).

Overall cognitive and intellectual abilities also decline in AD. Executive functioning, abstract reasoning, language abilities, as well as motor and perceptual systems all are affected. Executive function consists of judgment, planning, and cognitive flexibility, all of which appear decline (as measured by the Wisconsin Card Sorting Test). Abstract reasoning is the ability to conceptualize a higher order idea, is it also becomes a deficit, as measured by the Similarities subtest of the WAIS (Bondi, et al., 1994). Language difficulties, in the forms of anomia (word finding difficulties) and semantic fluency (the ability to put meaningful words together in a fluent manner), increase with the progression of AD (Zillmer, Spiers, & Culbertson, 2008). Both the motor and perceptual systems are affected by AD. Visuospatial scanning and fine motor skills decline (as measured by the Digit Symbol subtest on the WAIS, Trails A & B, Clock Drawing, and Grooved Pegboard; Bondi, et al., 1994).

Conclusions

Many resources are being devoted to discovering the causes of AD, as well as increasingly more sophisticated methods of diagnosing the disease. Because of the severity of the disease progression, the cost of treating it, and the increasing incidence of the disease (coupled with the expanding geriatric population), neuropsychological and neuropsychiatric breakthroughs in the causes and prevention of this disease are essential and, fortunately, just over the horizon.

References

Alzheimer's Association. Retrieved on April 23, 2009 from http://www.alz.org/.

Ashford, J. W. & Mortimer, J. A. (2002). Non-familial Alzheimer's disease is mainly due to genetic factors. *Journal of Alzheimer's Disease*, **4**, 169-177.

Bondi, M. W., Monsch, A. U., Galasko, D., Butters, N., Salmon, D. P., & Delis, D. C. (1994). Preclinical cognitive markers of dementia of the Alzherimer type. *Neuropsychology*, **8**(3), 374-384.

Boston, P. F., Dennis, M. S., & Jagger, C. (1999). Factors associated with vascular dementia in an elderly community population. *International Journal of Geriatric Psychiatry*, **14**, 761-766.

Boyd-Kimball, D., Sultana, R., Mohammad-Abdul, H., & Butterfield, D. A. (2004). Rodent AB(1-42) exhibits oxidative stress properties similar to those of human AB(1-42): Implications for proposed mechanisms of toxicity. *Journal of Alzheimer's Disease*, **6**, 515-525.

Buccione, I., Perri, R., Carlesimo, G. A., Fadda, L., Serra, L., Scalmana, S., & Caltagirone, C. (2007). Cognitive and behavioural predictors of progression rates in Alzheimer's disease. *European Journal of Neurology*, **14**, 440-446.

Dede, D. S., Yavuz, B., Yavuz, B. B., Cankurtaran, M., Halil, M., Ulger, Z., Cankurtaran, E. S., Aytemir, K., Kabakci, G., & Ariogul, S. (2007). Assessment of endothelial function in Alzheimer's disease: Is Alzheimer's disease a vascular disease? *JAGS*, **55**, 1613-1617.

Gallardo, G., Schluter, O. M., & Sudhof, T. C. (2008). A molecular pathway of neurodegeneration linking a-synuclein to ApoE and AB peptides. *Nature Neuroscience*, **11**(3), 301-308.

Ghanbari, H. A. (2000). Risk factors versus Alzheimer's disease or symptoms associated with Alzheimer's disease. *Journal of Alzheimer's Disease*, **2**, 117.

Grant, W. B., Campbell, A., Itzhaki, R. F., & Savory, J. (2002). The significance of environmental factors in the etiology of Alzheimer's disease. *Journal of Alzheimer's Disease*, **4**, 179-189.

Grazina, M., Pratas, J., Silva, F., Oliveira, S., Santana, I., & Oliveira, C. (2006). Genetic bases of Alzheimer's dementia: Role of mtDNA mutations. *Genes, Brain and Behavior*, **5**(2), 92-107.

Greenwood, P. M., Sunderland, T., Putnam, K., Levy, J., & Parasuraman, R. (2005). Change as a function of APOE genotype prior to old age: Results from NIMH BIOCARD study. *Neuropsychology*, **19**(6), 830-840.

Holden, R. J. (1999). Could a high cholesterol diet cause Alzheimer's disease in western society? *Human Psychopharmacology*, **14**, 185-188.

Kemp, S., Goulding, P., Spencer, J., & Mitchell, A. J. (2005). Unusually rapid and severe cognitive deterioration after mild traumatic brain injury. *Brain Injry*, **19**(14), 1269-1276.

Salib, E. (2000). Risk factors in clinically diagnosed Alzheimer's disease: A retrospective hospital-based case control study in Warrington. *Aging & Mental Health*, **4**(3), 259-267.

Salib, E. & Hillier, V. (1997). Head injury and the risk of Alzheimer's disease: A case control study. *International Journal of Geriatric Psychiatry*, **12**, 363-368.

Shcherbatykh, I. & Carpenter, D. O. (2007). The role of metals in the etiology of Alzheimer's disease. *Journal of Alzheimer's Disease*, **11**, 191-205.

Spear, J. (1995). Are professional footballers at risk of developing dementia? International *Journal of Geriatric Psychiatry*, **10**, 1011-1014.

Zillmer, E. A., Spiers, M. V., & Culbertson, W. C. (2008). *Principles of Neuropsychology* (2nd ed.). Belmont, CA: Thomson Wadsworth.

Zulli, R., Nicosia, F., Borroni, B., Agosti, C., Prometti, P., Donati, P., De Vecchi, M., Romanelli, G., Grassi, V., & Padovani, A.. (2005). QT dispersion and heart rate variability abnormalities in Alzheimer's disease and in mild cognitive impairment. *JAGS*, **53**, 2135-2139.

In: Handbook of Neuropsychiatry Research
Editor: Rebecca S. Davies, pp. 145-151

ISBN: 978-1-61668-138-8
© 2010 Nova Science Publishers, Inc.

Chapter 8

NEUROLOGY, PSYCHIATRY AND GENETICS: INTERRELATIONSHIP

Viroj Wiwanitkit
Wiwanitkit House, Bangkhae, Bangkok, Thailand 10160

Abstract

The study of the neurological system is defined as neurology and is an important branch of medicine. When talking about brain function, the fundamental relating topic is the mental status. The direct branch of medicine dealing with mental status is psychiatry. Hence, a close relationship between neurology and psychiatry can be expected, and this is the starting point for a new specific branch of medical science namely neuropsychiatry. In addition, several disorders in medicine have been shown to have their root cause in the genetic dimension. Here, the author focuses on the complex interrelationship among neurology, psychiatry and genetics.

Introduction

The neurological system is an important organ system in human beings. It can be said that we exist because our neurological systems are in control. Examining the neurological system function, a physician has to completely screen all aspects including sensory, motor and reflex. In addition, at present, an extensive investigation of the mental status is also practiced. Indeed, there is a classical specific branch of medicine studying mental status called psychiatry. The classical clinical correlation between neurological system and mental status can be expected. Several diseases manifest in both neurological deficit and mental status impairment. In the psychiatric view, an assessment of a mental disorder generally requires a complete explanation to discover an organic or neurological cause. The close relationship between psychiatry and neurology leads us to a new medical science namely neuropsychiatry. By easy definition, neuropsychiatry is a specific study of diseases or disorders that have both neurological and psychological manifestations [1]-[6].

Neurology and Genetics

In the present day, there are several pieces of evidence confirming that some neurological disorders are the result of genetic disorders. Indeed, in the present day, genetics is the approved contributing factor leading to several disorders in medicine. This is also true for neurological disorders. The genetics underlying epilepsy and movement disorders are the best example [7], [8]. It is accepted that two main things contributing to diseases are genetic and environmental factors. Indeed, in neurology, there is a specific subspecialty dealing with the developmental process of the neurological system called developmental neurology, which directly focuses on the developmental process of the neurological system of human beings [9]-[11]. There are several reports and evidences on genetic defects leading to disorders in developmental neurology [12], [13].

Psychiatry and Genetics

In the past, psychiatry was accepted as a specific study of mental status or the "mind". It was previously accepted that a psychological disorder is a mind disease, which is not an organic disease. Psychological disorders must have no organic cause. However, this belief has to be changed. Genetics is the new focus in psychiatry [14]-[16]. In the present day, evidence has emerged showing an underlying genetic dimension [14]-[16] to several psychological disorders such as schizophrenia [17]. Hence, the close relationship between genetics and psychiatry can be hereby noted. The new definition of a psychological disorder should be "a disorder presenting with alteration or abnormality of psychological status which might have a genetic root cause."

Genetics in Neuropsychiatry

The interrelationship among neurology, psychiatry and genetics can be mentioned. To help readers better realize and appreciate this topic, a summary of genetics in some important neuropsychiatric disorders are presented in Table 1.

Table 1. Summary of genetics in some important neuropsychiatric disorders.

Disorders	Details
Bipolar disorder	There are several evidences on the genetic aspects of bipolar disorder. From many genome-wide linkage assessments, it is noted that genome-wide linkage surveys revealed that chromosome 22q12 might pose a susceptibility locus for bipolar disorder (BPD) in the immediate region of the gene G protein receptor kinase-3 (GRK3) [18]. Basically, GRK3 is an excellent candidate risk gene for bipolar disorder since GRK3 is expressed mainly in the brain, and since GRKs play key roles in the homologous desensitization of G protein-coupled receptor signaling [18]. Barrett et al. noted that a dysregulation in GRK3 expression altered signaling desensitization, and thereby predisposed to the development of bipolar disorder [18]. The relationship of the gene GRK3, dopamine metabolism, and bipolar disorder is well and widely described [19]. Tiberi et al. [20] reported on differential regulation of dopamine D1A receptor responsiveness by various GRKs and this can directly resulted in the clinical appearance of bipolar disorder [21]. Research on the possible roles of epigenetics or analysis of genetic diseases, in which bipolar disorder is one of phenotypes, might also be possible [22]. GRKs are a family of serine/threonine kinases which are detected in the homologous desensitization of agonist activated G-protein coupled receptors [23]. G-protein coupled receptor supersensitivity, possibly as a result of decreased GRK, has been detected and proposed for its role in affective disorders [23]. Niculescu et al performed a study to identify a series of candidate genes for mania and psychosis and reported GRK3 as an important candidate [24]. They noted that GRK3, found by Western blot analysis, evidenced for decreased protein levels in a subset of patient lymphoblastoid cell lines that correlated with disease severity [24]. However, controversy on the role of GRK3 in bipolar disorder in some reports can be seen [25]. According to the present knowledge, mutations of GK3 can be seen in upto 10% of patients with bipolar disorder [18], [22]. The relevance of the association should also be mentioned. The identified positions can be the baseline for the presently undetected mutation in bipolar disorder.

148 Viroj Wiwanitkit

Table 1. Continued

Disorders	Details
Insomnia	The sleep-wake cycle is specifically under the control of the circadian clock [26]. Recent advances in rhythm biology shown molecular clocks and their key regulating genes [26]. A point mutation in the prion protein gene is found to be the cause of fatal familial insomnia [26]. Basically, fatal familial insomnia, first reported in 1986, is accepted as a hereditary prion disease with autosomal-dominant inheritance with a specific etiology by a missense-mutation at codon 178 of the prion-protein gene on chromosome 20 [27]. Molecular biology leads to an exact diagnosis of fatal familial insomnia although there is still no clear cutting on the phenotypal variability and physiopathogenic mechanisms [28]. Fatal Familial Insomnia is clinically defined by loss of sleep, oneiric stupor with autonomic/motor hyperactivity and somato-motor abnormalities (pyramidal signs, myoclonus, dysarthria/dysphagia, ataxia) [29]. Positon emission tomography disclosed thalamic hypometabolism and milder involvement of the cortex; neuropathology severe neuronal deficit in the thalamic nuclei variably resulting in the caudate, gyrus cinguli and fronto-temporal cortices [29]. The disease is extremely rare and there are approximately 60 cases reported worldwide since 1986 [30]. Incubation time of the disease may be as long as three decades; fatality generally occurs within 1 year of the onset of symptoms [30]. There is no known medical therapy treatment for delaying the onset of symptoms or tool for modifying the disease course [30].
Alzheimer 's disease	Alzheimer's disease and its relationship to genetics may be one of the most prolifically published areas in medicine and molcecular biology [31]. Three early-onset Alzheimer's disease genes with causative mutations (APP, PSEN1, PSEN2) and one late-onset Alzheimer's disease susceptibility gene, apolipoprotein E (APOE), are widely reported with biologic, genetic, and epidemiologic data [32]. Polygenic origin for Alzheimer's disease is mentioned [31]. Whether hereditary Alzheimer's disease in humans is existent or not still requires clarification. Analysis of gene expression in Alzheimer's disease is a present direction of neuropsychiatry research. Considering HADH2 gene on chromosome X, HADH2 is proved to be an enzyme involved in Alzheimer's disease [33]. Considering APBA1 gene on chromosome 9, a third member of the X11 protein family, has closed interaction with Alzheimer's beta-amyloid precursor protein [34]. Considering APBA2 gene on chromosome 15, encoding phosphotyrosine-binding domain proteins that has interaction with the Alzheimer's disease amyloid precursor protein is reported in the literature [35]. Considering GAL gene on chromosome 11, there is also no direct report. Considering APLP2 gene, APLP2 mRNAs had already reported for its existence in Alzheimer's disease specimen [36].

References

[1] Cobb, S. (1948) Review of neuropsychiatry for 1947. *Arch. Med. Interna.*, **81**(3):381-96.

[2] Lereboullet, J., Rosa, A., and Olivier-Martin, R. (1974) Neuropsychiatry in 1973. *Rev. Prat.*, **24**(15):1145-6, 1149-50.

[3] Raymondeaud-Castanet. (1965) Neuropsychiatry. *Gaz. Med. Fr.*, **72**(24):4353-64.

[4] Lereboullet, J. and Escourolle, R. (1965) Neuropsychiatry in 1965. *Rev. Prat.*, **15**(30):3889-908.

[5] Cobb, S. (1949) *Review of neuropsychiatry for 1948. Arch. Intern. Med. (Chic.),* **83**(4):454-69.

[6] Lereboullet, J., Rosa, A., and Olivier-Martin, R. (1975) Neuropsychiatry in 1975. *Rev. Prat.*, **25**(17):1235-55.

[7] Winawer, M. R. (2002) Epilepsy genetics. *Neurologist.*, **8**(3):133-51.

[8] Thyagarajan, D. (2001) Genetics of movement disorders: an abbreviated overview. *Stereotact. Funct. Neurosurg.*, **77**(1-4):48-60.

[9] Prechtl, H. F. (1988) Developmental neurology of the fetus. *Baillieres Clin. Obstet. Gynaecol.*, **2**(1):21-36.

[10] Hicks, S. P. (1957) Some aspects of developmental neurology: a review. *Cancer. Res.*, **17**(4):251-65.

[11] Visser, G. H., Mulder, E. J., and Prechtl, H. F. (1992) Studies on developmental neurology in the human fetus. *Dev. Pharmacol. Ther.*,**18** (3-4):175-83.

[12] Connors, S. L., Levitt, P., Matthews, S. G., Slotkin, T. A., Johnston, M. V., Kinney, H. C., Johnson, W. G., Dailey, R. M., and Zimmerman, A. W. (2008) Fetal mechanisms in neurodevelopmental disorders. *Pediatr. Neurol.*, **38**(3):163-76.

[13] Sheen, V. L. and Walsh, C. A. (2003) Developmental genetic malformations of the cerebral cortex. *Curr. Neurol. Neurosci. Rep.*,**3**(5):433-41.

[14] Abe, K. and Oda, N. (1991) Contributions of genetic studies to clinical psychiatry. *Jpn. J. Psychiatry Neurol.*, **45**(4):819-23.

[15] Kandel, E. R. (1998) A new intellectual framework for psychiatry. *Am. J. Psychiatry*, **155**(4):457-69.

[16] Giarelli, E. and Jacobs, L. A. (2000) Issues related to the use of genetic material and information. *Oncol. Nurs. Forum.*, **27**(3):459-67.

150   Viroj Wiwanitkit

[17] Williams, H. J., Owen, M. J., and O'Donovan, M. C. (2009) Schizophrenia genetics: new insights from new approaches. *Br. Med. Bull.*, [Epub ahead of print]

[18] Barrett, T. B., Hauger, R. L., Kennedy, J. L., Sadovnick, A. D., Remick, R. A., Keck, P. E., McElroy, S. L., Alexander, M., Shaw, S. H., and Kelsoe, J. R. (2003) Evidence that a single nucleotide polymorphism in the promoter of the G protein receptor kinase 3 gene is associated with bipolar disorder. *Mol. Psychiatry*, **8**:546-57.

[19] Beaulieu, J. M., Gainetdinov, R. R., and Caron, M. G. (2007) The Akt-GSK-3 signaling cascade in the actions of dopamine. *Trends Pharmacol. Sci.*, **28**:166-72.

[20] Tiberi, M., Nash, S. R., Bertrand, L., Lefkowitz, R. J., and Caron, M. G. (1996) Differential regulation of dopamine D1A receptor responsiveness by various G protein-coupled receptor kinases. *J. Biol. Chem.*, **271**:3771-8.

[21] Kummer, A. and Teixeira, A. L. (2008) Dopamine and bipolar disorder. *Acta Psychiatr. Scand.*, **117**:398.

[22] Kato, T., Kuratomi, G., and Kato, N. (2005) Genetics of bipolar disorder. *Drugs. Today (Barc.)*, **41**:335-44.

[23] Ertley, R. N., Bazinet, R. P., Lee, H. J., Rapoport, S. I., and Rao, J. S. (2007) Chronic treatment with mood stabilizers increases membrane GRK3 in rat frontal cortex. *Biol. Psychiatry*, **61**:246-9.

[24] Niculescu, A. B. 3rd, Segal, D. S., Kuczenski, R., Barrett, T., Hauger, R. L., and Kelsoe, J. R. (2000) Identifying a series of candidate genes for mania and psychosis: a convergent functional genomics approach. *Physiol. Genomics.*, **4**:83-91.

[25] Prata, D. P., Breen, G., Munro, J., Sinclair, M., Osborne, S., Li, T., Kerwin, R., St Clair, D., and Collier, D. A. (2006) Bipolar 1 disorder is not associated with the RGS4, PRODH, COMT and GRK3 genes. *Psychiatr. Genet.*, **16**:229-30.

[26] Hamet, P. and Tremblay, J. (2006) Genetics of the sleep-wake cycle and its disorders. *Metabolism*, **55**:S7-12.

[27] Friedrich, M., Körte, R., Portero, C., Arzberger, T., Kretzschmar, H. A., Zerr, I., and Nacimiento, W. (2008) Fatal familial insomnia - a rare differential diagnosis in dementia. *Fortschr. Neurol. Psychiatr.*, **76**:36-9.

[28] Ayuso Blanco, T., Urriza Mena, J., Caballero Martínez, C., Iriarte Franco, J., Munoz, R., García-Bragado, F. (2006) Fatal familiar insomnia: clinical, neurophysiological and histopathological study of two cases. *Neurologia*, **21**:414-20.

[29] Montagna, P. (2005) Fatal familial insomnia: a model disease in sleep physiopathology. *Sleep Med. Rev.*, **9**:339-53.

[30] Sundstrom, D. G. and Dreher, H. M. (2003) A deadly prion disease: fatal familial insomnia. *J. Neurosci. Nurs.*, **35**:300-5.

[31] Ertekin-Taner, N. (2007) Genetics of Alzheimer's disease: a centennial review. *Neurol. Clin.*,**25**(3):611-67.

[32] Schellenberg, G. D., D'Souza, I., and Poorkaj, P. (2000) The genetics of Alzheimer's disease. *Curr. Psychiatry Rep.*, **2**(2):158-64.

[33] Marques, A. T., Antunes, A., Fernandes, P. A., and Ramos, M. J. (2006) Comparative evolutionary genomics of the HADH2 gene encoding Abeta-binding alcohol dehydrogenase/17beta-hydroxysteroid dehydrogenase type 10 (ABAD/HSD10). *BMC Genomics*, **7**:202.

[34] Tanahashi, H. and Tabira, T. (1999) Genomic organization of the human X11L2 gene (APBA3), a third member of the X11 protein family interacting with Alzheimer's beta-amyloid precursor protein. *Neuroreport.*, **10**(12):2575-8.

[35] Blanco, G., Irving, N. G., Brown, S. D., Miller, C. C., and McLoughlin, D. M. (1998) Mapping of the human and murine X11-like genes (APBA2 and apba2), the murine Fe65 gene (Apbb1), and the human Fe65-like gene (APBB2): genes encoding phosphotyrosine-binding domain proteins that interact with the Alzheimer's disease amyloid precursor protein. *Mamm. Genome*, **9**(6):473-5.

[36] Johnston, J. A., Froelich, S., Lannfelt, L., Cowburn, R.F. (1996) Quantification of presenilin-1 mRNA in Alzheimer's disease brains. *FEBS Lett.*, **394**(3):279-84.

In: Handbook of Neuropsychiatry Research
Editor: Rebecca S. Davies, pp. 153-157

ISBN: 978-1-61668-138-8
© 2010 Nova Science Publishers, Inc.

Chapter 9

HOW CAN BIOINFORMATICS HELP STUDIES IN NEUROPSYCHIATRY?

Viroj Wiwanitkit
Wiwanitkit House, Bangkhae, Bangkok,
Thailand 10160

Abstract

Many acknowledge this to be the year of "bioinformatics". Bioinformatics has several advantages for both physical and biological sciences. In medicine, a branch of biological science, bioinformatics can be applied in all fields including neuropsychiatry. The fundamental functions of bioinformatics, including structural and functional manipulation, can be useful for studies in neuropsychiatry. The author will discuss the usefulness of bioinformatics in the study of neuropsychiatry. Brief examples are also available in this specific short paper.

Introduction

The present emerging of bioinformatics is raising hope for scientists around the world. This year has been accepted as the year of "bioinformatics". Bioinformatics has several advantages for both physical and biological sciences. Bioinformatics comes from two words, *bio* and *informatics*. Therefore, this means the use of information technology in biology, and there can be several areas for application. In medicine, a branch of biological science, bioinformatics can also be useful. This is the hope for present medicine.

Bioinformatics can be applied in all fields of medicine including neuropsychiatry. The fundamental functions of bioinformatics, including structural and functional manipulation, can be useful in neuropsychiatric studies. Indeed, neuropsychiatry, similar to other branches of medicine, involves the whole process starting from gene to expression. This matches the concept of bioinformatics as the approach starting from the genetic level to gross systematic level. The concept of stepwise manifestation from gene to actual visible expression can be adapted. The author will discuss the usefulness of bioinformatics in neuropsychiatric studies. Brief examples are also available in this specific short paper.

Usefulness of Bioinformatics in Neuropsychiatric Studies

There are many opportunities for the bioinformatics approach in neuropsychiatry. These include the studies in the stepwise manifestation from gene to expression as already mentioned. The author will discuss and give some important examples to help the readers follow the concept.

A. Study of the Mutation on Genetic and Protein Level

This is the basic study in bioinformatics. In structural genomics and structural proteomics, the finding of the structure of a gene or protein is the basic thing to be done. This is also useful for investigation of some genetic-based disorders in neuropsychiatry. A good example is the case of schizophrenia which is already classified as a genetic-based disorder. It is proposed to be a disease caused by multiple rare alleles. The role of many genes is noted. For example, DISC1 is the widely mentioned one [1]-[4]. The protocol used for the study of the mutation in DISC1 can be the one following standard protocol (as used in many previous published papers [5]-[8]). This will be further demonstrated as an example in Table 1. A similar technique can also be used for other neuropsychiatric disorders, such as the study of the mutation prone position within the PARKIN, a widely mentioned genetic component in Parkinsonism [13], [14].

How Can Bioinformatics Help Studies in Neuropsychiatry? 155

Table 1. Example of protocol to evaluate the mutation prone position within the DISC1 [9]-[12].

The standard data mining process can be performed using the first step in searching on standard proteomics server [such as those derived from the Swiss Institute of Bioinformatics (SIB), Expert Protein Analysis System (ExPASY)]. Then the amino acid sequence of DISC1 derived from the first step searching is the focused searched sequence and a standard bioinformatics technique (such as a widely used tool namely GlobPlot, a web service that allows the user to plot the tendency within the query protein for order/globularity and disorder) can be further used for identification for the weak linkage in derived DISC1.

B. Study on Physiogenomics

Psysiogenomics is a new approach to study the dimension of interrelationship between physiology and genome. This is actually a new area of bioinformatics and has limited reports in the literature. This can also be applicable in studies in neuropsychiatry—for example, any diseases with a possible underlying at the genome level. The author will use the example of the case of Alzheimer's disease. The protocol used for the study of the physiogenomics within Alzheimer's disease can be the one following standard protocol (as used in many previous published papers [15-16]). This will be further demonstrated as an example in Table 2.

Table 2. Example of protocol to assess the physiogenomics within Alzheimer disease [17]-[21].

The simulation study of the physiogenomics analysis can be based on a standard physiogenomics tool (such as by consomics technique, application of chromosomal substitution techniques in gene-function discovery; consomic strain is a technique in which an entire chromosome is introgressed into the isogenic background of another inbred strain using marker assisted selection) and standard simulation tool [such as PhysGen; this tool is for assessing functionality of relevant genes using a novel strategy, TILLING (Targeting Induced Local Lesions in Genomes) assay, a general reverse-genetic strategic tool, traditional chemical mutagenesis followed by high-throughput screening for point mutations, which provide the ability to detect allelic series of induced point mutations in focused interested genes]. In this approach, the human genome must be primarily used as a template and the assigned input ontology term is "Alzheimer's disease". Based on the mentioned protocol, the resulting identified gene accompanied with its specific physiogenomics score, which implies degree of correlation, is finally derived and this is the desired output.

Conclusion

It can be shown that the bioinformatics approach is very useful for studies in neuropsychiatry since neuropsychiatry can be accepted as the actual science that covers stepwise from gene level to gross expression level. The usefulness of bioinformatics in neuropsychiatric research can be seen in many aspects. Good examples, the protocols for important studies, are listed in this brief article, for the readers to further extend their work on this topic.

References

[1] Desbonnet, L., Waddington, J. L., and O'Tuathaigh, C. M. (2009) Mutant models for genes associated with schizophrenia. *Biochem. Soc. Trans.*, **37** (Pt 1):308-12.

[2] Verhoeven, W. M. and Tuinier, S.(2008) Clinical perspectives on the genetics of schizophrenia: a bottom-up orientation. *Neurotox. Res.*, **14** (2-3):141-50.

[3] Kalkman, H. O. (2009) Altered growth factor signaling pathways as the basis of aberrant stem cell maturation in schizophrenia. *Pharmacol. Ther.*, **121**(1):115-22.

[4] Golimbet, V. E. (2008) Molecular genetics of cognitive deficit in schizophrenia. *Mol. Biol. (Mosk.)*, **42**(5):830-9.

[5] Wiwanitkit, V. (2007) Identification of mutation-prone points in bile salt export pump. *HPB (Oxford)*, **9**(6):444-6.

[6] Wiwanitkit, V. (2008) Mutation-prone points in thrombin receptor. *J. Thromb. Thrombolysis*, **25**(2):190-2.

[7] Wiwanitkit, V. (2007) Weak linkage in androgen receptor: identification of mutationprone points. *Fertil. Steril.* [Epub ahead of print]

[8] Wiwanitkit, V. (2006) Where is the weak linkage in the globin chain? *Int. J. Nanomedicine*, **1**(1):109-10.

[9] Lee, C. and Wang, Q. (2005) Bioinformatics analysis of alternative splicing. *Brief. Bioinform.*, **6**:23-33.

[10] Levin, J. M., Penland, R. C., Stamps, A. T., and Cho, C. R. (2002) Using in silico biology to facilitate drug development. *Novartis. Found Symp.*, **247**:222-38

[11] Gasteiger, E., Gattiker, A., Hoogland, C., Ivanyi, I., Appel, R. D., and Bairoch, A. (2003) ExPASy: The proteomics server for in-depth protein knowledge and analysis. *Nucleic. Acids. Res.*, **31**:3784-8

How Can Bioinformatics Help Studies in Neuropsychiatry? 157

[12] Linding, R., Russell, R. B., Neduva, V., and Gibson, T. J. (2003) GlobPlot: Exploring protein sequences for globularity and disorder. *Nucleic. Acids. Res.*, **31**:3701-8.

[13] Lesage, S. and Brice, A. (2009) Parkinson's disease: from monogenic forms to genetic susceptibility factors. *Hum. Mol. Genet.*, **18**(R1):R48-59.

[14] Mochizuki, H. (2009) Parkin gene therapy. *Parkinsonism Relat. Disord.*, **15** Suppl., 1:S43-5.

[15] Williamson, J., Goldman, J., and Marder, K. S. (2009) Genetic aspects of Alzheimer disease. *Neurologist.*, **15**(2):80-6.

[16] Wiwanitkit, V. (2008) Physiological genomics analysis for central diabetes insipidus. *Acta Neurol. Taiwan*, **17**(3):214-6.

[17] Wiwanitkit, V. (2008) Difference in physiogenomics between male and female infertility. *Andrologia*, **40**(3):158-60.

[18] Isezuo, S. A. (2006) The metabolic syndrome: Review of current concepts. *Niger. Postgrad. Med. J.*, **13**(3):247-55.

[19] Cowley, A. W. Jr., Roman, R. J., and Jacob, H. J. (2004) Application of chromosomal substitution techniques in gene-function discovery. *J. Physiol.*, **554**(Pt 1):46-55.

[20] Cowley, A. W. Jr., Liang, M., Roman, R. J., Greene, A. S., and Jacob, H. J. (2004) Consomic rat model systems for physiological genomics. *Acta Physiol. Scand.*, **181**(4):585-92.

[21] Malek, R. L., Wang, H. Y., Kwitek, A. E., Greene, A. S., Bhagabati, N., Borchardt, G., Cahill, L., Currier, T., Frank, B., Fu, X., Hasinoff, M., Howe, E., Letwin, N., Luu, T. V., Saeed, A., Sajadi, H., Salzberg, S. L., Sultana, R., Thiagarajan, M., Tsai, J., Veratti, K., White, J., Quackenbush, J., Jacob, H. J., and Lee, N. H. (2006) Physiogenomic resources for rat models of heart, lung and blood disorders. *Nat. Genet.*, **38**(2):234-9.

In: Handbook of Neuropsychiatry Research
Editor: Rebecca S. Davies, pp. 159-192 © 2010 Nova Science Publishers, Inc.

ISBN 978-1-61668-138-8

Chapter 10

EXTRACTING DISCRIMINANT INFORMATION FROM NEUROIMAGES: A MULTIVARIATE COMPUTATIONAL FRAMEWORK TO ANALYZE THE WHOLE HUMAN BRAIN

Carlos E. Thomaz[1], Rafael D. Leão[1], João R. Sato[2] and Geraldo F. Busatto[3]

[1]Department of Electrical Engineering, Centro Universitário da FEI,
São Paulo, Brazil
[2]Center of Mathematics, Computation and Cognition,
Universidade Federal do ABC, São Paulo, Brazil
[3]Department of Psychiatry, Faculty of Medicine,
University of São Paulo, São Paulo, Brazil

Abstract

With the increasing anatomical resolution of the neuroimaging methods, clinicians are challenged nowadays, more than ever before, with the problem of detecting and interpreting statistically significant changes on neuroimages that are often distributed and involve simultaneously several structures of the human brain. In this chapter, we describe a general multivariate linear framework that analyses all the data simultaneously rather than segmented versions separately or feature-by-feature. This approach has been specially designed for extracting discriminative information from high dimensional data, dealing with the problem of small sample sizes, and it has been successfully applied in MR imaging analysis of the human brain. The multivariate linear framework is not restricted to any particular set of features and describes a simple and straightforward way of explaining multivariate changes of the whole brain on the original MR image domain, giving results that are statistically relevant to be further validated and interpreted by clinicians.

1. Introduction

The increasing anatomical resolution of neuroimaging methods nowadays has allowed the visualization of morphological changes of the human brain with impressive detail. For instance, the widely used method of magnetic resonance (MR) imaging affords superior soft-tissue contrast with high resolution, commonly less than 1mm. These advances have placed neuroimaging techniques as important tools for research and clinical purposes in neuropsychiatry. However, depending on the neurodegenerative disorder under investigation and its progression, neuroanatomical changes may be subtle, diffuse, or topologically complex to be detected by a simple visual inspection.

In the last decade, a considerable amount of effort has been devoted to the design of computational methods for morphological analysis of the human brain [11], [21], [2], [18], [37], [1], [27], [6], [28], [31], [26], [14], [41], [43], [35], [34], [4]. Traditionally, computational analysis of brain images has been based either on the definition of regions of interest given some a priori hypothesis about localization of pathological changes or on voxel-wise measurements with little prior knowledge [11], [21], [2], [18], [37], [1]. In practice, these traditional methodologies have shown limitations in their ability to identify previously unexplored relationships between a reference group of normal brain morphological patterns and the population under investigation.

Recently, multivariate pattern recognition methods [31], [26], [14], [4] have been proposed to extract and analyze morphological and anatomical structures of MR images of the human brain. Some of these techniques work in high-dimensional spaces of particular features such as shapes [26] or have overcome the difficulty of dealing with the inherent high dimensionality of medical data by using specific feature selection methods [31] that could no longer reconstruct the original brain, only certain aspects of it, limiting the general applicability of the method for detecting changes that are relatively more distributed and involve simultaneously several structures of the brain.

In this chapter, we describe a general multivariate linear framework that an-

Extracting Discriminant Information from NeuroImages   161

alyzes all the data simultaneously rather than segmented versions separately or feature-by-feature. This approach has been specially designed for extracting discriminative information from high dimensional data, dealing with the problem of small sample sizes, and it has been successfully applied in MR imaging analysis of the human brain [42], [41], [43], [35], [34]. The multivariate linear framework is not restricted to any particular set of features and describes a simple and straightforward way of mapping multivariate changes of the whole brain back into the original image domain, giving results that are statistically relevant and easy to be interpreted by clinicians.

The remainder of this chapter is divided as follows. In Section 2., we briefly introduce and contextualize a typical statistical pattern recognition system and its relation to the multivariate computational framework described here. Section 3. introduces the multivariate computational framework and its methods of pre-processing, feature extraction and classification of the samples of interest. In Section 4., we describe in detail how we can design the experiments of the multivariate computational framework in order to classify and extract the discriminant information from neuroimages. Section 5. presents experimental results of the framework on medical image analysis using two real case studies. Finally, in Section 6., we conclude the chapter, summarizing its main points and stating our opinion about the importance of using nowadays such multivariate pattern recognition methods for medical image analysis.

2. A Statistical Pattern Recognition System

Although a multivariate pattern recognition investigation may consist of several steps, a fairly typical statistical recognition system is commonly partitioned into components such as the ones shown in Figure 1 [13].

The pre-processing and feature extraction stages operate on the original (or new) samples (or images) in a way that normalizes the pattern of interest, diminishing noise, and removing redundant or irrelevant information. These stages attempt to transform data described in the original domain in a way that input vectors belonging to distinct classes should occupy as compact and disjoint regions as possible in a lower dimensional space, that is, in the feature space, for a subsequent classification. In the context of neuroimages, the pre-processing step is often refereed as the process of spatially normalizing the MR images. In the multivariate linear framework described in this chapter, the feature extraction stage is represented by the well-known multivariate statistical technique called

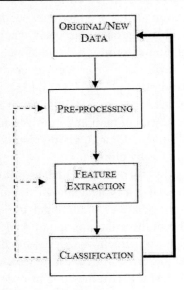

Figure 1. A typical statistical pattern recognition system with the direct connection from the output of the classification stage to the original input space for mapping the discriminant changes extracted by the system on the original data domain.

Principal Component Analysis [23], [29]. Both pre-processing stages will be better explained and contextualized in the next section.

The typical task of the classifier component, or the classification stage as illustrated in Figure 1, is to use the feature vectors provided by the previous stages to assign the object to a specific class or group. This assignment can be done directly, such as in the risk minimization-based approaches like Support Vector Machines [48], or indirectly such as in the spectral multivariate analysis of the data like the Fisher-based approaches [15], [16]. In the formal setting, an object is assumed to be a member of one, and only one, class and an error with an associated cost or loss is incurred if it is assigned to a different class [19]. In most pattern recognition problems, it is customary to consider as the loss function the 0/1 or symmetrical function, which assigns no loss to a correct decision and assigns a unit loss to any error [13]. Therefore, the symmetrical loss function assumes basically that all errors are equally costly and, consequently, the misclassification risk is then just the classification error rate, that is, the percent-

Extracting Discriminant Information from NeuroImages 163

age of new patterns that are assigned to the wrong class. Thus, it is common to evaluate the decision making process by seeking maximum classification accuracy or, equivalently, minimum error rate classification using separated and independent data subsets for training and testing the classifier. It can be seen from Figure 1 that to improve the classification results of both the original and new data, the feature extraction and pre-processing stages might often be revisited (feedback) during the decision-making process. This feedback procedure can essentially use the output of the classifier to recommend further adjustments on the statistical recognition system to improve its classification performance.

In this chapter, however, we would like to describe a new link in this typical statistical pattern recognition that connects directly the output of the classification stage, performed on the lower dimensional feature space, to the original input domain, as illustrated in Figure 1. Since statistical discrimination methods are suitable not only for classification but also for characterization of differences between a reference group of samples and the ones under investigation, the idea is to extract the discriminant information captured by the classifier and provide a simple and intuitive multivariate framework that allows a visualization and quantification of the differences between the groups on the original data space. In the context of neuroimages, such framework provides a way of mapping multivariate changes of the whole brain back into the original image domain, giving results that are statistically relevant and easier to be interpreted by clinicians.

3. The Multivariate Computational Framework

In this section, we describe the multivariate statistical framework that highlights the most discriminating difference between two populations. We are assuming that the number of samples per class is much less than the dimension of the original feature space. This situation is indeed quite common nowadays, especially in medical image analysis. For instance, patients and controls are presented by sample groups defined commonly by a small number of MR images but the features used for statistical analysis may be millions of voxels or hundreds of pre-processed image attributes.

3.1. Spatial Normalization (or Pre-Processing)

As mentioned in the previous section, the spatial normalization or pre-processing of the data is an important step for any pattern recognition analysis.

The purpose of the spatial normalization stage is to remove noisy effects from the data, especially the ones inherent to any data acquisition process, that are not relevant for the analysis. In the context of the classification of medical images this means that all images need to be mapped to a common coordinate system so that the voxel-wise features extracted from the images correspond ideally to the same anatomical location across all subjects [41].

The spatial normalization step is normally achieved by warping (or registering) each image to a common reference or template using a variety of registration techniques [24], [8], [9], [46], [3], [18], [40], [33], [7], [36]. It has essentially two goals [43]: (a) to reduce variability due to size, position and orientation of the brain and (b) to reduce variability due to differences in the brain shape. A feature extraction technique can then be categorized into techniques that deal with differences in brain shape (deformation-based morphometry, [2]) and those that deal with differences in the local composition of brain tissue after removing global shape differences (voxel-based morphometry, [1]). While both approaches require warping of images into a standard reference space using either elastic or fluid registration techniques, they differ fundamentally in the way the features are extracted from the aligned images. In deformation-based morphometry the deformation fields themselves are used to study similarities and differences, whereas in voxel-based morphometry these fields are used principally for normalization.

Each registered image then forms a pattern of interest consisting of n attributes or voxels which is then converted to an n-dimensional feature vector in the Euclidean original space. The goal is to analyze all the data simultaneously rather than feature-by-feature as in the pure deformation- or voxel-based morphometry approaches. Let us consider a 2D slice of an MR brain image, with intensity grey values between 0 and 2000, as an example to illustrate this standard procedure of converting images into vectors, as shown in Figure 2. In any image recognition task, an input image with n 2D pixels (or 3D voxels) can be viewed geometrically like a point in an n-dimensional space called the original image space. The Euclidean coordinates of this point represent the values of each intensity level of the image and form a vector $x^T = [x_1, x_2, \ldots, x_n]$ obtained by concatenating the rows (or columns) of the image matrix. Figure 2 shows an example of concatenating the rows of a 128x128 (or 16384) pixels image to represent a feature vector in the 16384-dimensional Euclidean space.

As pointed out by Lao et al. [31] in the context of MR images, it is unlikely that the image properties of individual voxels vary so dramatically among

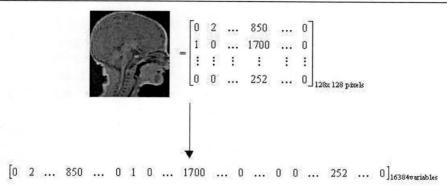

Figure 2. An example of concatenating the rows of an image matrix to form a vector.

patient populations that they can be used for classification. They have noted, however, that when those features are examined collectively the image properties of all voxels make clear distinctions among different groups. In other words, by using multivariate statistical methods we are able to characterize interregional dependencies necessarily present between the structures of the brain and consequently we can better explore the detail-rich information provided by neuroimages.

For this n-dimensional feature representation to make sense in classification problems, we are making implicitly the assumption that two images that look like one another correspond to two close points in the high dimensional original image space. In other words, the effectiveness of the registration algorithms and the multivariate statistical representation would be determined by how well patterns from different classes can be separated.

3.2. PCA (or Feature Extraction)

Principal Components Analysis, or simply PCA, is a feature extraction procedure concerned with explaining the covariance structure of a set of variables through a small number of linear combinations of these variables. It is a well-known statistical technique that has been used in several image recognition problems, especially for dimensionality reduction. A comprehensive description of this multivariate statistical analysis method can be found in [23], [29].

There are a number of reasons for using PCA to reduce the dimensionality of the 3D MR brain images. PCA is a linear transformation that is not only simple to compute and analytically tractable but also extracts a set of features that is optimal with respect to representing the data back into the original domain. Moreover, using PCA as an intermediate step will reduce dramatically the computational and storage requirements for the subsequent classification stage performed by an LDA-based covariance method. Since our application is a small sample size problem where the original variables (or voxels) are highly correlated and the number of training patterns (or images) is much smaller than the number of voxels, it is possible to transform data in a way that patterns occupy as compact regions in a lower dimensional feature space as possible with far fewer degrees of freedom to estimate.

Let an n x N training set matrix X be composed of N registered input images with n voxels. This means that each row of matrix X represents the values of a particular voxel observed all over the N images. Let this data matrix X have covariance matrix S with respectively P and Λ eigenvector and eigenvalue matrices, that is,

$$P^T S P = \Lambda, \tag{1}$$

where

$$S = \frac{1}{(N-1)} (X - \overline{X})(X - \overline{X})^T = \frac{1}{(N-1)} \sum_{j=1}^{N} (x_j - \overline{x})(x_j - \overline{x})^T, \tag{2}$$

and x_j is the n-dimensional pattern (or sample) j of the training set X, N is the total number of samples, and $\overline{x}$ is the grand mean vector given by

$$\overline{x} = \frac{1}{N} \sum_{j=1}^{N} x_j. \tag{3}$$

It is a proven result that the set of m $(m \leq n)$ eigenvectors of S, which corresponds to the m largest eigenvalues, minimizes the mean square reconstruction error over all choices of m orthonormal basis vectors [23]. Such a set of eigenvectors that defines a new uncorrelated Euclidean coordinate system for the training set matrix X is known as the principal components. In the context of image recognition, those $P_{pca} = [p_1, p_2, \ldots, p_m]$ components are frequently called most expressive features [38].

Although much of the sample variability can be accounted for by a smaller number of principal components, and consequently a further dimensionality reduction can be accomplished by selecting the principal components with the

Extracting Discriminant Information from NeuroImages 167

largest eigenvalues, there is no guarantee that such additional dimensionality reduction will not add any artifacts on the images when mapped back into the original image space. Thus, in order to reproduce the total variability of the training set matrix X, we can compose the PCA transformation matrix by selecting all principal components with non-zero eigenvalues. In other words, assuming that all the N training patterns are linearly independent the rank of the total covariance matrix S described in equation (2) is $N - 1$ and the number of principal components selected is $m = N - 1$.

Since one of our main concerns here is to map the classification results back to the image domain for further clinicians' validation and intepretation, we must be certain that any modification on the images, such as blurring or subtle differences, is not related to an "incomplete" or perhaps "misleading" feature extraction intermediate procedure. For example, Figure 3 illustrates on the top a reference image (shown on the left) reconstructed using several principal components and on the bottom the corresponding differences between these reconstructions to the original image. The values in parentheses represent the number of principal components used and corresponding total variance explained. We can see clearly that even when we use a set of principal components that represent more than 90% of the total sample variance we still have subtle differences between the reconstructed image and the original one.

Therefore, the multivariate framework has to use not only the major principal components with the largest eigenvalues but also all the principal components with small non-zero eigenvalues to extract the features from the MR brain images. Although some of these principal components, especially the ones with small eigenvalues, might represent non-discriminative information as noise, such feature extraction procedure is able to represent and further reconstruct the original images without adding any dimensionality reduction artifacts [41], [43].

3.3. LDA (or Hyperplane Classification)

In the generic classification problem, where the training set consists of the class membership and observations for N samples, the outcome of interest falls into g groups or classes and we wish to build a rule for predicting the class membership of an observation based on n variables or m features. However, as mentioned earlier, the multivariate framework's idea is not only to classify sample groups but also to extract and visually understand the discriminant infor-

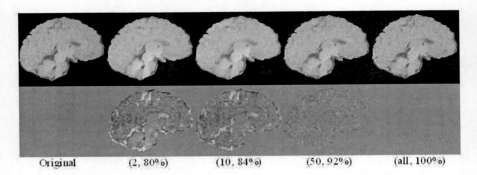

Figure 3. Reconstruction of a reference image (shown on the left) using several principal components. The row on the bottom illustrates the corresponding differences between the reconstructions to the original image. The number of principal components used and the corresponding total sample variance explained by each one of the sets of principal components are shown in parentheses. We can see clearly modifications on the reconstructed images where all principal components with non-zero eigenvalues are not selected [41].

mation captured by the classifier. Therefore, the well-known Fisher's discriminant approach [15], [16], that transforms multivariate observations in a way that the samples of the groups become as linearly separated as possible on a lower discriminant feature space, is an appropriate multivariate statistical method to perform both tasks simultaneously.

The primary purpose of Fisher Discriminant Analysis, often called as Linear Discriminant Analysis (LDA) as well, is to separate samples of distinct groups by maximizing their between-class separability while minimizing their within-class variability. Although LDA does not assume that the populations of the distinct groups are normally distributed, it assumes implicitly that the true covariance matrices of each class are equal because the same within-class scatter matrix is used for all the classes considered [29].

Let the between-class scatter matrix S_b be defined as

$$S_b = \sum_{i=1}^{g} N_i(\overline{x}_i - \overline{x})(\overline{x}_i - \overline{x})^T \qquad (4)$$

Extracting Discriminant Information from NeuroImages

and the within-class scatter matrix S_w be defined as

$$S_w = \sum_{i=1}^{g}(N_i - 1)S_i = \sum_{i=1}^{g}\sum_{j=1}^{N_i}(x_{i,j} - \overline{x}_i)(x_{i,j} - \overline{x}_i)^T \tag{5}$$

where $x_{i,j}$ is the m-dimensional pattern (or sample) j from class π_i, N_i is the number of training patterns from class π_i, and g is the total number of classes or groups. The vector $\overline{x}_i$ and matrix S_i are respectively the unbiased sample mean and sample covariance matrix of class π_i defined as [23]

$$\overline{x}_i = \frac{1}{N_i}\sum_{j=1}^{N_i}x_{i,j}, \tag{6}$$

$$S_i = \frac{1}{(N_i - 1)}\sum_{j=1}^{N_i}(x_{i,j} - \overline{x}_i)(x_{i,j} - \overline{x}_i)^T. \tag{7}$$

The grand mean vector $\overline{x}$ described in equation (3) can be rewritten as

$$\overline{x} = \frac{1}{N}\sum_{i=1}^{g}N_i\overline{x}_i = \frac{1}{N}\sum_{i=1}^{g}\sum_{j=1}^{N_i}x_{i,j}, \tag{8}$$

where N is, as described earlier, the total number of samples, that is, $N = N_1 + N_2 + \cdots + N_g$. It is important to note that the within-class scatter matrix S_w defined in equation (5) is essentially the standard pooled covariance matrix S_p multiplied by the scalar $(N - g)$, where S_p can be written as

$$S_p = \frac{1}{N-g}\sum_{i=1}^{g}(N_i-1)S_i = \frac{(N_1 - 1)S_1 + (N_2 - 1)S_2 + \cdots + (N_g - 1)S_g}{N - g}. \tag{9}$$

The main objective of LDA is to find a projection matrix W_{lda} that maximizes the ratio of the determinant of the between-class scatter matrix to the determinant of the within-class scatter matrix (Fisher's criterion), that is,

$$W_{lda} = \arg\max_{W}\frac{|W^T S_b W|}{|W^T S_w W|}. \tag{10}$$

The Fisher's criterion described in equation (10) is maximized when the projection matrix W_{lda} is composed of the eigenvectors of $S_w^{-1}S_b$ with at most

$(g-1)$ nonzero corresponding eigenvalues [23], [12]. In the case of a two-class problem, the LDA projection matrix is in fact the leading eigenvector w_{lda} of $S_w^{-1}S_b$, assuming that S_w is invertible.

However, in limited sample and high dimensional problems, such as in medical image analysis, S_w is either singular or mathematically unstable and the standard LDA cannot be used to perform the separating task. To avoid both critical issues, the multivariate computational framework calculates w_{lda} by using a maximum uncertainty LDA-based approach (MLDA) that considers the issue of stabilizing the S_w estimate with a multiple of the identity matrix [44], [45]. This approach has been successfully applied not only on medical imaging analysis [42], [35], [34] of the human brain but also on other similar high dimensional and limited sample size problems such as face images interpretation and reconstruction [30], [25] and DNA microarray analysis [22], [49].

The MLDA algorithm can be shortly described as follows:

1. Find the Φ eigenvectors and Λ eigenvalues of S_p, where $S_p = \frac{S_w}{N-g}$;

2. Calculate the S_p average eigenvalue $\overline{\lambda}$, that is,

$$\overline{\lambda} = \frac{1}{m}\sum_{j=1}^{m}\lambda_j = \frac{trace(S_p)}{m} \; ; \tag{11}$$

3. Form a new matrix of eigenvalues based on the following largest dispersion values

$$\Lambda^* = diag[max(\lambda_1, \overline{\lambda}), max(\lambda_2, \overline{\lambda}), \ldots, max(\lambda_m, \overline{\lambda})]; \tag{12}$$

4. Form the modified within-class scatter matrix

$$S_w^* = S_p^*(N-g) = (\Phi\Lambda^*\Phi^T)(N-g). \tag{13}$$

The MLDA method is constructed by replacing S_w with S_w^* in the Fisher's criterion formula described in equation (10). It is based on the idea that in limited sample size and high dimensional problems where the within-class scatter matrix is singular or poorly estimated, the Fisher's linear basis found by minimizing a more difficult but appropriate *inflated* within-class scatter matrix would also minimize a less reliable *shrivelled* within-class estimate [45].

Extracting Discriminant Information from NeuroImages 171

4. Design of the Experiments

In this section, we describe how we can design the experiments of the multivariate computational framework in order to classify and extract the discriminant information from neuroimages. Basically, we can divide the experiments into two main tasks: (1) classification of the training and test sets, and (2) visual analysis of the discriminant information extracted by the two-stage PCA+MLDA separating hyperplane, as illustrated in Figure 4.

Assuming that the neuroimages have already been spatially normalized and that there is a set of training examples with their corresponding labels to construct the MLDA classifier, firstly the average image vector of all the training images is calculated and subtracted from each n-dimensional vector, as shown in Figure 4. Then the training matrix composed of zero mean image vectors is used as input to compute the P_{pca} transformation matrix. The columns of this n x m transformation matrix are eigenvectors, not necessarily in eigenvalues descending order. The framework retains all the PCA eigenvectors with non-zero eigenvalues, that is, $m = N - 1$, to reproduce the total variability of the samples with no loss of information. It is important to emphasize, however, that this PCA intermediate step is necessary here because $n \gg N$, allowing the MLDA scatter matrices to be calculable in computers with a normal memory size. In situations where $N \gg n$, the multivariate computational framework may not need such PCA step for dimensionality reduction.

Thus, the zero mean image vectors are projected on the principal components and reduced to m-dimensional vectors representing the most expressive features of each one of the n-dimensional image vector. Afterwards, this N x m data matrix is used as input to calculate the W_{mlda} discriminant transformation matrix, as described in the previous section. Since in this chapter we have limited ourselves to two-group classification problems, there is only one w_{mlda} discriminant eigenvector. The most discriminant feature of each one of the m-dimensional vectors is obtained by multiplying the N x m most expressive features matrix by the m x 1 MLDA linear discriminant eigenvector. Hence, the initial training set of neuroimages consisting of N measurements on n variables is reduced to a data set consisting of N measurements on only 1 most discriminant feature.

Once the two-stage linear classifier has been constructed, we can move along its corresponding projection vector and extract the discriminant differences captured by the classifier. As illustrated in the Visual Analysis part of

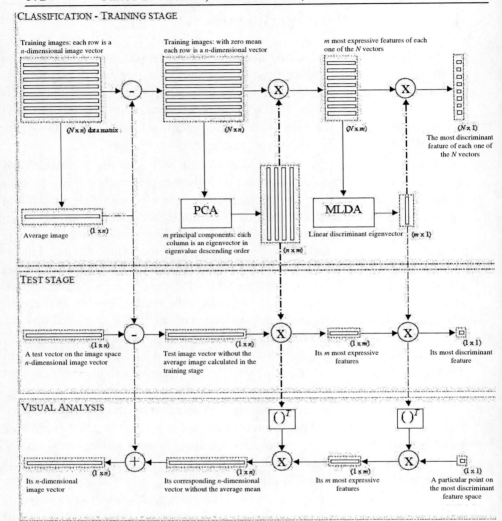

Figure 4. Design of the experiments of the multivariate computational framework [41], [43]. The experiments can be divided into two main tasks: (1) classification (training and test stages), and (2) visual analysis.

the framework shown in Figure 4, any point on the discriminant feature space can be converted to its corresponding n-dimensional image vector by simply: (1) multiplying that particular point by the w_{mlda} linear discriminant eigenvec-

Extracting Discriminant Information from NeuroImages 173

tor previously computed; (2) multiplying its m most expressive features by the P_{pca} transformation matrix; and (3) adding the average image calculated in the training stage to the n-dimensional image vector. Therefore, assuming that the spreads of the classes follow a Gaussian distribution and applying limits to the variance of each group, such as $\pm 3\sigma_i$, where σ_i is the standard deviation of each group $i \in \{1, 2\}$, we can move along the most discriminant hyperplane and map the results back into the image domain.

In fact, any neuroimage $x_{i,j}$ that followed the same acquisition and spatial normalization protocols can incorporate the discriminant information captured by the two-stage linear classifier. More specifically, this procedure of transferring the most discriminant feature can be generated through the following mathematical expression [45], [25], [35], [34]:

$$y_{i,j} = x_{i,j} + j\sigma_i \cdot P_{pca}w_{mlda}, \qquad (14)$$

where $j \in \{-3, -2, -1, 0, 1, 2, 3\}$. This operation is useful not only to transfer the most discriminant feature to any point on the original image space, but also, and most importantly, predict how the discriminant information can affect a particular sample that does not necessarily belong to the training set.

5. Case Studies

To illustrate the concepts and notions of the multivariate linear approach, we present in this section experimental results of the framework on medical image analysis using two real case studies.

5.1. MRI Differences in AD Patients Relatively to Controls

In this case study, we have used a data set that contains images of 14 patients with Alzheimer's disease (AD) and 14 healthy controls to illustrate the MRI statistical differences in AD patients relatively to an elderly healthy control group. The reader is referred to [6] for details on the demographic and clinical characteristics of these subjects. All these images were acquired using a 1.5T Philips Gyroscan S15-ACS MRI scanner (Philips Medical Systems, Eindhoven, The Netherlands), including a series of contiguous 1.2mm thick coronal images across the entire brain, using a T1-weighted fast field echo sequence (TE = 9ms, TR = 30ms, flip angle 30o, field of view = 240mm, 256 x 256 matrix). All

174 Carlos E. Thomaz, Rafael D. Leão, João R. Sato et al.

images were reviewed by a MR neuro-radiologist. Ethical permission for this study was granted by the Ethics Committee of the Clinical Hospital, University of São Paulo Medical School, São Paulo, Brazil.

5.1.1. Mass-univariate Statistical Analysis

For comparison purpose, Statistical Parametric Mapping (SPM, version SPM2) [21] analyzes were conducted using an optimized Voxel-Based Morphometry (VBM) protocol [27]. Detailed results of these optimized VBM analyzes have been reported previously in [6]. In contrast to the multivariate approach, SPM has been designed to enable voxel-by-voxel inferences about localized differences between the groups and consequently does not characterize interregional dependencies between the structures of the brain [20]. The optimized VBM involves essentially the following additional steps not present on the standard VBM approach: the construction of customized templates to reduce bias for spatial normalization; the segmentation and extraction of normalized whole brain images to remove non-brain tissues that could still remain outside the segmented images; and a further pre-processing step of modulation for correction for volume changes [27]. We describe next more details about these pre-processing steps and the brain differences between the patients with AD and healthy controls found by the SPM approach.

Template Customization, Tissue Segmentation and Smoothing

A template set was created specifically for this SPM analysis, consisting of a mean T1-weighted image, and a priori gray matter, white matter and cerebrospinal fluid (CSF) templates based on the images of all AD and healthy control subjects. The use of customized templates in VBM is aimed to match more closely the population under investigation and the image acquisition protocols used [27]. The inclusion of AD patients in our template set was intended to prevent biases during spatial transformations, as a template based exclusively on images from healthy controls would lead to a greater degree of warping of the AD scans during normalization. For example, it is expected that AD patients will present a greater degree of cortical atrophy than non-demented controls. Therefore, a template based exclusively on healthy brains might have introduced systematic bias, as images from AD subjects would always have to suffer a greater degree of warping on cortical brain region in order to be adjusted to the predominantly non-atrophied brains of healthy subjects.

Initially, images were spatially normalized to the standard SPM T1-MRI template [32], based on 152 health subjects from the Montreal Neurological Institute (MNI), using as matching criterion the residual sum of squared differences [27]. Such spatial normalization step was restricted to linear 12-parameter affine transformations, in order to minimize deformations of our original images. Spatially normalized images were then segmented into gray matter, white matter and CSF compartments, using a modified mixture model cluster analysis technique [27]. This technique used the MNI prior probability maps provided in the SPM2 package overlaid onto the images in order to classify voxels in terms of their probability of belonging to a particular tissue class, that is, gray matter, white matter or CSF. The segmentation method also included: an automated brain extraction procedure to remove non-brain tissue and an algorithm to correct for image intensity non-uniformity caused by different positions of the subjects' heads when acquiring the corresponding MR images. Details on the image intensity non-uniformity correction can be obtained in [1]. Finally, the segmented images were smoothed with an isotropic Gaussian kernel (8mm FWHM), and averaged to provide the gray, white matter and CSF templates in stereotactic space.

Then, to boost the signal-to-noise ratio, the image processing of the original images from all AD patients and controls was carried out, beginning by image segmentation. The segmented images were spatially normalized to the customized templates previously created by using 12-parameter linear as well as non-linear (7 x 9 x 7 basis functions) transformations. The parameters resulting from this spatial normalization step were reapplied to the original structural images. These fully normalized images were re-sliced using tri-linear interpolation to a final voxel size of 2 x 2 x 2 mm^3, and segmented into gray matter, white matter and CSF partitions. Voxel values were modulated by the Jacobian determinants derived from the spatial normalization, thus allowing brain structures that had their volumes reduced after spatial normalization to have their total counts decreased by an amount proportional to the degree of volume shrinkage [27]. Finally, images from AD patients and controls were smoothed with a 12-mm FWHM isotropic Gaussian kernel to remove the differences in sulcal/gyral patterns among individuals that may not be accounted for by normalization [1], and conform the images more closely to the SPM statistical assumption about normally distributed data. The 12-mm width was chosen in particular for the smoothing kernel to reduce the number of false positives. This 12-mm Gaussian smoothing filter promotes the detection of differences in structures of around 12-mm spatial extent [1].

Extracting Voxel-by-Voxel Differences from the MRI Samples

Figure 5 illustrates the results of regional brain volume comparisons between patients with AD and healthy controls, conducted using voxel-based morphometry with the SPM program [21]. The comparisons are shown separately for gray matter regions (top row), white matter regions (middle row), and CSF space (bottom row). For the three analyzes, the statistical results have been overlaid on segmented images of a reference brain spatially normalized into an approximation to the Tailarach and Tornoux stereotactic atlas [39].

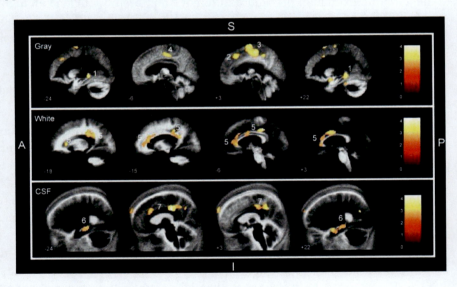

Figure 5. Brain regions where significant differences in AD patients relatively to controls were detected by the SPM voxel-wise statistical tests at $p < 0.01$. The foci of significance that were located in areas known to be critical to the pathophysiology of AD have been labeled as follows: (1) hippocampus/parahippocampal gyrus, (2) anterior cingulate gyrus, (3) parietal cortex, (4) posterior cingulate gyrus, (5) corpus callosum, (6) temporal horn of the lateral ventricle, and (7) anterior/posterior horns of the lateral ventricle. The numbers seen at the bottom of each frame represent the standard coordinate in x-axis (abbreviations: A= anterior; I= inferior; P= posterior; S= superior) [43].

The numbers seen at the bottom of each frame of Figure 5 represent the standard coordinate in the x-axis (abbreviations: A = anterior; I = inferior; P = posterior; S = superior). The images describing the analyzes for gray and white matter segments show, in yellow, foci where there were significant volume reductions in AD patients relative to controls, at a $Z > 2.33$ statistical threshold (corresponding to $p < 0.01$, one-tailed). Additionally, the images for the CSF analysis show areas of significant increases in CSF spaces, mainly ventricle enlargement, in AD patients relative to controls ($p < 0.01$). The foci of significance that were located in areas known to be critical to the pathophysiology of AD have been labeled with white-printed numbers, as follows: (1) hippocampus/parahippocampal gyrus; (2) anterior cingulate gyrus; (3) parietal cortex; (4) posterior cingulate gyrus; (5) corpus callosum; (6) temporal horn of the lateral ventricle; and (7) anterior/posterior horns of the lateral ventricle. These structures, especially where significant gray matter changes were observed, are among the regions thought to be the most prominently affected by atrophic changes in AD [6], [28].

5.1.2. Multivariate Statistical Analysis

The intensity features of all the MR images spatially normalized in the previous SPM analysis were used as input to the multivariate statistical analysis. As described earlier, the use of spatially normalized MRI data is an important step for any pattern recognition analysis, and the multivariate statistical framework in particular, because it removes confounding effects from the data, which are not relevant for the analysis.

Evaluating the Multivariate Separation between the AD and Control Sample Groups

In order to measure the similarity (or overlap) between the MRI samples of patients and controls projected on the multivariate separating hyper-plane, we have used the Bhattacharyya distance [5]. The Bhattacharyya distance measures the overlap between two distributions by calculating the class separability due to the mean (or prototype) and covariance (or spread) differences [23]. Our motivation for using the Bhattacharyya distance is based on the fact that it is a closed-form metric for evaluating classifier's performance and consequently its computational effort is reduced because we need only to evaluate a formula [23]. Assuming that the distributions of the two samples are Gaussian, the Bhattacharyya distance will also give us an estimate of the Bayes error of the multivariate statistical framework.

For two-class problems, the upper bound of the Bayes error e_u can be defined as [23]

$$e_u = (p_1 p_2)^{\frac{1}{2}} \exp(-d), \tag{15}$$

where p_1 and p_2 are the prior probabilities of classes π_1 and π_2 respectively, and d is the Bhattacharyya distance between the two classes. The Bhattacharyya distance d for the most discriminant one-dimensional samples can be written as

$$d = \frac{1}{4} \frac{(m_1 - m_2)^2}{\sigma_1^2 + \sigma_2^2} + \frac{1}{2} \ln \frac{\sigma_1^2 + \sigma_2^2}{2\sigma_1^2 \sigma_2^2}, \tag{16}$$

where m_i and σ_i^2 are respectively the unbiased one-dimensional sample mean and covariance of class π_i ($i = 1, 2$).

Since the dataset under investigation comes with the same proportion of patient images relatively to controls, we have assumed that the prior probabilities of both groups are equal. Thus, assuming $p_1 = p_2 = 0.5$ and calculating the Bhattacharyya distance d using leave-one-out parameter estimation, the multivariate statistical classifier achieves a Bayes error of 1.57% (with standard deviation of 0.5%). This result indicates the classifier's ability of separating the brains of controls from those of patients with an estimate of 98.43% on average for the classification rate, using the closed-form method for the error probability.

Evaluating the Diagnostic Coherence of the Separating Hyper-Plane

Although the multivariate statistical framework has been able to fairly separate the AD and control sample groups, it is important to examine the coherence of the most discriminant direction defined by the separating hyper-plane on practical methods or evidences used by the clinicians for grading the cognitive state of patients.

Figure 6 presents the scatter plot of the Mini-Mental State (MMSE) [17] versus the most discriminant feature captured by the multivariate statistical approach. The MMSE index is a practical method commonly used by clinicians to grade the cognitive state of patients [17]. As can be seen, the MRI patient samples with lower MMSE and consequently higher cognitive decline tend to be far away from the classifier's decision boundary. In other words, the most discriminant information extracted by the multivariate statistical hyper-plane correlates

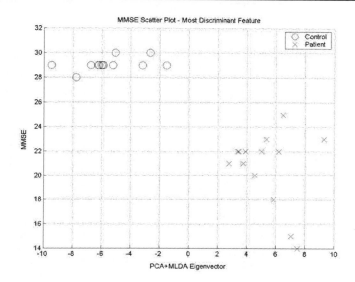

Figure 6. Scatter plot of the MMSE versus the most discriminant feature captured by the separating hyper-plane [43].

well (with the exception of two subjects) with MMSE and might highlight differences between the two populations that would help to understand the underlying causes of the AD abnormalities.

Additionally, Figure 7 illustrates the scatter plot of the age of each MRI sample versus the most discriminant feature captured by the multivariate statistical approach. We can see that when we move from the patient (right) to control (left) samples there is a decrease on average of the age of the patients but not necessarily of the age of the controls. Although this is not a surprising result because we know that AD is a neurodegenerative disorder most prevalent in elderly population [CB03], this result shows other evidences about the coherence and plausibility of the most discriminant direction found by the multivariate statistical approach.

Extracting Multivariate Discriminative Information from the MRI Samples

The statistical differences between the control and AD MRI samples captured by the multivariate statistical framework are illustrated in Figure 8. As

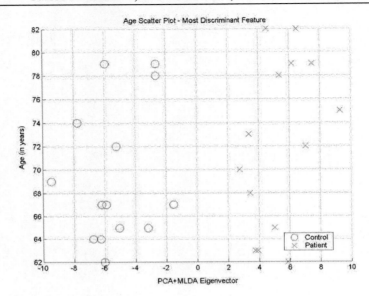

Figure 7. Scatter plot of the age of each subject versus the most discriminant feature captured by the separating hyper-plane [43].

mentioned earlier, the one-dimensional vector found by the multivariate statistical approach corresponds to a hyper-plane on the original image space which direction describes statistically the most discriminant differences between the control and patient images used for training.

Figure 8 shows the differences between the control (on the left column) and patient (on the right column) images captured by the multivariate statistical classifier using MR intensity features as inputs and all the spatially normalized samples for training. These images correspond to one-dimensional points on the PCA+MLDA space projected back into the image domain following limits to the variance of each sample group (± 3 standard deviations), as described in the Section 4.. The label 'boundary' represents the decision boundary of the multivariate classifier assuming equal prior probabilities and misclassification costs for both groups. We can interpret this mapping procedure as a way of defining intensity changes that come from "definitely control" and "definitely patient" samples captured by the statistical classifier [41]. We can see the following brain differences in the AD patients relatively to the controls: (1) enlargement of the ventricular system, (2) atrophy of the hippocampus, (3) cortical

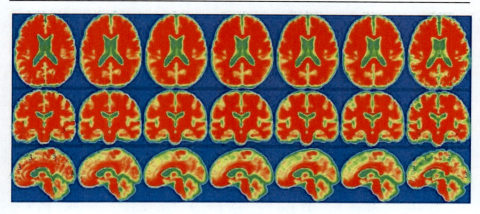

Figure 8. Statistical differences between the control (group 1, on the left) and AD patient (group 2, on the right) images captured by the multivariate statistical classifier and mapped back into the image domain as follows: $[-3\sigma_1, \overline{x}_1, +2\sigma_1, boundary, -2\sigma_2, \overline{x}_2, +3\sigma_2]$. We can see the following brain differences in the AD patients relatively to the controls: (1) enlargement of the ventricular system, (2) atrophy of the hippocampus, (3) cortical degeneration of the occipital, parietal, and frontal lobes, (4) enlargement of the inter-hemispheric fissure, and (5) atrophy of the corpus callosum and hypothalamus [43].

degeneration of the occipital, parietal, and frontal lobes, (4) enlargement of the inter-hemispheric fissure, and (5) atrophy of the corpus callosum and hypothalamus. These multivariate results are consistent with the SPM between-group differences presented previously and with other common findings of patients who have developed the pathology [47], [6], [28].

5.2. MRI Multi-linear Analysis of Normal Subjects

In the previous case study, the detection of the multivariate changes has been based essentially on a visual inspection of the most discriminant features of a single two-group separation task. In this case study, however, we illustrate how the multivariate computational framework can be generalized to extract and quantify multiple two-group separation differences in MR images, such as linear demographic differences by gender and age in normal subjects.

MR Images Description, Normalization and Segmentation

We have used a subset of the IXI database that contains T1-weighted MR images of 169 normal subjects between the age of 20 and 80 years to carry out these experiments. The IXI database is a cross-sectional brain imaging study and has been freely available for download[1] subject to a license agreement to ensure appropriate end usage and comply with ethical requirements. For these experiments, we have analyzed only the data acquired at the site of the Hammersmith Hospital in London, United Kingdom. All images are anonymous but contain basic demographic information collected from the subjects such as height, smoking habits, gender, age, weight and etc. The images have size of 256 x 256 x 150 with a voxel size of 0.9375 x 0.9375 x 1.2 mm^3, and have been converted to the NIFTI (NeuroImaging Informatics Technology Initiative[2]) file format.

Analogously to the normalization and segmentation steps of the previous case study, all the images were initially registered to the standard SPM T1-MRI template [32], using as matching criterion the residual sum of squared differences [27]. Such spatial normalization step was restricted to linear 12-parameter affine transformations, in order to minimize deformations of the original IXI MR images. The spatially normalized images were then segmented into gray matter, white matter and CSF compartments, using a modified mixture model cluster analysis technique [27]. This technique used the MNI-152 prior probability maps provided in the SPM5 package overlaid onto the images in order to classify voxels in terms of their probability of belonging to a particular tissue class, that is, gray matter, white matter or CSF. In this case study, we have used only the gray matter and white matter segmented images to performing the experiments. The segmentation method also included an automated brain extraction procedure to remove non-brain tissue and an algorithm to correct for image intensity non-uniformity caused by different positions of the subjects' heads when acquiring the corresponding MR images. Finally, the segmented images were smoothed with an isotropic Gaussian kernel (8mm FWHM) to improve the signal-to-noise ratio.

---

[1] http://www.brain-development.org
[2] http://nifti.nimh.nih.gov

Extracting Discriminant Information from NeuroImages 183

Performing and Evaluating the Multi-linear Discriminant Analyzes

We have performed the following six multi-linear two-group analyzes of the 169 spatially normalized and segmented MR images: (1) height (94 tall versus 75 short subjects); (2) ever smoked (73 smokers versus 96 non-smokers); (3) gender (84 males versus 85 females); (4) hypertension (35 hypertensive versus 134 non-hypertensive subjects); (5) age (84 young versus 85 elderly subjects); and (6) obesity (97 obese versus 72 non-obese subjects). For the height, ageing and obesity experiments, we have composed the corresponding two-group samples in order to achieve a fairly homogeneous distribution between the classes of interest. That is, subjects that have height of 1.70m (or above), 46 years of age (or over) and body mass index of 24 (or above), have been considered tall, elderly and obese, respectively, whereas short, young and non-obese otherwise. Starting with the same registered and segmented 169 images, the multivariate computational framework determines the most discriminant direction of change by organizing the training data according to the analysis of interest and constructing distinct PCA+MLDA linear classifiers for each one of the six characteristics. Figure 9 shows the box plots of the 10-fold cross validation of the classification accuracy of the gray matter (top) and white matter (bottom) multi-linear discriminant analyzes. It is possible to see that the multivariate framework achieved the highest classification accuracies ($> 80\%$) in the two-group discriminant analysis of the characteristic of age, obtaining good ($> 75\%$) linear separation in the two-group multivariate analyzes of the height, gender and hypertension characteristics. Analyzes of the discriminant features extracted by the multivariate framework from the ever smoked and obesity experiments, however, should be done with caution because in both experiments the multivariate computational framework achieved classification accuracies lower than 75% on average. This is an important information provided by the multivariate computational framework that is based on a pattern recognition system rather than a hypothesis-driven approach and considers the whole brain structures simultaneously to evaluate statistical significant changes between the sample groups of interest rather than feature-by-feature.

In order to quantify and rank the statistical significance of the multivariate changes and avoid the use of raw units that are quite arbitrary or lack meaning outside the investigation, we have calculated the t-values of the differences between the statistical mean points from each sample group on the corresponding two-group PCA+MLDA separating hyperplane and projected back on the orig-

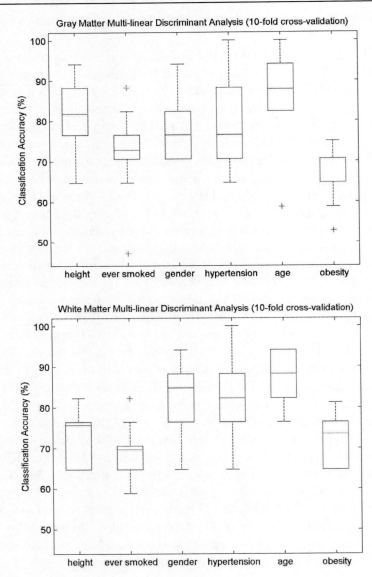

Figure 9. Box plots of the classification accuracy (10-fold cross validation) of the gray matter (top) and white matter (bottom) multi-linear discriminant analyzes performed by the multivariate computational framework.

inal image space. Figure 10 shows the spatial distribution of the discriminant voxels extracted by each PCA+MLDA separating hyperplane superimposed on a reference image chosen randomly. From top to bottom, it highlights only the most discriminant voxels which correspond to the 5% (first two rows) and 1% (last two rows) largest (in absolute values) t-values that are mutually exclusive for all the two-group characteristics considered (i.e., present in one only one characteristic), minimizing their inherent confounding effects. Gray matter differences are shown on the first row and white matter differences on the second row of each corresponding 5% and 1% t-maps of Figure 10. It is clear that the resulting t-maps of the multivariate computational framework mitigate the multiple comparison problem commonly present on the mass-univariate analyzes [10], [20]. In fact, according to the classification accuracy previously reported and the consistency of the spatial distribution of the most discriminant voxels, the two-group discriminant analysis of the age characteristic seems to illustrate the most robust MRI changes of all the characteristics considered, given the limited number of MRI samples available.

6. Conclusion

In this chapter, we described and implemented a general multivariate linear framework that analyzes all the voxel-based information provided by MR images of the human brain simultaneously rather than segmented versions separately or feature-by-feature. This multivariate computational framework has been specially designed for extracting discriminative information from high dimensional data, dealing with the problem of small sample sizes. The two case studies carried out in this work indicated that discriminant information can be efficiently extracted and evaluated by multivariate linear classifiers in the original neuroimage space. In both case studies, the experimental results showed that the multivariate computational framework, based on a pattern recognition system rather than a hypothesis-driven approach, provides an intuitive interpretation of the differences between the groups, highlighting and reconstructing the most discriminant statistical changes between the sample groups analyzed.

With the increasing anatomical resolution of the neuroimaging methods and consequently the increasing information on the details of the human brain, clinicians have been challenged with the problem of detecting and interpreting statistically significant changes on neuroimages that are often distributed and involve simultaneously several structures of the human brain. We believe that

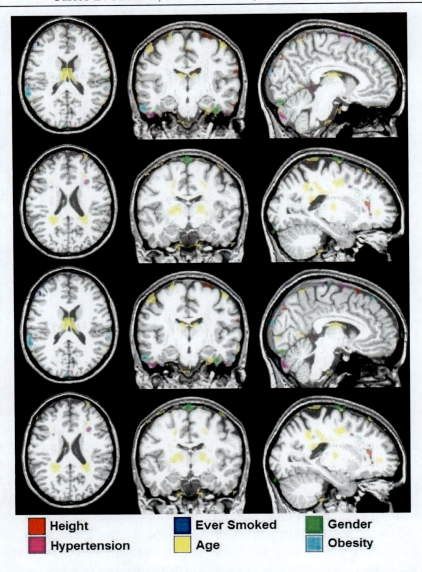

Figure 10. Statistical significance of mutually exclusive changes extracted by the multivariate computational framework described as follows (from top to bottom): (1) 5% t-maps of gray matter, (2) 5% t-maps of white matter, (3) 1% t-maps of gray matter, and (4) 1% t-maps of white matter.

Extracting Discriminant Information from NeuroImages 187

pattern recognition models, such as the one described in this chapter, make the best possible use of these detail-rich data, because multivariate statistical pattern recognition approaches not only mitigate the multiple comparison problem inherent to the mass-univariate methods, but also provide explicitly a measure of error prediction for the model selection, considerably important for clinical diagnosis.

Acknowledgment

The authors would like to acknowledge Fabio L. S. Duran for his scientific support on carrying out some of the experimental results shown in the first case study of this chapter. Also, the authors would like to thank Professor Daniel Rueckert from the Department of Computing, Imperial College London, for providing the subset of the IXI database used in this work. Additionally, the authors would like to thank the support provided by the Brazilian agencies Fundação de Amparo à Pesquisa do Estado de São Paulo (FAPESP: 95/9446-1, 99/12205-07, 2005/02899-4) and Conselho Nacional de Desenvolvimento Científico e Tecnológico (CNPq: 303976/2008-0).

References

[1] Ashburner, J. and Friston, K. J. (2000) Voxel-based morphometry - the methods. *NeuroImage*, **11**(6):805–821.

[2] Ashburner, J., Hutton, C., Frackowiak, R., Johnsrude, I., Price, C., and Friston, K. (1998) Identifying global anatomical differences: Deformation-based morphometry. *Human Brain Mapping*, **6**:638–657.

[3] Bajcsy, B. and Kovacic, S. (1989) Multiresolution elastic matching. *Computer Vision, Graphics and Image Processing*, **46**:1–21.

[4] Batmanghelich, N., Taskar, B. and Davatzikos, C. (2009) A general and unifying framework for feature construction, in image-based pattern classification. In *Proceedings of Information Processing in Medical Imaging (IPMI'09)*, pp. 423–434. Springer-Verlag.

[5] Bhattacharyya, A. (1943) On a measure of divergence between two statistical populations defined by their probability distribution. *Bulletin of Calcutta Mathematical Society*, **35**:99–110.

188 Carlos E. Thomaz, Rafael D. Leão, João R. Sato et al.

[6] Busatto, G. F., Garrido, G. E. J., Almeida, O. P., Castro, C. C., Camargo, C. H. P., Cid, C. G., Buchpiguel, C. A., Furuie, S. and Bottino, C. M. (2003) A voxel-based morphometry study of temporal lobe gray matter reductions in alzheimer's disease. *Neurobiology of Aging*, **24**:221–231.

[7] Christensen, G. E. and Johnson, H. J. (2001) Consistent image registration. *IEEE Transactions on Medical Imaging*, **20**:568–582.

[8] Collins, D. L., Neelin, P., Peters, T. M., and Evans, A. C. (1994) Automatic 3d intersubject registration of mr volumetric data in standardized talairach space. *Journal of Computer Assisted Tomography*, **18**(2):192–205.

[9] Davatzikos, C. (1997) Spatial transformation and registration of brain images using elastically deformable models. *Computer Vision and Image Understanding*, **66**:207–222.

[10] Davatzikos, C. (2004) Why voxel-based morphometric analysis should be used with great caution when characterizing group differences. *NeuroImage*, **23**:17–20.

[11] Davatzikos, C., Vaillant, M., Resnick, S. M., Prince, J. L., Letovsky, S., and Bryan, R. N. (1996) A computerized approach for morphological analysis of the corpus callosum. *Journal of Computed Assisted Tomography*, **20**(1):88–97.

[12] Devijver, P. A. and Kittler, J. (1982) *Pattern Classification: A Statistical Approach.* Prentice-Hall.

[13] Duda, R. O., Hart, P. E., and Stork, D. G. (2001) *Pattern Classification.* John Wiley and Sons, New York.

[14] Fan, Y., Shen, D., Gur, R. C., Gur, R. E. and Davatzikos, C. (2007) Compare: Classification of morphological patterns using adaptive regional elements. *IEEE Transactions on Medical Imaging*, **26**(1):93–105.

[15] Fisher, R. A. (1936) The use of multipled measurements in taxonomic problems. *Annals of Eugenics*, **7**:179–188.

[16] Fisher, R. A. (1938) The statistical utilization of multiple measurements. *Annals of Eugenics*, **8**:376–386.

Extracting Discriminant Information from NeuroImages 189

[17] Folstein, M. F., Folstein, S. E. and McHugh, P. R. (1975) Mini-mental state: A practical method for grading the cognitive state of patients for the clinician. *Journal of Psychiatric Research*, **12**:189–198.

[18] Freeborough, P. A. and Fox, N. C. (1998) Modeling brain deformations in alzheimer disease by fluid registration of serial mr images. *Journal of Computer Assisted Tomography*, **22**:838–843.

[19] Friedman, J. H. (1989) Reguralized discriminant analysis. *Journal of the American Statistical Association*, **84**(405):165–175.

[20] Friston, K. J. and Ashburner, J. (2004) Generative and recognition models for neuroanatomy. *NeuroImage*, **23**:21–24.

[21] Friston, K. J., Holmes, A. P., Worsley, K. J. Poline, J. P., Frith, C. D., and Frackowiak, R. S. J. (1995) Statistical parametric maps in functional imaging: A general linear approach. *Human Brain Mapping*, **2**:189–210.

[22] Fujita, A., Gomes, L. R., Sato, J. R., Yamaguchi, R., Thomaz, C. E., Sogayar, M. C., and Miyano, S. (2008) Multivariate gene expression analysis reveals functional connectivity changes between normal/tumoral prostates. *BMC Systems Biology*, **2**:106.

[23] Fukunaga, K. (1990) *Introduction to Statistical Pattern Recognition*. Academic Press, New York.

[24] Gee, J. C., Reivich, M., and Bajcsy, R. (1993) Elastically deforming 3d atlas to match anatomical brain images. *Journal of Computer Assisted Tomography*, **17**:225–236.

[25] Giraldi, G. A., Rodrigues, P. S., Kitani, E. C., Sato, J. R., and Thomaz, C. E. (2008) Statistical learning approaches for discriminant features selection. *Journal of the Brazilian Computer Society*, **14**(2):7–22.

[26] Golland, P., Grimson, W., Shenton, M., and Kikinis, R. (2005) Detection and analysis of statistical differences in anatomical shape. *Medical Image Analysis*, **9**:69–86.

[27] Good, C. D., Johnsrued, I. S., Ashburner, J., Henson, R. N., Friston, K. J., and Frackowiak R. S. (2001) A voxel-based morphometric study of ageing in 465 normal adult human brains. *NeuroImage*, **14**:21–36.

[28] Grossman, M., McMillan, C., Moore, P., Ding, L., Glosser, G., Work, M., and Gee, J. (2004) What's in a name: voxel-based morphometric analyses of mri and naming difficulty in alzheimer's disease, frontotemporal dementia and corticobasal degeneration. *Brain*, **127**:628–649.

[29] Johnson, R. A. and Wichern, D. W. (1998) *Applied Multivariate Statistical Analysis*. New Jersey: Prentice Hall.

[30] Kitani, E. C., Thomaz, C. E., and Gillies, D. F. (2006) A statistical discriminant model for face interpretation and reconstruction. In *Proceedings of XIX Brazilian Symposium on Computer Graphics and Image Processing (SIBGRAPI'06)*, pp. 247–254. IEEE CS Press.

[31] Lao, Z., Shen, D., Xue, Z., Karacali, B., Resnick, S., and Davatzikos, C. (2004) Morphological classification of brains via high-dimensional shape transformations and machine learning methods. *NeuroImage*, **21**:46–57.

[32] Mazziotta, J. C., Toga, A. W., Evans, A., Fox, P., and Lancaster, J. (1995) A probabilistic atlas of the human brain: theory and rationale for its development. *NeuroImage*, **2**:89–101.

[33] Rueckert, D., Sonoda, L. I., Hayes, C., Hill, D. L. G., Leach, M. O., and Hawkes, D. J. (1999) Non-rigid registration using free-form deformations:application to breast mr images. *IEEE Transactions on Medical Imaging*, **18**(8):712–721.

[34] Sato, J. R., Fujita, A., Thomaz, C. E., Morais-Martin, M. G., Mourao-Miranda, J., Brammer, M. J., and Junior, E. A. (2009) Evaluating svm and mlda in the extraction of discriminant regions for mental state prediction. *NeuroImage*, **46**(1):105–114.

[35] Sato, J. R., Thomaz, C. E., Cardoso, E. F., Fujita, A., Morais-Martin, M. G., and Junior, E. A. (2008) Hyperplane navigation: A method to set individual scores in fmri group datasets. *NeuroImage*, **42**(4):1473–1480.

[36] Shen, D. and Davatzikos, C. (2002) Hammer: Hierarchical attribute matching mechanism for elastic registration. *IEEE Transactions on Medical Imaging*, **21**(11):1421–1439.

[37] Sowell, E. R., Thompson, P. M., Holmes, C. J., Batth, R., Jernigan, T. L., and Toga, A. W. (1999) Localizing age-related changes in brain structure

Extracting Discriminant Information from NeuroImages   191

between childhood and adolescence using statistical parametric mapping. *NeuroImage*, **9**(6):587–597.

[38] Swets, D. and Weng, J. (1996) Using discriminants eigenfeatures for image retrieval. *IEEE Transactions on Patterns Analysis and Machine Intelligence*, **18**(8):831–836.

[39] Talairach, J. and Tornoux, P. (1998) *Co-Planar Stereotaxic Atlas of the Human Brain*. New York: Thieme Medical Publishers Inc.

[40] Thirion, J. P. (1998) Image matching as a diffusion process: An analogy with maxwell's demons. *Medical Image Analysis*, **2**(3):243–260.

[41] Thomaz, C. E., Boardman, J. P., Counsell, S., Hill, D. L. G., Hajnal, J. V., Edwards, A. D., Rutherford, M. A., Gillies, D. F., and Rueckert, D. (2007) A multivariate statistical analysis of the developing human brain in preterm infants. *Image and Vision Computing*, **25**(6):981–994.

[42] Thomaz, C. E., Boardman, J. P., Hill, D. L. G. Hajnal, J. V., Edwards, A. D., Rutherford, M. A., Gillies, D. F., and Rueckert, D. (2004) Using a maximum uncertainty lda-based approach to classify and analyse mr brain images. In *Proceedings of the 7th International Conference on Medical Image Computing and Computer Assisted Intervention (MICCAI'04)*, pp. 291–300. Springer Verlag.

[43] Thomaz, C. E., Duran, F. L. S., Busatto, G. F., Gillies, D. F., and Rueckert, D. (2007) Multivariate statistical differences of mri samples of the human brain. *Journal of Mathematical Imaging and Vision*, **29**(2-3):95–106.

[44] Thomaz, C. E., Gillies, D. F., and Feitosa, R. Q. (2004) A new covariance estimate for bayesian classifiers in biometric recognition. *IEEE Transactions on Circuits and Systems for Video Technology, Special Issue on Image- and Video-Based Biometrics*, **14**(2):214–223.

[45] Thomaz, C. E., Kitani, E. C., and Gillies, D. F. (2006) A maximum uncertainty lda-based approach for limited sample size problems - with application to face recognition. *Journal of the Brazilian Computer Society*, **12**(2):7–18.

[46] Thompson, P. M., MacDonald, D., Mega, M. S., Holmes, C. J., Evans, A. C., and Toga, A. W. (1997) Detection and mapping of abnormal brain

192   Carlos E. Thomaz, Rafael D. Leão, João R. Sato et al.

structure with a probabilistic atlas of cortical surfaces. *Journal of Computer Assisted Tomography*, **21**:567–581.

[47] Thompson, P. M., Moussai, J., Zohoori, S., Goldkorn, A., Khan, A., Mega, M. S., Small, G., Cummings, J., and Toga, A. W. (1998) Cortical variability and asymmetry in normal aging and alzheimer's disease. *Cerebral Cortex*, **8**:492–509.

[48] Vapnik V. N. (2000) *The nature of statistical learning theory.* Springer-Verlag New York, Inc..

[49] Xu, P., Brock, G. N., and Parrish, R. S. (2009) Modified linear discriminant analysis approaches for classification of high-dimensional microarray data. *Computational Statistics and Data Analysis*, **53**(5):1674–1687.

INDEX

A

acetylcholine, 118, 126, 129
acid, 2, 8, 13, 31, 32, 33, 104, 118, 131, 134, 155
ACTH, 118, 119
activity level, 101
adaptation, 89, 134
adipocyte, viii, 1, 8, 9, 11, 12, 14, 21, 31
adiponectin, viii, 2, 14, 21, 33
adipose, viii, 1, 2, 7, 8, 9, 10, 11, 12, 13, 14, 21, 23, 28, 29, 30, 31, 32, 33
adipose tissue, viii, 1, 2, 7, 8, 9, 10, 11, 12, 13, 14, 21, 23, 28, 29, 30, 31, 32, 33
adiposity, 36
adjustment, ix, 71, 72, 73, 74, 75, 77
adolescence, 37,191
adrenal gland, 119, 120
adrenocorticotropic hormone, 121, 123
affective disorder, 122, 147
aggregation, 67
aggression, 75, 126, 131
agnosia, 45, 51, 52, 54
agonist, 5, 20, 131, 132, 133, 147
AIDS, 78
alcohol, 73, 78, 151
alcoholism, 19
aldosterone, 121
algorithm, 170, 175, 182
allele, 138
ALS, 59, 60, 65
alternatives, 86, 88
alters, 30, 61
aluminum, 139
ambivalence, 86

amenorrhea, 5, 24, 25
American Psychiatric Association, 108
amino acids, 3
amnesia, 63, 134
amphetamines, ix, 97
amygdala, 55, 104, 110, 118
amylase, vii, x, 113, 114, 115, 117, 121, 123
amyotrophic lateral sclerosis, 42, 43, 59, 61, 64, 67
androgen, 11, 156
androgens, 13
anger, 76, 87, 92
antagonism, 28
antibody, 128
antidepressant, 15, 102, 107, 111
antipsychotic, 15, 17, 19, 20, 21, 34, 35, 37, 129, 130, 133
antipsychotic drugs, 17, 19, 21, 35, 133
antisocial personality, 73
anxiety, ix, x, 72, 73, 75, 76, 77, 78, 88, 97, 98, 106, 113, 114, 115, 116, 117, 118, 120, 121, 122, 126, 132, 134
anxiety disorder, ix, x, 113, 114
apathy, ix, 45, 46, 49, 50, 72, 75, 91, 97, 98, 107
aphasia, viii, 39, 40, 51, 52, 65, 67
appetite, viii, 2, 6, 7, 13, 14, 15, 16, 19, 20, 21
apraxia, ix, 40, 43, 44, 45, 49, 50, 52
arginine, 17, 26
arousal, 75, 118
assessment, 55, 83, 88, 101, 111, 121, 140, 146
asthma, 123
asymmetry, 192
asymptomatic, 59, 62

194 Index

ataxia, 148
atrophy, viii, 40, 41, 44, 54, 55, 56, 57, 58, 59, 60, 64, 68, 174, 180, 181
autonomic activity, 117
autonomic nervous system, 114
autopsy, viii, 40, 68, 69, 140
autosomal dominant, 59

B

baby boomers, x, 137, 138
barbiturates, 109
baroreceptor, 126, 134
basal forebrain, 118
basal ganglia, 55, 56, 127
behavior, 3, 19, 34, 37, 90, 93, 99, 100, 101, 102, 103, 105, 106, 107, 108, 111, 118, 119, 132
behavioral aspects, 106
beliefs, 82
beneficial effect, vii, 1, 6, 21
benign tumors, 4
benzodiazepine, 135
bias, 58, 174
bile, 156
binding, 3, 10, 11, 13, 30, 34, 119, 129
bioinformatics, x, xi, 153, 154, 155, 156
biological markers, x, 113
biomarkers, 122
biopsy, 140
bipolar disorder, 147, 150
birds, 3, 8
birth, 23, 119
bladder, 4
blame, 73
blocks, 4
blood, ix, 26, 28, 113, 114, 115, 118, 119, 126, 139, 157
blood pressure, 114, 118
blood vessels, 118, 139
bloodstream, 118
body composition, vii, viii, 1, 5, 7, 31
body fat, vii, 1, 6, 7, 11, 17, 19, 20, 21, 31, 36, 38
body mass index, vii, 1, 16, 19, 28, 183
body weight, viii, 2, 6, 7, 11, 13, 15, 16, 17, 19, 20, 21, 27, 28, 30, 32, 35, 38
bone, vii, 1, 3, 4, 5, 11, 24, 31, 42, 68
bone marrow, 3, 4, 11, 31

bone mass, 5, 24
brain structure, 115, 183, 190
brainstem, x, 55, 125, 127, 128, 129, 134, 135
breast cancer, 35

C

caloric intake, 139
cardiac activity, 116
cardiovascular risk, 6, 22, 28
caregivers, 77
case study, 173, 181, 182
caspases, 135
catecholamines, 4, 117, 118
cation, 126
CBS, 63
cell, 3, 4, 9, 12, 14, 16, 128, 139, 147, 156
cell death, 128
cell line, 12, 14, 147
cell lines, 147
central nervous system, 119, 125, 126, 129
cerebellum, 127, 128
cerebral cortex, 46, 61, 118, 149
cerebrospinal fluid, 59, 64, 67, 174
childhood, 4, 35, 191
children, 37, 123
cholesterol, 20, 38, 139, 142
chromosome, 42, 43, 61, 65, 147, 148, 155
circadian rhythm, 17, 30, 101
classes, 161, 165, 167, 168, 169, 173, 178, 183
classification, 41, 57, 58, 132, 161, 162, 163, 164, 165, 166, 167, 171, 172, 178, 183, 184, 185, 187, 190, 192
clients, 79, 85, 86, 87, 88, 89
clinical diagnosis, 43, 44
clinical symptoms, ix, 40, 45, 52
clinical syndrome, viii, ix, 39, 40, 43
clonus, 45, 46
clozapine, 19, 130
cluster analysis, 175, 182
clusters, 85
CNS, 32, 126, 129, 133
cocaine, 130
codon, 43, 148
cognition, 127
cognitive deficit, 156
cognitive flexibility, 141
cognitive impairment, 140, 143

coherence, 178, 179
components, 77, 81, 83, 161, 166, 167, 168, 171
composition, 2, 7, 164
comprehension, viii, 40, 45, 46, 49, 51, 52, 60, 115
compulsive behavior, 19
computed tomography, 120
concentration, viii, 2, 9, 10, 59, 116, 139
conceptual model, 89
conceptualization, 81
concussion, 74, 92, 93
conditioning, 104
confidence, 87
confrontation, 88
confusion, 81, 83
connectivity, 189
consciousness, 81
consensus, ix, 7, 62, 65, 71, 77
construction, 174, 187
contingency, 81
contracture, ix, 40, 45, 46, 52, 60
control, viii, 2, 4, 6, 7, 13, 17, 18, 19, 20, 21, 28, 32, 33, 35, 36, 59, 76, 104, 120, 126, 129, 130, 131, 132, 134, 135, 142, 145, 148, 173, 174, 178, 179, 180, 181
control group, 7, 76
controlled trials, 75
conversion, 12, 31
coping strategies, 73, 76, 86, 88
corneal transplant, 117
corpus callosum, 176, 177, 181, 188
correlation, 13, 21, 67, 116, 117, 146, 155
correlations, x, 62, 82, 116, 117, 125
cortex, 4, 41, 42, 43, 44, 46, 51, 53, 55, 58, 59, 106, 118, 127, 129, 148, 177
corticobasal degeneration, 41, 64, 65, 190
corticotropin, 123
cortisol, vii, ix, 8, 10, 35, 113, 114, 115, 117, 118, 119, 120, 121, 122, 123
counseling, 83, 87, 88, 92
coupling, 6
CSF, 59, 60, 174, 175, 176, 177, 182
cycles, 23, 99, 101
cytokines, 14, 118
cytoplasm, 127

D

data analysis, 82
data mining, 155
data set, 171, 173
database, 182, 187
death, 45, 46, 49, 51, 134
decision-making process, 163
decisions, 78
defects, 22
deficiency, 17, 24, 131
deficit, 91, 141, 146, 148
definition, 56, 146, 160
deformation, 164
delinquency, 78
delivery, 83
delusion, 45
delusions, 103
dementia, viii, 39, 40, 41, 42, 43, 44, 49, 52, 57, 61, 62, 63, 64, 65, 66, 67, 68, 69, 130, 131, 139, 141, 142, 143, 150, 190
denial, 87, 92
density, vii, 1, 25, 31
deposition, 6, 8, 11, 17, 19, 21, 29, 68
depression, ix, x, 72, 73, 75, 76, 77, 87, 91, 92, 97, 98, 102, 105, 106, 107, 108, 110, 112, 113, 114, 119, 120, 121, 122, 129, 132, 135
deprivation, 5
derivatives, 37
desensitization, 147
detection, vii, 1, 175, 181
developmental process, 146
diabetes, 157
diagnostic criteria, 40
diet, 36, 100, 139, 142
dietary fat, 139
differential diagnosis, 150
differentiation, viii, 1, 8, 9, 11, 12, 21, 24, 29, 31, 60
diffusion, 191
diffusion process, 191
dilation, 55, 56
dimensionality, 160, 165, 166, 167, 171
disability, 88, 92
discriminant analysis, 183, 185, 189, 192
discrimination, 163
disease gene, 148
disease progression, 51, 141

Index

disequilibrium, 19
disorder, 19, 94, 119, 120, 122, 123, 146, 147, 150, 154, 155, 157, 160, 179
dispersion, 143, 170
distress, 72, 73, 77, 114, 115
distribution, vii, 1, 4, 6, 7, 21, 31, 36, 53, 58, 173, 183, 185
divergence, 187
DNA, 170
dopamine, viii, 2, 4, 5, 6, 7, 10, 13, 16, 17, 18, 19, 20, 21, 22, 24, 25, 28, 34, 35, 37, 38, 107, 109, 111, 126, 129, 147, 150
dopamine agonist, viii, 2, 5, 7, 10, 13, 17, 19, 20, 21, 22, 25, 28, 35, 38
dopaminergic, 4, 7, 16, 18, 19, 20, 21, 22, 24, 35, 36, 37, 38, 107, 110, 130, 131, 133
dosage, 101, 110
dosing, 101
drug abuse, 98
drug abusers, 98
drug action, 134
drug dependence, 109, 110
drug history, 110
drug treatment, 98, 99, 100, 106, 108
drug use, 107
drug withdrawal, 103, 105
drugs, ix, 5, 15, 19, 97, 98, 106, 120, 129, 130, 133
DSM, 72
duodenum, 4
duration, 45, 46, 47, 49, 51, 53, 54, 55, 56, 57, 58, 76
dysarthria, 45, 49, 148
dysphagia, 148

E

eating disorders, 78
economic crisis, x, 137
elderly, 46, 141, 173, 179, 183
emission, 148
emotional distress, 72, 73, 77, 90
emotional reactions, 86
emotions, 77, 88, 118
empathy, 87
employment, 72, 91
enantiomers, 132
encoding, 141, 148, 151
endocrine, 35, 37, 119

endothelial cells, 11
energy, viii, 2, 16, 20, 34, 80, 86, 118
engagement, 75
enlargement, 177, 180, 181
environment, 4, 80, 86, 100, 101, 119
environmental change, 4, 18
environmental factors, 142, 146
enzymatic activity, 10
enzymes, 8, 11, 32
epigenetics, 147
epilepsy, 146
epinephrine, 116
episodic memory, 43
estrogen, 8, 11, 16, 24, 30, 31
ethanol, 109
etiology, 19, 142, 148
Euclidean space, 164
euphoria, 45, 46, 49, 50
evolution, 51, 64
excitation, 116
excretion, 112
exercise, 107, 117
exposure, 4, 78, 114
extraction, 161, 163, 164, 165, 167, 174, 175, 182, 190

F

false positive, 175
family, 4, 43, 44, 47, 57, 58, 59, 62, 74, 77, 79, 87, 89, 92, 138, 139, 147
family functioning, 77
family history, 44, 47, 57, 58, 59, 138, 139
family members, 62, 74, 77, 79, 89, 92
family system, 77
FAS, 2, 13
fasting, 35, 36, 38
fat, vii, viii, 1, 6, 8, 11, 12, 13, 17, 27, 28, 29, 32
fatigue, ix, 74, 97, 98, 102, 105, 107, 110
fatty acids, 10, 20
feature selection, 160
feedback, ix, 4, 7, 13, 88, 113, 118, 119, 163
feelings, 73, 86, 87, 88
females, 14, 73, 100, 115, 183
fetal growth, 23
fetus, 24, 149
fibers, 128
fibroblasts, 3, 11, 31

Index

fibrosis, 5
filament, viii, 40, 41
fluid, 164, 189
focusing, 8, 60, 76
food intake, 11, 12, 14, 15, 16, 19, 21, 27, 32, 33, 34
forebrain, 110
freedom, 166
freezing, 104, 118
frontal cortex, 44, 51, 53, 150
frontal lobe, 40, 58, 59, 63, 181
frustration, 87

G

gait, 45, 49, 51, 52
galactorrhea, vii, 1, 24
gambling, 19
gastrointestinal tract, 4
gender, 6, 115, 181, 182, 183
gender differences, 115
gene, viii, ix, 2, 3, 4, 5, 8, 10, 12, 22, 23, 28, 29, 32, 37, 39, 40, 41, 43, 58, 59, 61, 64, 65, 66, 67, 122, 147, 148, 150, 151, 154, 155, 156, 157, 189
gene expression, 4, 10, 12, 23, 28, 29, 122, 148, 189
gene therapy, 157
generalization, 89
generation, 36, 133
genes, 42, 139, 147, 148, 150, 151, 154, 155, 156
genetic defect, 146
genetic disease, 147
genetic disorders, 146
genetic factors, 141
genetics, x, 139, 145, 146, 147, 148, 149, 150, 151, 156
genome, 147, 155
genomics, 150, 151, 154, 157
genotype, 37, 142
gestation, 3, 24, 128
gland, 3, 7, 10, 28, 29
globus, 55
glucagon, 26
glucocorticoid receptor, 119
glucose, 6, 10, 11, 20, 26, 30, 33, 38
glucose tolerance, 33, 38
goals, 74, 75, 77, 87, 89, 164

grading, 178, 189
grains, 61
granules, 16
gray matter, 57, 118, 174, 175, 176, 177, 182, 183, 184, 186, 188
grief, 83, 87, 88
groups, 10, 55, 57, 58, 59, 73, 81, 88, 89, 109, 115, 117, 128, 163, 165, 167, 168, 169, 174, 178, 180, 183, 185
growth, 3, 8, 22, 23, 24, 25, 26, 27, 29, 30, 31, 33, 34, 35, 36, 89, 118, 156
growth factor, 31, 156
growth hormone, 3, 22, 23, 24, 26, 27, 29, 30, 31, 33, 34, 35, 36

H

habituation, 101
hair follicle, 23
hallucinations, 103
head injuries, 92, 139
head injury, 85, 90, 91, 92, 93, 94
health, 80, 90, 93, 139, 175
heart rate (HR), 114, 115, 116, 139, 143
height, 19, 37, 182, 183
hemianopsia, 5
hemiparesis, 45
hemiplegia, 46
hepatocytes, 30, 38
heterogeneity, 24, 57
hip, 17
hippocampus, 118, 129, 133, 176, 177, 180, 181
histamine, 19
histology, 43, 47, 57, 65
homeostasis, 10, 126, 129, 131
hormone, ix, 3, 5, 8, 11, 13, 19, 22, 26, 29, 36, 113, 115, 118, 121, 123
hostility, 76
House, 145, 153
HPA axis, 111, 115, 118, 119, 120
human brain, xi, 127, 128, 159, 160, 161, 170, 185, 189, 190, 191
human genome, 155
hydrolysis, 129, 134
hyperactivity, 148
hyperglycemia, 38
hyperinsulinemia, 10, 17, 18, 33
hyperplasia, 16

hyperprolactinemia, vii, viii, 1, 2, 4, 5, 6, 7, 10, 13, 14, 17, 18, 19, 20, 21, 24, 25, 26, 28
hypertension, 183
hypertrophy, 119
hypoglycemia, 17, 36
hypogonadism, vii, 1, 5, 18, 31
hypothalamus, 15, 16, 17, 20, 27, 119, 122, 181
hypothesis, 4, 7, 17, 21, 82, 85, 106, 107, 110, 122, 131, 133, 160
hypoxia, 35

I

identification, 21, 72, 87, 155, 156
identity, 170
image, xi, 160, 161, 163, 164, 165, 166, 167, 168, 170, 171, 172, 173, 174, 175, 180, 181, 182, 185, 188, 191
image analysis, 161, 163, 170
images, 56, 160, 161, 163, 164, 165, 166, 167, 168, 170, 171, 173, 174, 175, 176, 177, 178, 180, 181, 182, 183, 185, 188, 189, 190, 191
immune response, 118
immunohistochemistry, 47, 64, 128
impairments, 49, 73, 75, 76
implementation, 74, 75
impulsive, 106
impulsivity, 72, 79
in vitro, 3, 12, 26, 27, 33, 131
in vivo, 9, 12, 33, 60, 131
incidence, x, 25, 137, 138, 141
inclusion, viii, 40, 41, 42, 46, 63, 64, 67, 174
independence, 75
indicators, 72
indices, 115
individual differences, 122
induction, 3, 6, 14, 15, 16, 19, 21, 30, 117
inefficiency, 74
inferences, 174
infertility, vii, 1, 3, 157
information processing, 75
information technology, 153
ingestion, 19
inheritance, 148
inhibition, 4, 5, 22, 100, 103, 105, 109, 110, 111, 131, 132
inhibitor, 18, 23

initiation, 129
injections, 9, 27, 100, 103, 104, 107
insight, 27, 75, 79, 87, 88
insomnia, 148, 150, 151
instability, 73
instruments, 72
insulin, viii, 2, 6, 9, 10, 11, 14, 17, 20, 21, 23, 26, 29, 30, 33, 38
insulin resistance, 6, 14, 17, 33
integration, 72
intentions, 106
interaction, viii, x, 2, 13, 18, 21, 34, 37, 73, 115, 125, 129, 148
interactions, 8, 29, 32, 33, 116, 126
interface, 3
internal consistency, 82, 85
interpersonal relations, 73, 75
interpersonal relationships, 73, 75
interval, 100
intervention, 76, 77, 78, 79, 80, 82, 83, 85, 88, 92, 93
intoxication, 109
intravenously, 100, 110, 119
intrinsic motivation, 86
ions, 139
irritability, 45

K

kidney, 4

L

labeling, 133, 138
lactation, 3, 4, 8, 10, 11, 12, 28, 29, 30, 31
latency, 27, 117
learning, 131, 134, 189, 192
learning task, 134
leptin, viii, 2, 13, 15, 18, 20, 21, 28, 29, 32, 33, 36
libido, 5
lifestyle, 73
ligand, 3, 126, 131
limbic system, 118
linkage, 19, 147, 155, 156
lipid metabolism, 13, 20, 30
lipids, 8, 20, 28
lipolysis, 12, 29, 32

Index

liver, 4, 8, 23, 28
localization, 125, 129, 160
locomotor, 16, 100, 101, 104, 105, 107, 133
locus, 42, 65, 147
LSD, 129
luteinizing hormone, 32, 36
lymphocytes, 3
lymphoid, 3, 4
lymphoid tissue, 4
lysergic acid diethylamide, 129

M

machine learning, 190
macrophages, 11
magnetic resonance, vii, 1, 160
magnetic resonance imaging (MRI), ix, 40, 42, 56, 58, 64, 68, 173, 176, 177, 178, 179, 181, 185
major depression, 120, 134
major depressive disorder, 117, 118, 119, 120, 121, 123
males, 25, 31, 73, 115, 183
mammography, 78
management, 24, 37, 76, 81, 92, 107, 114
mania, 147, 150
manipulation, x, 153, 154
mapping, 33, 161, 162, 163, 180, 191
marrow, 11
matrix, 164, 165, 166, 167, 168, 169, 170, 171, 173
maturation, 8, 156
measurement, 101
measures, 76, 77, 81, 98, 106, 107, 108, 116, 139, 177
medical care, 60
medication, 78
medication compliance, 78
membership, 167
memory, 45, 49, 51, 52, 68, 75, 94, 127, 129, 130, 132, 133, 134, 138, 140, 171
memory formation, 134
mental arithmetic, 116, 122
mental disorder, vii, 108, 146
mental health, 91
mental state, 190
messenger RNA, 2, 13, 29, 31, 110, 118, 119, 130, 151
messengers, 126

metabolic dysfunction, viii, 2, 38
metabolic syndrome, 37, 157
metabolism, viii, 1, 5, 6, 7, 8, 10, 11, 12, 20, 21, 26, 27, 32, 109, 112, 130, 147
metals, 139, 142
methylphenidate, 75, 93, 94, 95
mice, 8, 10, 11, 12, 13, 20, 22, 23, 26, 28, 29, 31, 32, 34, 38, 101, 102, 103, 105, 107, 109, 111, 112, 128, 131, 134, 135
microdialysis, 131
military, 119
minority, 7
model, ix, 71, 78, 79, 80, 81, 82, 83, 85, 89, 90, 93, 94, 98, 105, 108, 132, 133, 151, 157, 175, 182, 187, 190
model system, 157
modeling, 23
models, ix, 97, 98, 105, 106, 107, 108, 109, 111, 119, 132, 156, 157, 187, 188, 189
mood, 75, 109, 120, 126, 150
mood disorder, 126
mood states, 120
morphology, 123
morphometric, 188, 189, 190
motivation, 75, 104, 177
motor activity, ix, 97, 98, 107
motor control, 135
motor neuron disease, 42, 48, 65
motor neurons, 42
motor skills, 141
movement, 82, 129, 146, 149
movement disorders, 146, 149
mtDNA, 142
muscles, 4
mutagenesis, 155
mutant, 68
mutation, 4, 22, 41, 42, 43, 59, 61, 62, 63, 65, 66, 67, 147, 154, 155
myoclonus, 148
myopathy, 42, 68

N

necrosis, 2, 5, 14
nervous system, vii, 4, 126, 127
neurobiology, 110
neurodegeneration, 138, 142
neuroendocrine system, 115
neurofibrillary tangles, 46, 140

neuroimaging, xi, 159, 160, 185
neuroleptics, 35
neuronal circuits, 122
neurons, 15, 16, 34, 55, 110, 122, 128, 129, 140
neuropsychiatry, vii, x, xi, 137, 145, 146, 148, 149, 153, 154, 155, 156, 160
neuropsychology, 137, 138
neurotransmission, 102, 106, 107, 131, 132
neurotransmitter, 4, 15, 125, 131
nicotine, 131
noise, 103, 161, 167
non-smokers, 183
norepinephrine, 102, 116, 117
normal aging, 133, 138, 192
nuclei, 15, 127, 128, 129, 148
nucleus, 16, 17, 34, 55, 56, 111, 118, 122, 127, 129, 131, 134
nucleus tractus solitarius, 134
null hypothesis, 83

O

obesity, viii, 2, 6, 10, 14, 17, 18, 19, 20, 21, 22, 26, 27, 28, 32, 33, 34, 35, 36, 37, 38, 78, 183
obesity prevention, 20
observations, 98, 101, 102, 103, 104, 107, 167, 168
olanzapine, 20, 38
old age, 142
oligomenorrhea, 5
openness, 86
opiates, 109
opioids, 19
order, ix, x, 3, 7, 10, 15, 16, 74, 79, 80, 81, 97, 98, 125, 139, 140, 141, 155, 161, 167, 171, 174, 175, 177, 182, 183
ores, 38
organ, 145
organic disease, 146
orientation, 156, 164
outpatients, 93
ovariectomy, 29
overtime, 74
overweight, 6, 18, 21, 36
oxidation, 11, 30, 33
oxidative stress, 142

P

pain management, 78
pancreas, 4
panic disorder, 78, 117, 119, 130
parameter, 178
parameter estimation, 178
parameters, 31, 98, 99, 100, 115, 117, 175
paranoia, 72, 103
paranoid schizophrenia, 103
parietal cortex, 54, 176
parietal lobe, 59, 66
parkinsonism, ix, 40, 44, 45, 51, 52, 60, 61
parotid, 116
parotid gland, 116
passive, 132
pathogenesis, 4, 6, 19, 20, 21
pathology, 42, 47, 57, 59, 60, 61, 62, 64, 68, 69, 181
pathophysiology, 121, 131, 132, 135, 176, 177
pathways, 18, 19, 20, 21, 22, 108
pattern recognition, 160, 161, 162, 163, 177, 183, 185, 187
pedigree, 42
peer support, 88
peptides, 142
peripheral nervous system, 16
persecutory delusion, 49
personality, 45, 72, 73, 94
personality disorder, 72
pharmacotherapy, ix, 37, 97, 98, 107, 108, 110, 131
phenotype, 29, 44, 47, 61
phospholipids, 8
phosphorylation, 26, 129
physical environment, 86
physiology, 155
physiopathology, 151
pica, 45, 46, 49, 50
pituitary gland, 3, 118, 119
pituitary tumors, vii, 1, 4, 28
placebo, 75, 130
plasma, 23, 32, 33, 38, 59, 62, 116, 117
plasma levels, 116
plasticity, 110
plausibility, 80, 179
point mutation, 148, 155
polymorphisms, 19, 150
polypeptide, 4

pons, 128
positive correlation, 116
positive feedback, 4
posttraumatic stress, 122
post-traumatic stress disorder, 119
posture, 102
prediction, 60, 121, 187, 190
predictors, 91, 138, 142
prefrontal cortex, 129, 131, 133, 134
pregnancy, 4, 8, 12, 23, 26, 29, 31, 78
pressure, 115, 117, 126
preterm infants, 191
prevention, 78, 138, 141
primate, 131
Principal Components Analysis, 165, 166, 167, 171, 180, 183, 185
prior knowledge, 160
probability, 138, 139, 175, 178, 182, 187
probability distribution, 187
problem-solving, 73, 75, 76, 77, 88, 89, 93
problem-solving strategies, 75
prodromal symptoms, 105
prodrome, 111
production, 4, 5, 14, 16, 19, 33, 129
progesterone, 8, 27, 29
program, 31, 76, 77, 93, 176
progressive supranuclear palsy, viii, 39, 41
prolactin, vii, 1, 22, 23, 24, 26, 27, 28, 29, 30, 31, 32, 33, 34, 35, 36
proliferation, 3, 4, 11, 12, 25, 26, 29
promoter, 11, 12, 13, 150
prostacyclins, 129
prostaglandins, 129
prostate cancer, 31
prostate gland, 22
protective factors, 139
protein family, 148, 151
protein kinase C, 129
protein sequence, 157
proteins, 41, 140, 148, 151
proteomics, 154, 155, 156
protocol, 101, 154, 155, 174
prototype, 177
psychiatric disorders, 92
psychoeducational intervention, 74
psychological distress, 77
psychological stress, 115, 116, 117, 123
psychological well-being, 73
psychometric properties, 82
psychopathology, 73, 91

psychosis, 103, 105, 108, 111, 112, 140, 147, 150
psychosocial functioning, 76, 93
psychosocial stress, 116, 117, 122
psychostimulants, 109
psychotherapy, 78, 81, 83, 85, 86, 88, 89, 92
puberty, 13

R

radon, 78
range, 13, 72
reactivity, 122
reason, 83
reasoning, 141
receptors, vii, viii, x, 2, 3, 4, 9, 10, 11, 14, 15, 16, 19, 23, 24, 25, 28, 29, 30, 32, 35, 116, 117, 118, 125, 126, 127, 128, 129, 130, 131, 132, 133, 134, 135, 147
recognition, 45, 80, 132, 135, 161, 163, 164, 165, 166, 189, 191
reconstruction, 166, 170, 190
recovery, 26, 72, 74, 75, 77, 88, 95, 120
recurrence, 112
region, 11, 12, 13, 15, 51, 57, 118, 128, 147, 174
regulation, viii, 1, 2, 8, 10, 13, 14, 15, 16, 19, 20, 21, 23, 28, 29, 30, 31, 32, 34, 75, 115, 121, 130, 131, 147, 150
regulators, 12
rehabilitation, 75, 83, 85, 90, 91, 93, 94
rehabilitation program, 75, 85
relationship, x, 6, 13, 18, 21, 22, 35, 87, 88, 92, 116, 120, 122, 145, 146, 147, 148
remediation, 75, 89
remission, ix, 113, 119
reproduction, 8, 13, 16, 31, 32
resistance, 30, 79, 87
resolution, xi, 159, 160, 185
resources, x, 137, 138, 141, 157
respiration, 131
respiratory, 134
responsiveness, 29, 30, 115, 116, 117, 118, 119, 147, 150
rhinorrhea, 5
rhythm, 116, 148
ribonucleic acid, 2, 32, 134
risk, 6, 22, 35, 138, 139, 142, 143, 147, 162
risk factors, 138, 139

S

saliva, 115, 116, 122
salivary glands, 116
sample mean, 82, 169, 178
sample variance, 167, 168
sampling, 77
satisfaction, 77
scatter, 168, 169, 170, 171, 178, 179
scatter plot, 178, 179
schizophrenia, 49, 103, 105, 111, 112, 129, 133, 135, 146, 154, 156
schizophrenic patients, 105
school activities, 74
sclerosis, 66
scores, 82, 190
search, 93, 139
secretion, vii, viii, 1, 2, 3, 4, 5, 6, 9, 10, 11, 13, 14, 16, 17, 18, 19, 20, 21, 23, 26, 28, 30, 32, 33, 34, 35, 36, 116, 117, 118, 123
sedentary lifestyle, 78
selecting, 85, 166, 167
selectivity, 135
self-awareness, 73, 77, 89
self-esteem, 76
self-regulation, 76
semantic memory, viii, 40, 45, 46, 49, 50, 51, 52, 60
semen, 26
sensation, 129
senses, 118
sensitivity, 29, 31, 109
sensitization, 105, 108, 109, 110, 111, 112
separation, 119, 181, 183
serine, 147
serotonin, 17, 19, 106, 110, 118, 125, 126, 128, 129, 130, 131, 132, 133, 134, 135
serum, vii, 1, 4, 6, 13, 14, 18, 23, 115
severe stress, 103
severity, 61, 68, 72, 76, 87, 110, 121, 141, 147
sex, 15, 25, 29, 30
sex differences, 15
sex steroid, 30
sexual behavior, 104, 106, 108
shape, 164, 189, 190
sheep, 8, 9, 29
short term memory, 95, 138
side effects, 35
signal transduction, 22, 23

signaling pathway, 14, 156
signals, 3, 15, 129
signal-to-noise ratio, 175, 182
signs, ix, 6, 40, 45, 46, 52, 60, 69, 148
silver, 46
simulation, 155
skills, 75, 76, 77, 89, 90
skills training, 89
skin, 4
smokers, 78, 183
smoking, 19, 78, 182
smoothing, 175
snakes, 118
social anxiety, 123
social network, 74
social stress, 114
social support, 89
socialization, 121
space, 161, 162, 163, 164, 165, 166, 167, 168, 172, 173, 175, 176, 180, 185, 188
spatial learning, 134
species, 3, 10, 15, 38, 101, 102, 106, 111, 127, 128
spectrum, 94
speech, viii, ix, 40, 45, 46, 49, 51, 52, 60, 114
spine, 100
spleen, 3
stabilizers, 150
standard deviation, 173, 178, 180
starvation, 13
steroids, 11, 13, 18, 126
stimulant, 109, 110
stimulus, 4, 103
storage, 11, 118, 141, 166
strain, 155
strategies, ix, 71, 73, 74, 75, 77, 86, 88, 89, 91
stress, vii, ix, x, 73, 76, 77, 88, 89, 102, 104, 113, 114, 115, 116, 117, 118, 119, 120, 121, 122, 123
stressful life events, 121
stressors, x, 114, 116, 119
striatum, 57, 106
stroma, 31
stromal cells, 11
stupor, 148
subgroups, 72
substance abuse, 72, 73, 78
substance use, 72, 73
substitution, 155, 157
substrates, viii, ix, 40, 41

Index

sudden infant death syndrome, 127
suicide, 130
supervision, 77
suppression, 121, 123
susceptibility, 65, 105, 147, 148, 157
sympathetic nervous system, 116
symptom, ix, 45, 49, 51, 71, 72, 73, 74, 76, 118, 120
symptoms, ix, 37, 43, 44, 45, 46, 48, 49, 51, 54, 60, 72, 73, 74, 75, 76, 77, 90, 97, 98, 101, 102, 104, 105, 106, 107, 108, 138, 142, 148
syndrome, ix, 22, 40, 44, 48, 52, 65, 67, 91, 92, 94, 98, 107, 108, 109, 134
synthesis, viii, 2, 4, 7, 10, 11, 16, 20, 32, 83, 112

T

tamoxifen, 20
targets, 120, 131
tau, viii, 39, 41, 42, 43, 57, 58, 59, 62, 64, 67, 135, 140
TBI, 74, 75, 76
temporal lobe, 40, 57, 58, 59, 129, 188
tension, 73
testosterone, 11, 18
therapeutic interventions, 122
therapeutics, x, 125, 135
therapists, 86, 87
therapy, 25, 26, 28, 31, 75, 78, 79, 81, 84, 88, 89, 90, 92, 93, 130, 148
thermoregulation, 9
threonine, 147
threshold, 6, 177
thrombin, 156
thymus, 3
thyrotropin, 36, 123
tissue, viii, 1, 5, 8, 9, 10, 11, 13, 24, 29, 68, 104, 106, 107, 140, 164, 175, 182
TNF, 2, 14
toxicity, 142
training, 75, 111, 163, 166, 167, 169, 171, 172, 173, 180, 183
trait anxiety, 115
transcription, 2, 3, 5, 10, 12, 15, 31, 32
transcription factors, 12
transducer, 2, 3
transformation, 166, 167, 171, 173, 188

transformation matrix, 167, 171, 173
transformations, 174, 175, 182, 190
transition, 139
transmission, 122
traumatic brain injury, 74, 90, 91, 92, 93, 94, 95, 142
treatment methods, 83
tremor, 46
trial, 76, 93, 94, 95
triglycerides, 20
trust, 86
TSH, 36
tumor, vii, 1, 14, 25, 26
tumorigenesis, 16
tumors, vii, 1, 5
tyrosine, 4

V

validation, 167, 183, 184
variability, 58, 64, 65, 98, 106, 139, 143, 148, 164, 166, 167, 168, 171, 192
vascular dementia, 63, 141
vasoactive intestinal peptide, 34
vasopressin, 18, 118, 119, 122
vector, 164, 165, 166, 169, 171, 172, 173, 180
ventricle, 55, 56, 176, 177
vertebrates, 3, 4, 6, 128, 129
visualization, 160, 163
vulnerability, 111, 119

W

weight control, 16, 32
weight gain, vii, viii, 1, 2, 6, 7, 14, 15, 16, 17, 19, 20, 21, 22, 24, 27, 28, 35, 36, 37, 38
weight loss, 7, 10, 17, 18, 21
weight reduction, 20, 35
white matter, 174, 175, 176, 177, 182, 183, 184, 185, 186
withdrawal, ix, 34, 97, 98, 99, 100, 101, 102, 103, 104, 105, 106, 107, 108, 109, 110, 111, 112
working memory, 138, 140